SO-AEM-914

SYMBOLIC INTERACTIONISM

SYMBOLIC INTERACTIONISM

An Introduction, An Interpretation, An Integration

NINTH EDITION

Joel M. Charon

PROFESSOR EMERITUS
MINNESOTA STATE UNIVERSITY MOORHEAD

PEARSON
Prentice
Hall

Upper Saddle River, New Jersey 07458

Library of Congress Cataloging-in-Publication Data

Charon, Joel M.
  Symbolic interactionism : an introduction, an interpretation, an
integration / Joel M. Charon.— 9th ed.
      p. cm.
  Includes bibliographical references and index.
  ISBN-13: 978-0-13-227691-7 (paper back)
  ISBN-10: 0-13-227691-7 (paper back)
  1. Symbolic interactionism.   I. Title.
  HM499.C46 2007
  302—dc22

                                                                    2006003623

Editorial Director: Leah Jewell
Publisher: Nancy Roberts
Editorial Assistant: Lee Peterson
Executive Marketing Manager: Marissa Feliberty
Marketing Assistant: Anthony DeCosta
Production Liaison: Fran Russello
Manufacturing Buyer: Brian Mackey
Cover Art Director: Jayne Conte
Cover Design: Bruce Kenselaar
Composition/Full-Service Project Management: Chitra Ganesan/GGS Book Services
Printer/Binder: RR Donnelley and Sons Company
Cover Printer: RR Donnelley and Sons Company

Credits and acknowledgments borrowed from other sources and reproduced, with permission,
in this textbook appear on appropriate page within text.

**Copyright © 2007, 2004, 2001, 1998, 1995, 1992 by Pearson Education, Inc., Upper Saddle
River, New Jersey 07458.**
Pearson Prentice Hall. All rights reserved. Printed in the United States of America. This
publication is protected by Copyright and permission should be obtained from the publisher
prior to any prohibited reproduction, storage in a retrieval system, or transmission in any form
or by any means, electronic, mechanical, photocopying, recording, or likewise. For information
regarding permission(s), write to: Rights and Permissions Department.

Pearson Prentice Hall™ is a trademark of Pearson Education, Inc.
Pearson® is a registered trademark of Pearson plc
Prentice Hall® is a registered trademark of Pearson Education, Inc.

Pearson Education LTD. London
Pearson Education Singapore, Pte. Ltd
Pearson Education, Canada, Ltd
Pearson Education–Japan
Pearson Education Australia PTY, Limited

Pearson Education North Asia Ltd
Pearson Educación de Mexico, S.A. de C.V.
Pearson Education Malaysia, Pte. Ltd
Pearson Education, Upper Saddle River, New Jersey

10 9 8 7 6 5 4 3 2
ISBN: 0-13-227691-7

CONTENTS

PREFACE

For many students a book entitled "symbolic interactionism" might be too academic, or too much like jargon, or a forbidding mystery. To me, however, it is exactly on the money. That is because this whole book is a description of a social psychology that focuses on the importance of interaction as the basis for what individuals and societies are made of, and that interaction is always symbolic.

I like symbolic interactionism because it addresses so many of the issues that are important for those people who wrestle with what the human being is and why the human being acts. It is a unique perspective in that it is part of what we call social science, yet it is very probabalistic in its predictions. That is, it does not normally identify a single "cause" when it understands human action. Instead, its studies focus on the history of action, the many decisions and choices people make as they act. Interaction with others is almost always important, but interaction takes us one way, then the other.

It treats the human being not as a passive responder to the environment, a being who is conditioned, who is pushed around by environment and biology. Instead, people are active in their environment, determining to a great extent what they do, think, and become. Symbolic interactionism is a context within which we can understand both the uniqueness of humankind and the ways human beings are similar to other animals.

The first edition of this book attempted to fulfill a promise I made to myself in graduate school: to write a clear, organized, and interesting introduction to symbolic interaction, a perspective that seemed to have interesting ideas and studies, but did not seem to hold together. Integration of the ideas became central to this book. I hope you will find this perspective interesting, organized, and useful.

This is the ninth edition. Each time I attempt to improve on what I have written before, it brings a certain humility to my work. Each time I revise I wonder how in the world I could ever have written what I had previously. The publisher this time chose excellent reviewers, and many of their suggestions were accepted. I try to update, correct errors and ambiguities, and reorganize chapters so that they make better sense. In this edition I have made changes in almost every chapter, and I have redone large parts of Chapters 4 (The Meaning of Symbols), 6 (The Nature of the Self), 9 (Human Action) and 10 (Social Interaction).

Because of a suggestion by a reviewer I decided to add interesting and relevant introductions to each chapter, highlighting the importance of what the chapter is. I believe this makes the book far more attractive to the student and is a good pedagogical tool.

Always I try to appeal to students who think sociologically and students who are attracted to the world of ideas. This book is an attempt to contribute to the mystery of what human beings are, their essence.

I dedicate this book to my wife, Susan, who continues to be my best friend and greatest supporter.

Joel M. Charon
Professor Emeritus
Minnesota State University Moorhead

CHAPTER ONE

The Nature of Perspective

The O.J. Simpson trial was very hard for me to ignore. There were many issues that had real importance to me. Indeed, many of the values I give lip service to and try to pursue in my life were challenged, questioned, put at risk. As a sociologist and teacher I have tried very hard to care about people, to seek justice, truth, equality. The trial forced me to ask many questions about these values, their importance to me, and their importance to others. I experienced a lot of conflict, because the issues involved were very complex to me.

One of the issues, of course, had to do with truth. Who has truth, and how can we tell who has truth? Indeed, is there a real truth to be found? What do the lawyers on both sides really believe? Which jury found the truth: the first, which determined that he was not guilty, or the second, which decided he was guilty? What is the best way to find the truth? Indeed, is the purpose of a trial in democracy not really to find the truth at all but simply to ensure that innocent people are never found guilty, recognizing that real truth is not attainable? What is the truth that O.J. Simpson really believes? Why is there so much disagreement between the African-American community and the white community in what constitutes the truth? Very often, in this case and in most others that people develop strong opinions about, we wonder: does the other side lie, do others know they are lying, are their conclusions inaccurate because they do not understand as much as we do, are they poorer thinkers than we are, are we simply seeing the same reality in a different way, are their values or emotions getting in the way of understanding, or perhaps are all of us really equally ignorant of the truth? These questions about truth bother most of us on occasion, and they bother some of us all the time.

It occurred to me that many of my questions made much more sense if I introduced the concept of "perspective," especially the division between the two communities. If I bring in perspective in trying to unravel this mystery, everything begins to make a lot more sense. People interact over a period of time; out of that interaction they come to share a perspective; what they see will be interpreted through that perspective; often each perspective tells us something very important about what is really true.

The word *perspective* has a long history with me. Many years ago, I read the following story by A. Averchenko. It underscores the difficulty the human has in knowing what is really happening "out there." When I first read it, I thought that it illustrated well how people could be so close-minded, narrow, and less than truthful. Eventually, it, like my questions about the Simpson trial, led me to see the importance of understanding the big role that perspective plays in all of our lives.

"Men are comic," she said, smiling dreamily. Not knowing whether this indicated praise or blame, I answered noncommittally: "Quite true."

"Really, my husband's a regular Othello. Sometimes I'm sorry I married him." I looked helplessly at her. "Until you explain—" I began.

"Oh, I forgot that you haven't heard. About three weeks ago, I was walking home with my husband through the square. I had a large black hat on, which suits me awfully well, and my cheeks were quite pink from walking. As we passed under a street light, a pale, dark-haired fellow standing nearby glanced at me and suddenly took my husband by his sleeve."

"'Would you oblige me with a light,' he says. Alexander pulled his arm away, stooped down, and quicker than lightning, banged him on the head with a brick. He fell like a log. Awful!"

"Why, what on earth made your husband get jealous all of a sudden?" She shrugged her shoulders. "I told you men are very comic."

Bidding her farewell, I went out, and at the corner came across her husband.

"Hello, old chap," I said. "They tell me you've been breaking people's heads."

He burst out laughing. "So, you've been talking to my wife. It was jolly lucky that brick came so pat into my hand. Otherwise, just think: I had about fifteen hundred rubles in my pocket, and my wife was wearing her diamond earrings."

"Do you think he wanted to rob you?"

"A man accosts you in a deserted spot, asks for a light and gets hold of your arm. What more do you want?"

Perplexed, I left him and walked on.

"There's no catching you today," I heard a voice from behind.

I looked around and saw a friend I hadn't set eyes upon for three weeks.

"Lord!" I exclaimed. "What on earth has happened to you?"

He smiled faintly and asked in turn: "Do you know whether any lunatics have been at large lately? I was attacked by one three weeks ago. I left the hospital only today."

With sudden interest, I asked: "Three weeks ago? Were you sitting in the square?"

"Yes, I was. The most absurd thing. I was sitting in the square, dying for a smoke. No matches! After ten minutes or so, a gentleman passes with some old hag. He was smoking. I go up to him, touch him on the sleeve and ask in my most polite manner: 'Can you oblige me with a light?' And what do you think? The madman stoops down, picks up something, and the next moment I am lying on the ground with a broken head, unconscious. You probably read about it in the newspapers."

I looked at him and asked earnestly: "Do you really believe you met up with a lunatic?"

"I am sure of it."

Anyhow, afterwards I was eagerly digging in old back numbers of the local paper. At last I found what I was looking for: a short note in the accident column.

UNDER THE INFLUENCE OF DRINK

Yesterday morning, the keepers of the square found on a bench a young man whose papers show him to be of good family. He had evidently fallen to the ground while in a state of extreme intoxication, and had broken his head on a nearby brick. The distress of the prodigal's parents is indescribable.

The seeker of truth wants to know: "What really happened?" The police, of course, will investigate situations such as this one in order to determine who is telling the truth. Usually they conclude "someone must be lying" or "someone is twisting the truth to fit his or her own selfish needs." It is difficult for the police— and for most of the rest of us—to believe that all may be telling what they believe to be the truth, and, indeed, each one may actually be capturing part of the truth. If we place ourselves in the positions of the people involved, however, and try very hard to imagine what they were seeing from their particular angle, we might begin to appreciate the powerful role that "perspective" plays as we try to see reality "as it really is." It actually may be that some of these perspectives bring the actor closer to reality than the others, but none of them is able to capture the whole of it. Not a single one of these is omniscient or all-inclusive.

The story is called "Point of View," and, in a sense, that is the very best definition of what a perspective is. A perspective is an angle on reality, a place where the individual stands as he or she looks at and tries to understand reality. An angle will always limit what one sees, since other angles—many of which may also be accurate—cannot be considered at the same time.

Human beings always see reality through perspectives. Once we begin to learn perspectives as children we are doomed—or blessed—to use them as our angle of vision. If we recognize this fact, then we must also admit there is no possible way that any individual can see all aspects of any situation simultaneously. Perspectives force us to pull out certain stimuli from our environment and to totally ignore other stimuli. Perspectives force us to make sense out of those stimuli in one way rather than another. Perspectives sensitize the individual to see parts of reality, they desensitize the individual to other parts, and they guide the individual to make sense of the reality to which he or she is sensitized. Seen in this light, a perspective is an absolutely basic part of everyone's existence, and it acts as a filter through which everything around us is perceived and interpreted. There is no possible way that the individual can encounter reality "in the raw," directly, as it really is, for whatever is seen can be only part of the real situation.

Whatever happened in the trial of O.J. Simpson, those involved are going to see it differently, and those observing it from the outside will inevitably disagree about what is and is not true about it. It becomes clearer to me why those in the African-American community will see it differently from me. What they see comes from a perspective that arose out of oppression. For hundreds of years there has been an ongoing discussion about events affecting people in that community. Learning about their own history and seeing how friends and neighbors are treated by many outside their community, including and especially the police and the courts, they develop a perspective that causes many individuals who hold it to notice a racist system of justice, to be skeptical of police officers, to wonder about the good intentions of white judges, white middle-class jurors, and white reporters. Does their perspective allow them to see the truth? Sometimes a part of it—never the full truth. And how about those who come from the perspective of whites outside of that community—will their perspective allow them to see the truth? Sometimes a part of it—never the full truth. Can those of us trying to understand reality benefit from the fact that there are many perspectives that people can use to see the reality of the O.J. Simpson trial? Of course we can. It is important for all of us who seek the truth to understand why some people, because of their perspective, will see the criminal justice system as unjust, while others will think of it as democratic and fair. It is probably both of these, and for the pursuer of truth to understand it well, both perspectives may be important to understand.

Perspectives are made up of words; it is these words that are used by the observer to make sense out of situations. In a way, the best definition of perspective is a *conceptual framework*, which emphasizes that perspectives are really interrelated sets of words used to order physical reality. The words we use cause us to make assumptions and value judgments about what we are seeing (and not seeing).

Reality, for the individual, depends on the words used to look at situations. If we examine the story by Averchenko in this light, it becomes obvious that the differences between actors' viewpoints depend on the words they used to *see*. The woman uses "Othello," "married," "black hat" ("which suits me"), "pale, dark-haired fellow," all of which reveal that in that situation she was "seeing" according to a perspective associated with a woman concerned with her attractiveness. Her husband, fearful of losing his money, uses these words: "fifteen hundred rubles," "diamond earrings," "accosts," "deserted," "gets hold of your arm." In the O.J. Simpson and Averchenko examples, and in all other cases, too, certain aspects of the situation were pulled out, emphasized, and integrated, according to each person's *perspective*, each person's conceptual framework. And in each case, the conceptual framework led to various value judgments and assumptions.

In this same way, whites who look at the O.J. trial might use words such as *evidence, DNA, science, injustice, biased jurors, ruthless lawyers,* and *abuse* to describe what took place in the first trial, in which he was found not guilty. In the African-American community words such as *planted evidence, racist police,* and *discrimination* might be used by people who saw the same reality. There is probably some truth in each perspective, and there may be ideas that are downright false. However, if we focus on people's personal life experiences, as well as on the words they use among one another, we can begin to see why people differ in how they see reality, and it is not simply that one side is correct and the other is wrong or that one side is telling the truth and the other is lying.

It is also a mistake to believe that individuals have simply one perspective that is important to them. There may have been nine African Americans on the jury, and the African-American perspective may have been important to some of them, but other perspectives also came to be important to them, and sometimes even more important. Being on the jury became a perspective. Each individual therefore brought an occupational perspective, and each had a perspective associated with age and gender and class. It is a mistake to claim that this jury was simply made up of nine African Americans and three other persons; perspectives are complex in every situation, and being African American may not have been as important to people on the jury as it was for those people who were in the wider community and who did not have to see the situation from the perspective of jury member.

A college education, in many ways, is an introduction to a variety of perspectives, each telling us something about what is going on around us. Sociology, psychology, history, humanities, art, George Orwell, Machiavelli, Freud, James Joyce, and Malcolm X—each represents a perspective that we might adopt as our own, integrate with others we have, or forget entirely after our final exam. Each perspective is a different approach to "reality," and each, therefore, tells us something but cannot include everything.

It seems that the most difficult aspect of "perspective" to grasp is that perspectives cannot capture the whole of physical reality. It is probably because we want so desperately to know that what we believe is true that we cannot face the fact that whatever we know must be seen only as a truth gained from a certain *perspective*. We cannot, for example, even agree totally on what a simple object is. One day in the middle of winter, I went outside and picked up something from the ground and brought it to class. I asked, "What is this?" The answers were snow, a snowball, ice crystals, frozen water, something you are showing us to make some point, something little boys use to frighten little girls, the beginning of the world's biggest snowman, molecules, dirty snow, a very interesting shape to draw, the symbol of cold weather. Of course, my response was, "What is this really?" And, of course, the response by them was that it is all of those things, and probably many, many more things. Indeed, that physical reality was interpreted in many ways, depending entirely on the perspective the students used to see it. No one of those perspectives could ever claim to have grasped the true essence of that which was brought in from outside. And even if we might try to claim that all of those perspectives together captured the object completely, we would be missing the point: perspectives are almost infinite; thus, we can never claim to have found all the possible perspectives we might use to see anything.

Human beings are limited by their perspectives; they cannot see outside of their perspectives. Yet, perspectives are vitally important: they make it possible for human beings to make sense out of what is "out there."

It is important for me to emphasize that I am *not* saying here that there is no truth at all or that all opinions about reality are equally correct. Unfortunately, many people do in fact believe that there is no truth at all, and many will try to interpret my discussion as a way to support their position. My view is that reality does in fact exist—that is, there is something actually happening out there in the world—but we cannot know it completely or in any perfectly accurate way because we always see it through filters we are here calling perspectives.

NEW PERSPECTIVES MEAN NEW REALITIES

The Autobiography of Malcolm X is a fascinating book and movie about an important leader in the Civil Rights movement during the 1960s. Here is an individual whose life situations caused him to see the reality around him in very different ways. He changed because his truths changed, and his truths changed because each perspective he took on as he interacted with others opened up whole new worlds for him. In seventh grade, for instance, he was elected class president, and in looking back, he reports:

> And I was proud: I'm not going to say I wasn't. In fact, by then, I didn't really have much feeling about being a Negro, because I was trying so hard, in every way I could, to be white....remember one thing that marred this time for me: the movie "Gone With the Wind." When it played in Mason, I was the only Negro in the theater, and when Butterfly McQueen went into her act, I felt like crawling under the rug.[1]

---

[1]From *The Autobiography of Malcolm X*, by Malcolm X, with the assistance of Alex Haley, pp. 31–32. Copyright © 1965 by Alex Haley and Betty Shabazz. Reprinted by permission of Random House, Inc., New York, and the Hutchinson Publishing, Random Century Group Ltd., London.

Malcolm remembers his perspective changing in school:

> It was then that I began to change—inside. I drew away from white people. I came to class, and I answered when called upon. It became a physical strain simply to sit in Mr. Ostrowski's class. Where "nigger" had slipped off my back before, wherever I heard it now, I stopped and looked at whoever said it. And they looked surprised that I did. (p. 37)

Then in New York:

> "Man, you can't tell him nothing!" they'd exclaim. And they couldn't. At home in Roxbury, they would see me parading with Sophia, dressed in my wild zoot suits. Then I'd come to work, loud and wild and half-high on liquor or reefers, and I'd stay that way, jamming sandwiches at people until we got to New York. Off the train, I'd go through the Grand Central Station afternoon rush-hour crowd, and many white people simply stopped in their tracks to watch me pass. The drape and the cut of a zoot suit showed to the best advantage if you were tall—and I was over six feet. My conk was fire-red. I was really a clown, but my ignorance made me think I was "sharp." My knob-toed, orange-colored "kick-up" shoes were nothing but Florsheims, the ghetto's Cadillac of shoes in those days....And then, between Small's Paradise, the Braddock Hotel, and other places—as much as my twenty- or twenty-five dollar pay would allow, I drank liquor, smoked marijuana, painted the Big Apple red with increasing numbers of friends, and finally in Mrs. Fisher's rooming house I got a few hours of sleep before the "Yankee Clipper" rolled again. (p. 79)

Malcolm has been seeing the world from the perspective of zoot suits, reefers, conk, Cadillac of shoes, but he is suddenly exposed to a new perspective, which opens up a new world to him:

> When Reginald left, he left me rocking with some of the first serious thoughts I had ever had in my life: that the white man was fast losing his power to oppress and exploit the dark world; that the dark world was starting to rise to rule the world again, as it had before; that the white man's world was on the way down, it was on the way out. (p. 162)

Because of this new perspective, Malcolm X becomes sensitive to things in his world he never really saw before. His past takes on a new meaning, and the many situations that took place between blacks and whites in his past are seen differently. He joins the Black Muslims, and he becomes a great leader in that movement. At the height of his activity in that movement, the words he preaches reflect his perspective:

> No *sane* black man really wants integration! No *sane* white man really wants integration. No *sane* black man really believes that the white man ever will give the black man anything more than token integration. No! The Honorable Elijah Muhammed teaches that for the black man in America the only solution is complete *separation* from the white man! (p. 248)

And, finally, Malcolm's perspective changes once more, as a result of a pilgrimage he makes to Mecca. As his perspective changes, the world around him becomes transformed:

> It was in the Holy World that my attitude was changed, by what I experienced there, and by what I witnessed there, in terms of brotherhood—not just brotherhood toward me, but brotherhood between all men, of all nationalities and complexions, who were there. And now that I am back in America, my attitude here concerning white people has to be governed by what my black brothers and I experience here, and what we witness here—in terms of brotherhood. The *problem* here in America is that we meet such a small minority of individual so-called "good," or "brotherly" white people. (p. 368)

Malcolm X's autobiography is an excellent description of an individual's undergoing profound changes in perspective. His story is not unique, but how one's perspective can change is probably more obvious to us in his story than it would be in many others.

Not only do we all undergo *basic* change in our perspectives many times throughout our lives, but our perspectives also change from situation to situation, often many times during the same day. Few of us have one perspective that we can apply to every situation we encounter. Perspectives are situational: in the classroom my perspective is that of teacher-sociologist; in my home it becomes father or husband; on a fishing trip it changes to "seasoned fisherman." Each situation calls forth a different role, which means a different perspective. Some roles we play may have more than one perspective we can use (there are many different *student* perspectives we might draw on, depending on the situation we encounter), and some perspectives may apply to more than one role we play (e.g., a Christian may apply his or her perspective as a Christian to several roles). Perspectives are a complex matter.

Some of us confuse a perspective with an opinion. We might say: "My perspective is that I don't want to go to war in Iraq!" It is critical to realize that an opinion about Iraq arises *from* your perspective. It is the eyeglasses you use to see war in Iraq. It is the point of view that you are taking in examining Iraq. What we actually see (our perceptions) and what we believe (our beliefs) are embedded in perspectives we use. (See Figure 1–1)

A perspective, then, by its very nature, is a bias; it contains assumptions, value judgments, and ideas; it orders the world; it divides it up in a certain way; and, as a result, it influences our action in the world. A father and his son see each other from at least two perspectives (one the father's and the other the son's) and thus define a situation that affects them both (e.g., the use of the car) in two very different ways. Neither is necessarily wrong nor in error, although they may certainly disagree. A candidate for president of the United States may see the society as in need of change and promise all kinds of possibilities, but once that person is in office, his or her perspective will change and his or her behavior will be affected. It is not, as may appear to us, that the new president is dishonest, but rather that the definition of the situation has

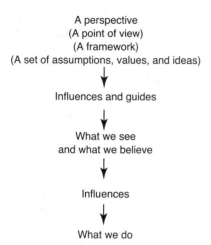

A perspective
(A point of view)
(A framework)
(A set of assumptions, values, and ideas)

↓

Influences and guides

↓

What we see
and what we believe

↓

Influences

↓

What we do

FIGURE 1–1

changed because that person now sees the world from the perspective of president, not of candidate.

PERSPECTIVES ARE SOCIALLY CREATED

The Autobiography of Malcolm X highlights another important quality of perspective. In every case his perspective changed as he entered into and out of various groups of people and took on new roles in life. As a junior high student he had one perspective, as an African American in a junior high with mostly whites he had another, then as a young man on the make in the big city another, then as a Black Muslim still another. In each case here we see someone changing as he changes groups or roles; likewise, almost all of our own perspectives change with our roles. Examine the points of view we take on the world. Examine why we believe them: "Because they are true?" Maybe. But are we encouraged to believe them by our particular place in society? Definitely. Groups and roles are what give most of us the filters through which we see reality. Not only do our biases come from our perspectives, but our perspectives in turn are not simply chosen by each of us; they are products in large part of the social worlds within which we move.

ARE ALL PERSPECTIVES CREATED EQUAL?

Of course, almost all of us will believe that our perspectives are the right ones. It is extremely difficult to evaluate one's own perspective. And in a discussion with someone who is getting the best of the argument, we are sometimes tempted to assert that "all of us are equally right—we just have different perspectives!"

Whose perspective is better—a medical doctor, a minister, or a philosopher? The Jewish, Islamic, Christian, or atheist? It depends in part on what is being understood. It also may depend on whether or not one is open minded. If we are careful we might evaluate its limits, assumptions, focus, its history of understanding, its honesty, and whatever else that might determine its ability to understand.

Most of us do little in evaluating perspectives. Too often we simply reject perspectives we know little about or we have some irrational reason to stay away. It is very difficult to evaluate perspectives in a rational way. Some of us do not even try; we even accept "all perspectives" as valid. Sometimes we wonder: is the human world simply a place where everyone has his or her own perspective and no one is right or wrong? Although some academics believe that we should treat all perspectives equally, most academics certainly do not, and symbolic interactionists normally do not.

Yes, our social life creates perspectives that influence our perception and action. Yes, our perspectives are always limited and biased. Yes, it is rare for us to critically evaluate our own perspectives as well as why we continue to believe them. However, human beings have gone a long way in understanding the universe despite their dependence on perspective. If we are serious about understanding something, we need to establish standards for judging perspectives, such as using careful observation, good thinking, objectivity, recognizing the possibility of error, and reputation for successful accumulation of knowledge. We will never know exactly what reality is, but we can get closer and closer to it if we use good perspectives and are careful.

Most natural and social scientists defend their perspectives because they make efforts to discipline their personal bias. The fruits of science also support the fact that the scientific perspective is accurate in studying and understanding the natural and social worlds.

Of course, there are problems with science also. For example, many questions we seek answers to cannot be studied by science. Or, sometimes scientists do not follow the disciplined rules laid out for purposes of understanding; some scientists simply do not do good science. Sometimes scientists mistakenly think they have the "truth" rather than simply a way of understanding reality. Yet, even for its limitations, science has clearly delivered a great deal of understanding of the universe.

Philosophy too has helped us to understand many issues because it has rules that attempt to determine the truth or falsehood of its conclusions. Some brilliant individuals and groups have created reliable perspectives. Some who have had firsthand experience as a soldier, an artist, a businessperson, a teacher—for example—can contribute to understanding in many matters.

Comparing perspectives is a difficult task, but it is not impossible if we are careful. If we simply think that all perspectives are equally good or bad, we are missing a great deal. And if we uncritically believe that our perspective is the full truth we are also missing a great deal.

Summary

It may be beneficial to summarize this chapter by simply restating the basic points and by listing some examples of perspectives:

1. Perspectives are points of view—eyeglasses, sensitizers—that guide our perceptions of reality.
2. Perspectives can further be described as conceptual frameworks—a set of assumptions, values, and beliefs used to organize our perceptions and control our behavior.
3. The individual has many perspectives. Each acts as a filter and therefore does not allow the individual to see all of reality. Each perspective is created in the individual's social life. Each also changes as the individual's groups and roles change.
4. No object can simply be understood from only one perspective. Many perspectives can be used to see the same object, and each might tell us something important about that object.
5. It is important to be careful which perspective we use for understanding. Some perspectives will help us understand and some will actually stand in the way.

Some Examples of Perspectives: Informal and Formal Perspectives

One way of understanding how important perspectives are is to list many examples. We might divide all perspectives into informal everyday perspectives and formal written ones. In a given day, I might use many informal perspectives: male, instructor, husband, consumer, opera fan, friend, poker player, homeowner, amateur counselor, past chair of the Department of Sociology and Criminal Justice, employee and then retiree of Minnesota State University Moorhead. I may use other formal perspectives, however: sociologist, scientist, and existentialist, for example. Furthermore, we might also divide up sociologist, scientist, and existentialist into several subperspectives, each one causing us to see a slightly different focus on reality. We can briefly illustrate the diversity of perspectives individuals might use. Of course, this list is not all-inclusive, only suggestive of the diversity of perspectives possible.

1. Some informal everyday perspectives:
   student
   daughter
   mother
   pedestrian
   unemployed
   stranger
   shopper

2. Some formal perspectives—nonscientific:
    stamp collector
    artist
    poet
    Chinese
    Jewish
    religious
    Republican
    left fielder
3. Some formal perspectives—scientific:
    biologist
    physicist
    chemist
    astronomer
    psychologist
    anthropologist
    economist
    sociologist
4. Some perspectives within sociology:
    Marxist
    symbolic interactionist
    Weberian
    Durkheimian
    postmodern
    conflict
    positivist

Any one individual is made up of several of these kinds of perspectives and may enter any one of them in a situation. Indeed, once in the situation, the individual can change perspectives or even find that the initial perspective is being transformed as he or she interacts with others. A person may in a single day be student, daughter, mother, artist, Asian, American, Jewish, biologist, sociologist, Marxist, and Parsonian. In each perspective a different world will be seen, and perhaps a new way of looking at old things will be revealed.

Perspective is a wonderful word to understand. It is also, I believe, a wonderful way to introduce this book. The title of this book is *Symbolic Interactionism*, and its purpose is to focus on one perspective within social psychology. Symbolic interactionism—as are physics, chemistry, sociology, existentialism, psychology—is a perspective, and that means it is *one way of understanding reality*. Because it is part of social science, it focuses on the human being and tries to understand human behavior. Because it is part of sociology, it attempts to uncover the significance of our social life. Yet, it is incomplete, it exaggerates certain qualities of the human being, and it ignores other qualities. It is therefore limited, but so are all other perspectives. The real question we need to ponder is how much does it accurately tell us about the human being and how much does it ignore?

Symbolic interactionism is a very unusual perspective, in my opinion. It is unlike psychology and much of sociology. For some people it may seem like common sense because we recognize that its ideas explain so well what we all do in the situations we encounter. Yet, to most of us the ideas here will be new and will sometimes seem strange. After all, we have been exposed to other social sciences in our search for truth—psychology, sociology, and anthropology, for example—and these have become familiar to us. Symbolic interactionism will often cause us to question some of the assumptions we have come to accept from those other perspectives, and it is difficult to break away, even temporarily, from them. You are, however, invited to give this perspective a chance. It is far from perfect, but it promises much, as you will undoubtedly recognize. We will begin to look at it in Chapter 3. Before that, however, it is important to examine briefly some other perspectives in social science in order to see symbolic interactionism in a larger context and to better recognize its uniqueness as we describe it through the rest of the chapters.

The Perspective
of Social Science

Science is a perspective. It is one way people are able to understand the universe. It is not "Truth," but scientific understanding has changed what we know about the world, and it continues to show us that its accuracy allows us to build, fly, make our lives longer, help us be healthy, go into space, and create technology that many of us depend on.

Most of us do not use science as our perspective. We get our understandings by other means. Think of yourself. Where do you gain your understanding? How do you know that your ideas are actually true? How do you know what to believe?

FIVE WAYS OF KNOWING

There are probably five ways we all find our "truths." Some of us simply accept what others teach us. *We accept authority.* Someone who we love, idolize, respect, even fear tells us what to believe and we accept it. Of course, accepting authority is not necessarily bad, especially if the authority understands something important, if the authority has arrived at his or her ideas carefully, is able to somehow prove his or her points. Authority, on the other hand, can manipulate us, trick us, overwhelm us, teach us misunderstandings, and so on.

The second way we find our "truths" is *from our culture.* All of us live in a social world that teaches us what we should believe. Sometimes we are taught great understandings that have been passed down through the ages; sometimes we continue to accept ideas that are not true but since others all around us believe them we accept them.

The third way is *from personal experience.* Because "we were there" in the "actual situation" we believe that we are able to understand. Yet, personal experience is always interpreted through a perspective that may or may not help us understand what we are experiencing. And, if we are honest, we must be wary of personal experience since it is one experience by one person that may or may not be generalizable to anyone else. On the other hand, experience allows us to see parts of reality that others do not.

The fourth way is *from carefully and rationally thinking through the ideas* we come to believe. From what we learn and from what we experience, we carefully create understanding. We are able to apply evidence to what we come to believe, evidence that is governed by rules of good thinking. Good thinking becomes a measuring stick that we use to test the truth or falsehood of our ideas.

The fifth way is *careful observation.* Science is a perspective that relies on empiricism to understand reality. This does not make science perfect, or always the best. It simply asks us to examine reality according to the measuring stick of carefully observing nature in order to understand nature. Like thinking, scientists are supposed to use evidence to test the truth or falsehood of an idea.

This book is an attempt to introduce you to an interesting and useful perspective in social science. Because it claims to be a part of social science, its conclusions are based on careful observation. It does not claim to be truth with a capital T, but it does claim that by carefully observing human beings we can understand why they think and act as they do.

SCIENCE AS A PERSPECTIVE

Although the roots of science go back to the ancient world, science as a dominant way of understanding is a recent development in human history. For much of history, culture (including religious thought), personal experience, and authority were the major guides to understanding. By the seventeenth century science was becoming a major perspective, and by the eighteenth century social science was important for many. Social science studied human beings as individuals and as part of society. It actually had a difficult time convincing people that science could be used to understand human beings. It also came in direct conflict with religion which emphasized authority rather than critical thinking or careful observation.

It was Immanuel Kant (1724–1804), an important philosopher who reminded us that there does not have to be a conflict between religion and science. Kant was a believer in God, a Christian who was concerned about the assault of reason and science on traditional religious belief. He was also critical of those religious thinkers who believed that religion must be defended by rational and scientific evidence. Kant wanted to make it explicit: science and religion are two perspectives on the universe, and each has something important to say.

Kant argued that there are two worlds in the universe: a world he called *phenomena* and a world he called the *noumena.* The world of phenomena is the world we can experience with our senses; it is open to scientific and rational investigation. Science observes the world of phenomena—the natural world—and reason orders those observations. The world of noumena is above scientific investigation; it cannot be approached by empirical observation, because it is not physical or empirical. Although many people have attempted to approach this world through reason, they have failed. Kant stated in the preface to the second edition of *The Critique of Pure Reason:* those who try to use reason or science, or both, to understand the world of noumena are engaged in "mock-contests," never "gaining an inch of ground." Kant believes that reason and science, as good as they are for understanding many things, are not able to understand God, immortality, soul, free will, sin, and whatever else that does not belong in the world of phenomena. We can imagine such things, but it is impossible to investigate them in the same way as we can investigate nature. Science and reason are important ways to understand reality, but they are limited. Science is but one perspective, and that perspective allows us to understand nature—the phenomenal world—but science is unable to sensitize us to the other world—the noumena—nor should we use it to try.

Physical objects such as plants, livers, wastepaper baskets, dogs, CD players, and computers are clearly in the world of phenomena and therefore subject to scientific investigation. God, heavenly angels, and the devil are clearly noumena and therefore beyond science. But how about human beings? Can science be used to investigate them, or are they above nature? Can science uncover the secrets of human life? Or, are we simply engaged in "mock-contests" since humans are not part of nature. Human beings, Kant proposed, are both part of nature and above nature. To the scientist, the study of the human being is part of the phenomenal universe, understandable through careful observation, measured by scientific tools, physical like all other things in nature. Yet, many scientists and others believe that the study of the human being is part of the noumenal universe, and that science cannot really capture or understand whole layers of the human being. We are subject to laws of nature, open to scientific investigation, and subject to natural cause. We may also be beings with a "soul," perhaps possessing "free will," perhaps born with a "conscience," perhaps having "everlasting life."

The debate between freedom and determinism is central to religion, philosophy, the humanities, and certainly social science. Social science as science tends to make the human being subject to natural causation. There are reasons humans do what they do. There are reasons that people become religious, criminal, intellectual, or revolutionary. There are reasons why wars exist, democracy develops, globalization occurs, and terrorism increases throughout the world. Social science, by its very nature, tends to ignore free will. If we follow Kant, however, we can still believe in free will even though we cannot understand freedom scientifically. It is a quality that is not physical, not part of the world of phenomena.

This is also true of morality. To the social scientist, conscience, goodness, evil are a result of society, something that results of socialization. To many peoples these concepts are universally true and to be accepted, and are much more than something that humans learn.

To some of us social science ignores whole levels of reality. In some cases when we treat human as part of the physical world, we come to ignore some important qualities and end up missing the essence of the human being. Even some social scientists are critical of those who only look at the physical human.

However, in the end, science must be understood as a perspective, and therefore limited, incomplete, based on a set of assumptions, a viewpoint from which we can understand many things. If we are honest, I think, we should probably agree that science has expanded our understanding of a great deal of our natural world, even though some technology arising from science can sometimes have negative consequences. There is every reason to believe that science will continue to bring us many new understandings. Its evidence of usefulness is all around us.

SOCIAL SCIENCE AS A PERSPECTIVE

Since its beginning, social science has attempted to apply the tools of science to understand the human being. As a perspective, it assumes that humans are part of nature, the phenomenal world. What we think and do is caused by forces that are understandable. Although we often try very hard to capture free will in our work, we almost always end up showing that free will is limited by factors we have identified. Our goal is almost always to understand causality to the neglect of free will.

Peter Berger (1963) clearly presents the problem of finding a place for freedom in social science:

> Freedom is not empirically available. More precisely, while freedom may be experienced by us as a certainty along with other empirical certainties, it is not open to demonstration by any scientific methods. If we wish to follow Kant, freedom is also not available rationally, that is, cannot be demonstrated by philosophical methods based on the operations of pure reason ... the elusiveness of freedom with regard to scientific comprehension does not lie so much in the unspeakable mysteriousness of the phenomenon ... as in the *strictly limited scope of scientific methods*. An empirical science must operate within certain assumptions, one of which is that of universal causality. Every object of scientific scrutiny is presumed to have an anterior cause. An object, or an event, that is its own cause lies outside the scientific universe of discourse. Yet freedom has precisely that character. For this reason, no amount of scientific research will ever uncover a phenomenon that can be designated as free. Whatever may appear as free within the subjective consciousness of an individual will find its place in the scientific scheme as a link in some chain of causation....
>
> In terms of social-scientific method, one is faced with a way of thinking that assumes a priori that the human world is a causally closed system. The method would not be scientific if it thought otherwise. Freedom as a special kind of cause is excluded from this system a priori. In terms of social phenomena, the social scientist must assume an infinite regress of causes, none of them holding a privileged ontological status.

The scientist, Berger continues, might try to explain an event through one sociological concept, and, if it cannot be explained that way, the scientist will try to explain it by another. If that is unsatisfactory, there are political causes to be investigated, or economic, psychological, or biological ones. The explanation, however, will still be within the scientific perspective. Within this perspective, the scientist cannot "encounter freedom. There is no way of perceiving freedom, either in oneself or another human being, except through a subjective inner certainty that dissolves as soon as it is attacked with the tools of scientific analysis" (p. 124).

Social scientists recognize this issue, and if pushed, most would agree that social science is only one way to understand the human being. If we are to understand the human being, social science is a tough path, but so long as we argue that there are reasons why humans think and act as they do, we must do what we can to measure and understand such concepts.

Some social scientists are critical of the bias that science creates when we try to understand humans scientifically. We tend to ignore too much. Indeed, Hampden-Turner (1970:1–15) argues that without realizing it, we have created a view of the human being that "concentrates on the repetitive, predictable, invariable, aspects of the human." We concentrate on "visible externalizes" that is "exposed to the general gaze," rather than the subjective world of dreams, philosophies and the whole mental life of those whose physical movements we observe. We concentrate on the various parts of the person, analyzing the parts in order to understand the whole. We ultimately miss the whole.

Clearly, social science is a perspective. I think of myself as a social scientist. My purpose for writing this book is to introduce you to symbolic interactionism, an important perspective within social science. Social science has produced much that has helped us predict, control, improve, and sometimes even mess up the condition of the human being. Social science is useful although it—like all perspectives—is a bias. Authorities that I read and evaluate tend to be social scientists. I tend to believe that humans are part of the natural universe which includes society. I also tend to believe that social science, as difficult as it is, continues to bring an important understanding of the human being.

Within social science there are many perspectives (we might call these subperspectives), and each one is somewhat unique in its approach to the human being. Each one concentrates on a different aspect of reality, and must naturally ignore other aspects picked up by other social sciences. Anthropology, economics, political science, perhaps history and geography are considered social sciences, but because my interest here is in symbolic interactionism, I will spend a short time introducing three: sociology, psychology, and social psychology.

Sociology As a Perspective

Sociology is the study of society. It is the study of how society works and how society is an important cause of human action. In fact, it is not just the study of society, but the study of all organized life, from small groups and formal organizations to communities and society. It begins with the assumption that humans have always existed within society, that society is the source of our qualities as a species (for example, conscience, language, mind, self), and that it is the source of our qualities as individuals (interests, values, talents, ideas, and so on).

Society is external to the human being, yet through socialization society is internalized and becomes part of each actor. Society is made up of social patterns, developed in the past and important to us living in society.

For example, social structure is a social pattern in society. Social structure was formed in the past, and we are all placed in it at birth and as we go through life. We are placed in a class position in social structure, and gender and ethnic group membership are also positions. We live within a political structure, and in every organization we encounter an authority structure. Even the small groups we exist in develop structures that influence us.

Another social pattern that exists in society is culture. Culture is the consensus developed by people over a long history. It is their shared view of reality, the basic ideas, values, and rules they have come to believe in. That culture is something we are born into and are socialized to accept. Its ideas become our truths; its rules become our morals, customs, and laws; its values become what we regard as important in life.

We are also born into a society that has developed a particular set of social institutions. These are the grooves that are there for us to follow and participate in. We live within hundreds of institutions: some, for example, are political institutions; others might be economic, familial, religious, military, criminal justice, educational, health care, or recreational. So, in U.S. society, the corporation, private health insurance, a volunteer army, and public education exist as social institutions. How the individual acts in society is shaped by such grooves.

In *Invitation to Sociology,* Peter Berger describes the power of society in his conclusion to Chapter 4:

> We are located in society not only in space but in time. Our society is a historical entity that extends temporally beyond any individual biography. Society antedates us and it will survive us. It was there before we were born and it will be there after we are dead. Our lives are but episodes in its majestic march through time. In sum, society is the walls of our imprisonment in history (p. 92).

To the sociologist, therefore, humans exist within a massive reality—society— developed historically, regarded by us as legitimate, telling us what to do and what to think, and shaping our behavior through a variety of mechanisms.

But society also exists within all of us. In a sense, we agree to this imprisonment precisely because the society has penetrated us through socialization; we have, in a real sense, become what society has demanded. This is the role of socialization, and it is an important part of what sociology examines. Berger continues:

> Society not only controls our movements, but shapes our identity, our thought and our emotions. The structures of society become the structures of our own

consciousness. Society does not stop at the surface of our skins. Society penetrates us as much as it envelopes us. Our bondage to society is not so much established by conquest as by collusion ... The walls of our imprisonment were there before we appeared on the scene, but they are ever rebuilt by ourselves. We are betrayed into captivity with our own cooperation (p. 121).

Sociology is a perspective that thinks of the human being as an actor. We act out roles. Think of roles as scripts handed out to us in the positions we fill in an organization. A male in society, a student, a sociology major, an employee at a department store, and an unemployed shoe salesman are all positions in society, and all of them direct what the actor does in the organization. This concept is significant because sociologists tend to see actors as changing all through life, from situation to situation, because we change our roles in society and because society itself changes. How we act in life, then, is tied, once again, to society.

There is, in this perspective, a lot of determinism. That is, humans are thought to be linked to society, products of society, controlled by society. The purpose of sociology is to understand this link and to understand how society itself works. Many sociologists will claim that I am exaggerating the determinism of sociology, and perhaps I am, but it is important to see this determinism as central to any social-scientific perspective that seeks to understand *why* humans act the way they do. Sociology describes society as an important cause of human action. Its whole conceptual framework aims at this relation between society and individuals, as do its studies. Sociology has a different perspective than other social sciences, such as psychology, since its focus is society. Sociology's perspective is useful because it does help explain a great deal about human behavior. Its perspective, however, can sensitize us to only part of the picture, and it is really up to other social-scientific perspectives to help us understand the other parts.

Psychology As a Perspective

If sociology is most easily defined as the study of society, then psychology is most easily defined as the study of the person. It is an understanding of how the person works and how the characteristics of the person influence what he or she does.

Psychology is similar to sociology in some ways. It has a particular perspective, and it is a social science. As a science, it attempts to apply the tools developed in natural science. More than sociology, it has relied heavily on the controlled laboratory experiment (indeed, some psychologists will define a perspective as scientific only if the controlled laboratory experiment is the norm), and it has usually considered the human being as part of nature, in the world of phenomena, moved by natural laws, created, shaped.

Because there are many schools of psychology (each can be called a perspective), there are differences among psychologists. Psychologists, however, as do sociologists, seem to share certain assumptions, ideas, and concepts, sensitizing the investigator to certain aspects of the human being while neglecting others. Let us emphasize again that a focus is not a fault; it is a limitation of every perspective, and there seems to be no way to escape it. Perspectives are absolutely essential for understanding, but by their very nature they do not capture the whole of reality.

The threads of the psychological perspective are not always clear, and there is always a danger that someone who is not a psychologist will mistake the perspective. However, it seems that all schools of psychology emphasize the following:

1. The *individual* organism, shaped by various combinations of heredity and environment, social and nonsocial forces.

2. An underlying belief that a person's performance at any point is tied to previous experience. This can be labeled a *predispositional orientation.* For example, the brain developed earlier predisposes behavior. In psychoanalysis as well as various other personality theories, early childhood training causes one to act later on in a certain manner. In learning theory previous conditioning causes behavior; in Gestalt psychology it may be the person's conceptual framework or cognitive structure developed in the past that is all-important.

3. An attempt to explain behavior in relation to the *organism.* Change is explained in relation to change in the organism (if we change the "person," behavior will change); stability of behavior is explained in the structure of the person ("that is simply the way the person is; people don't really change").

4. A focus on *personality traits,* qualities of the person, developed over time, such as aggressiveness, shyness, lack of self-confidence, and compulsiveness. Some psychologists would call a person's attitude a trait, and some would even call intelligence and habit traits. Whatever these qualities are called, they are similar in that they have been developed earlier in the person's life, become a part of the person, and are brought into a situation, causing behavior. The term *personality* or *person* implies that these traits constitute a system, a network of qualities, an interrelated set of qualities. A stability within the person is assumed: from past to present and from situation to situation. One's actions are thought to be the result of "the way the person is."

5. The idea that behavior is not a result of situation or social patterns but is personal and trait related, even though traits might be developed over the long run by social influences.

Commonalities and Differences Between Sociology and Psychology

It should be emphasized here that the psychological perspective differs significantly from the sociological. Although both emphasize studying human behavior, one (psychology) focuses on how the person develops, how the person works, and how the person's qualities influence behavior from situation to situation. The other (sociology) focuses on how society develops, how society works, and how society's qualities influence the individual in different situations. In psychology, change happens to or within the organism, whereas in sociology change occurs in society, in the individual's roles in society, in different organizations one belongs to.

In both cases, the focus is on the human being's behavior, behavior that is caused by forces beyond the individual's own will. The individual is conceptualized as passive in relation to these forces; that is, we are shaped, we are not actively shaping our behavior or our environment as individuals. By taking a scientific perspective, social science has focused on those aspects of the human being molded by the biological, physical, and social worlds. The purpose of social science has been to try to identify those forces.

There are, of course, exceptions to a deterministic and passive view of human beings in both sociology and psychology. Erich Fromm provides one such exceptional view in psychology, as do such psychologists as Carl Rogers and Abraham Maslow. Indeed, clinical psychology emphasizes the active human more than academic psychology does. Cognitive psychology in recent years has taken psychology more in the direction of an active conception of the human being. In sociology, Max Weber is a fine example of someone who takes a more active approach, as do phenomenology and dramaturgical sociology.

It is, in my opinion, the passive, determined, and nonreflective human being who has been portrayed in both psychology and sociology for the past two hundred years. We sometimes will claim that humans really are active beings, but in our academic pursuits determinism is usually at work. This approach seems perfectly understandable since the goals of social science have always been to examine the human as part of the natural universe, governed by laws that can be discovered through careful research. A liberal education in social science tends to create an image of the human as being caused or shaped by factors in the natural world, as are all other living organisms. Indeed, other social science perspectives (such as anthropology, economics, geography) do seem not to question this image but, on the contrary, to reinforce it. And, in most recent years, the continuing emphasis on human biology adds considerably to psychological determinism. Increasingly, we have come to believe that the key to human behavior lies in DNA, that it all comes down to what we inherit before we are even born.

The Perspective of Social Psychology in Psychology

Of all perspectives in social science, social psychology is the most difficult to describe. Some would argue that it is not a perspective at all but a conglomeration of topics and studies with little unity. Others will argue that it is a discipline in its own right, with roots in both psychology and sociology but with its own distinct history and subject matter.

It is useful to realize that two social psychologies have developed, sometimes influencing each other but often developing as parallel and without overlap. We might call one "psychological social psychology" and the other "sociological social psychology."

Psychological social psychology has its roots, to a large extent, in Gestalt psychology, an important perspective in psychology first developed in the late-nineteenth and early-twentieth centuries. Gestalt psychology emphasizes the central importance of *perception* in human behavior: the human being acts according to how the situation is perceived. Gestalt psychologists have attempted to isolate various principles of perception in order to better understand how the individual organizes the stimuli he or she confronts. Gestalt psychology as such is entirely psychological in its orientation, but because of the work of some Gestaltists—especially Solomon Asch and Kurt Lewin—a social dimension was added to the framework, which greatly influenced the direction of social psychology.

The social psychology that developed out of Gestalt psychology focuses on interpersonal influence. "Social psychology," writes Elliot Aronson (1992), is the study of social influence, "the influences that people have upon the beliefs and behavior of others" (p. 6). The basic question to be answered is how other people around us influence our thoughts, feelings, attitudes, and behaviors. The focus is neither society nor the person, but on the present situation one is in. Besides our past and society's control the individual is influenced by forces in the immediate environment, most importantly other people. The study of social influence includes how speakers, including media, influence our thoughts and actions, how groups form our attitudes, and what makes people attractive.

By far the most important focus investigated in psychological social psychology has been the development of attitudes and attitude change. An attitude is usually conceptualized as a person's set of beliefs and feelings toward an object that predisposes the person to act in a certain manner when confronted by that object (or class of objects). Attitudes are really developed in social situations, they are difficult to change and when they do change it is also usually due to social influence. For many people—social scientists, teachers, journalists, ministers, and political leaders, for example—attitudes are the key to changing people's behavior. There is often an optimistic view of the future, if we can educate the people to change their attitudes.

Psychological social psychology is also the study of how other people directly influence behavior (irrespective of attitudes). Conformity, obedience, power, leaders, and attraction are some of the topics covered in this perspective. Interpersonal communication, group decision making, and propaganda are also important. The key to this perspective seems to be, as Aronson states, interpersonal influence, both in attitudes and in behavior. The human is a "social animal" in the sense that he or she adjusts his or her attitudes and behaviors to the action of others in the situation.

There is a great similarity between the perspective described here as psychological social psychology and the sociological and psychological perspectives discussed earlier. That similarity is that there is a continuing focus on cause, the assumption being that something inside or outside the actor influences what he or she does. The purpose of all three perspectives is to uncover that cause. Social psychology looks at other people in the situations we act in. Others influence us through what they say and how they say it, by persuading us and manipulating us, by acting as models or by teaching us directly. Others form our attitudes and influence our behavior despite our attitudes. Whatever we bring to the situation (our traits) must be balanced with the social situation itself if we are going to understand human behavior. Whatever social patterns of society play themselves out in what we do, the social situation will still matter. Together, these three perspectives explain a lot of why human beings act as they do. Together, they tell us to look at the social situation, who the person is, and the society within which the person exists. There is overlap among them, but each has a different focus, and whichever one we study or use will lead us down a path that emphasizes one of these three aspects rather than the others.

The Perspective of Social Psychology in Sociology

Another approach to social psychology has developed within the discipline of sociology. Besides studying the topics of psychological social psychologists (attitudes and behavior influenced by others), they look at issues more related to sociology: the socialization into groups, organizations, and society, development and maintaining social inequality, group dynamics, social patterns in groups, elements of social interaction, family interaction, social power.

Morris Rosenberg and Ralph Turner (1981) argue that the real focus of sociological social psychology to be *social interaction,* the ongoing action that actors take toward one another back and forth. It is not a one-way causal influence of other people or groups on the individual that matters as much as what takes place between and among actors as they organize their action in relation to one another. This would include for example, deviance, identity, culture, roles, negotiation, and inequality.

Rosenberg and Turner also draw attention to the fact that sociological social psychology places emphasis on *researching real-life events,* such as interaction at a bar or on a team, or in a kindergarten class. Psychological social psychologists, on the other hand, are far more likely to use surveys or laboratory experiments. Related to this distinction is the fact that sociological social psychology emphasizes *socialization,* the various ways that individuals learn to become members of society—learn the patterns of society in face-to-face-interaction. Thus, for example, *identity* becomes a central concept, since the creation of identity is thought to arise through social interaction, and ongoing social interaction is understood as central to the whole socialization process.

There is, however, one school—or perspective—within the sociological social psychology that has become for many sociologists the most important perspective. This is called *symbolic interactionism.* Its history is different from most other social-scientific perspectives, and its goals and insights are also different. It, of course, is limited because it too, is a perspective, and whether it is useful depends on how well it helps us to understand the human being. Although it is part of the social-scientific tradition, it also tries to stand apart from the determinism that characterizes most social scientists. The rest of the book is an attempt to introduce this perspective.

Here I introduce the contents of this book. It is a picture of the ideas, it gives some idea of how the ideas fit together. After the whole book is read, it is also a good review.

1. *Background: The perspective of symbolic interactionism grows out of the work of George Herbert Mead and other pragmatists. It is also heavily influenced by Charles Darwin's work.* It emphasizes the *uniqueness* of the human being in nature, especially the fact that human beings *act back* on their environment rather than passively respond to that environment. The phrase *symbolic interactionism* gives us the key to the perspective: to understand the human being, we need to study interaction, and interaction of human beings relies heavily on the use of symbols (Chapter 3).

2. *Centrality of symbols: Human beings create and depend on symbols.* Mead describes the use of symbols to be our very essence. Symbolic communication both between people and within the person is the core to our reality, our society, and our distinctly human qualities (Chapters 4 and 5).

3. *Centrality of self: Human beings possess a self.* Self is socially created and makes it possible for the actor to act back on himself or herself. The actor becomes the object of his or her own actions, and this makes possible a vast array of actions of which we are capable (Chapter 6).

4. *Centrality of mind: Human beings engage in continuous mind action in almost every situation.* We talk to ourselves, we understand our environment, we make decisions about how to act toward the environment, and we organize our actions according to goals we determine for ourselves. We work out in our heads how to deal with problems we encounter (Chapter 7).

5. *Centrality of taking the role of the other: Human beings continuously take account of people around them, and in doing so they regularly try to understand the others' perspective on the situation.* This is a central part of mind action, and it alters considerably the nature of how we act in relation to others (Chapter 8).

6. *Centrality of action: Human beings act along a continuous stream of action,* interacting with others and engaging in mind action, determining goals and defining objects in relation to goals. Instead of responding to stimuli in our environment, *we continuously define our situation and make decisions as we go along* (Chapter 9).

7. *Centrality of social interaction: Human beings interact with one another, and this ongoing interaction influences both what we do in situations and it also becomes the source of human society.* Social interaction does not mean that others simply influence us, but that it is a mutual social process toward one another that matters (Chapter 10).

8. *Centrality of society: Society is any instance of social interaction in which actors cooperate over time, and develop culture.* Each individual exists in many societies.

Instead of society being an entity created in the past and imprisoning the actor, *society is dynamic,* continuously being created and recreated, shaped through social interaction, and held together not by force but by the voluntary commitment of the actors involved (Chapter 11).

9. *Erving Goffman* is one of the most important theorists in sociology whose ideas are built on the principles outlined in this perspective. Goffman's ideas are central to understanding the human being as an active player in situations, social interaction as central to what we all do in situations, as well as the creation and perpetuation of human society (Chapter 12).

10. *Centrality of science and the usefulness of the symbolic interactionist perspective:* Research in symbolic interactionism is guided by certain scientific principles, and it is a perspective that is applicable to many issues and situations—everyday and academic (Chapter 13).

Summary

This chapter described social science and its view of the human being. It emphasized that social science itself is a perspective and that within social science there are several unique perspectives. Each is an example of how some scholars attempt to understand the human being. Each is a focus and makes assumptions about reality. Each is limited, yet useful, for examining reality.

Kant's work was used as a reminder to us that science itself assumes certain things about the universe. It does not study everything because it too is limited. Social science, in its acceptance of a scientifc approach to understanding the human being, is therefore also limited. One of the very basic elements of science examined here is the assumption of natural cause, which tends to lead social science to take a deterministic perspective in attempting to understand the human being.

This chapter briefly examined sociology, psychology, and social psychology to underline the tendency for social science to attempt to isolate the reasons for or causes of human behavior. Although each emphasizes a different set of causal factors, all tend to take a deterministic stance. Sociology focuses on society, psychology on the person's development resulting from heredity and environment, and social psychology on the social situations we encounter.

This chapter also introduced the rest of the book by highlighting a unique perspective in social psychology called *symbolic interactionism.*

Figure 2–1 attempts to illustrate the relationships between the perspectives described in this chapter.

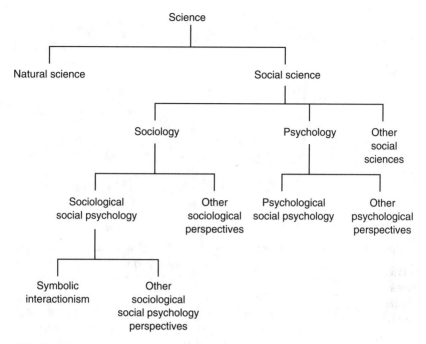

FIGURE 2–1

CHAPTER THREE

Symbolic Interactionism
As a Perspective

What is it that we should be teaching and learning in a university? Reading, writing, and math. Computers. Career preparation. Facts that sometime may come in handy. How to survive in society. How to make friends. Maybe respect for one another. How to continue to learn when we leave the university. As you probably know the list can go on and on. I know I am leaving out a lot.

I remember that in my freshman year at the University of Minnesota I read *Heart of Darkness*. I was introduced to Shakespeare, British and American poetry, European history, biology, psychology, sociology. I studied music, philosophy, and political science. I took a speech class where everyone had to give several talks during the quarter, and I wrote a theme every week for English. For what purpose? What is it that I studied and learned?

I realize now that the Ancient Greeks were right: it is the human being that is the object we must seek to understand. All of us at one time or another look back on our lives and the lives of others and try to understand what living is all about. And I now see that the real excitement of my university experience was studying the mystery of the human being. Every one of my classes and discussions with other students and friends pointed to my place in the universe and the nature of the human condition.

What does it mean to be a human? Are we different from other animals? Is there purpose in our existence? How is human society possible? Why do humans do what they do? Why do I do what I do? How do they create, and what do their creations tell us about ourselves? Is there truth? What is justice and can it be achieved? Is there right and wrong? Is it all right to judge other people? Is it right to be judged? Is there anything beyond physical existence? Here are the questions that began actually in high school, continued throughout my studies at the university, and then through 42 years of teaching.

Never did I find final answers; only understandings that I have found exciting and maybe pushed me toward capturing the essence of the human being.

The perspective presented in this book, symbolic interactionism, directly deals with many of these issues. What are we? What are our qualities?

Why do we do what we do? How is it possible to live together in a society? Why do some succeed? Why do some get into trouble? This is what this perspective tries to deal with. Its ideas are worth understanding alongside many of the other perspectives in the university and throughout our adult lives.

INTRODUCTION: FIVE CENTRAL IDEAS

We begin with the five central ideas in symbolic interactionism. Before we examine the individual concepts and details, it is important to get a general preview. Each one of these key ideas give us an inkling as to how symbolic interactionists view the human being.

1. The human being must be understood as a social person. *It is ongoing constant lifelong social interaction which leads us to do what we do.* Instead of focusing on the individual and his or her personality characteristics, or on how the society or social situation causes human behavior, symbolic interactionism focuses on the activities that take place between and among actors. *Interaction* is the basic unit of study. Individuals are created through *interaction*; society too is created through *social interaction*. What we do depends on *interaction* with others earlier in our lifetimes, and it depends on our *interaction* right now. *Social interaction* is central to what we do. If we want to understand cause, focus on *social interaction*.

Thus, if someone commits a crime it is his or her interaction with others that is emphasized as cause.

2. *The human being must be understood as a thinking being.* Human action is not only caused by interaction among individuals but also *interaction within the individual*. It is not our ideas or attitudes or values that are as important as the constant active ongoing process of *thinking*. We are not simply conditioned, we are not simply beings who are influenced by those around us, we are not simply products of society. We are, to our very core, *thinking* animals, always conversing with ourselves as we interact with others. If we want to understand cause, focus on human *thinking*.

Thus, whatever else is happening in a given situation, the actor who is committing a crime is described as someone who is thinking as he or she acts—sometimes very quickly, often very carefully and deliberate.

3. Humans do not sense their environment directly; instead, *humans define the situation they are in.* An environment may actually exist, but it is our *definition* of it that is important. *Definition* does not simply randomly happen; instead, it results from ongoing social interaction and thinking.

Thus, the actor commits the crime largely because of how he or she sees and defines the situation—past, future, other people in the situation, whether or not the situation is safe, the intentions and emotions others are giving off, and so on.

4. *The cause of human action is the result of what is occurring in our present situation.* Cause unfolds in the *present* social interaction, *present* thinking, and *present* definition. It is not society's encounters with us in our past that causes

action, nor is it our own past experience that does; it is, instead, social inter-action, thinking, definition of the situation takes place in the *present*. Our past enters into our actions because we think about it and apply it to the definition of the *present* situation.

Thus, the actor commits a crime because of factors he or she is defining in the immediate situation. The actor commits a crime because of what is going on in his or her present social interaction as well as his or her present definition of the situation.

5. *Human beings are described as active beings in relation to their environment.* Words such as "conditioning," "responding," "controlled," "imprisoned," "formed" are not used to describe the human being in symbolic interaction-ism. In contrast to other social-scientific perspectives humans are not thought of as being passive in relation to their surroundings, but *actively involved* in what they do. To a great extent we control what we do (based on our social in-teraction, thinking, and definition of the situation). Although it is probably impossible to state that we are free beings, symbolic interactionism examines the preconditions necessary for human freedom and normally tries to explain an *active* being that is able to overcome whatever forces that the environment pushes on us. We ultimately form our own action rather than responding to the physical environment.

Thus, to a great extent the actor commits a crime because of making de-cisions out of choices he or she is considering. Never is self control complete.

Although there is much else to remember and understand about sym-bolic interactionism, try to recall this point: *To understand human action, we must focus on social interaction, human thinking, definition of the situation, the pre-sent, and the active nature of the human being.*

These five ideas are not difficult to understand on the surface. You have no reason to believe them at this point, because the perspective has not yet been explained. However, here is the broad outline, and we go back to these ideas again and again in the chapters that follow. Hopefully, you will come to under-stand more fully their meaning, and come to appreciate their importance.

GENERAL HISTORICAL BACKGROUND OF SYMBOLIC INTERACTIONISM

Symbolic interactionism is usually traced back to the work of George Herbert Mead (1863–1931), who was a professor of philosophy at the University of Chicago. Mead wrote many articles, but much of his influence on symbolic interactionists comes through the publishing of his lectures and notes by his students, as well as through interpretation of his work by various other sociologists, especially one of his students, Herbert Blumer.

Blumer draws not only from Mead but also from others who pioneered symbolic interactionism. The perspective goes back to the work of John Dewey, William James, Charles Peirce, William Thomas, and Charles Cooley, to name a few. Blumer, writing primarily in the 1950s and 1960s, integrated much of their work. After Blumer, many others have drawn from these early interactionists and contributed to the perspective. In the past twenty years, the study of emotions, the attraction of qualitative research methodology, the integration of the perspective into mainstream sociology, and the writings of Erving Goffman have considerably made symbolic interactionism more important than ever, and have led many social thinkers and researchers in new and productive directions.

One way of understanding the general position of the symbolic interactionist perspective is to summarize the major influences on Mead, its principal founder. (The following draws from Strauss, 1964 and Desmonde, 1957.) There were three such influences, each one being central to all the symbolic interactionists since.

1. The philosophy of pragmatism
2. The work of Charles Darwin
3. Behaviorism

Mead and Pragmatism

Mead was a member of that school of philosophy known as *pragmatism.* The ideas of this school are especially important to Mead's approach to understanding the nature of truth. As we shall see, pragmatism becomes an important foundation for the whole perspective of symbolic interactionism. Basically, four ideas are important here.

First, pragmatists believe that humans do not respond to their environment; instead, they almost always interpret their environment. What we see as real almost always depends on our active intervention, our own definition. *The world does not tell us what it is; we actively reach out and understand it and decide what to do with it.* Reality does not simply impose itself on us without our taking a role in interpreting it. A fish is not simply a fish to the human being; it is not simply a physical stimulus that we respond to. Instead, in looking at a fish we must engage in an interpretive process. We might call it an animal, a fish, a dead fish, a pike, something to eat, or something to set free or put up on our wall as a trophy. Objects that exist in our environment do not simply reveal themselves to us; we ourselves must make decisions as to what they are to us. We see nothing "in the raw": nothing for humans ever "speaks for itself." "Read my lips" assumes there is only one way of understanding someone's words, but there are always many ways. "The thing is plain as day" assumes that everyone sees something exactly the same. This is far from the truth no matter what we are referring to.

Second, pragmatists argue that humans believe something according to its usefulness in situations that they encounter. We do not believe that which is actually true or because we have carefully eliminated falsehoods. *Knowledge is learned, remembered, and believed in relation to our ability to successfully apply it.* Each attempt to apply what we know is a test—if it works for us we tend to remember it and use it again in another situation. You may be familiar with the pronouncement "People see what they want to see and remember what they want to remember." The pragmatist is not disagreeing but is trying to explain why this is so: We remember that which works for us. Perspectives, facts, definitions, experiences, evidence, ideas—are all judged by the individual in terms of applicability. Right now, whatever we believe may or may not be actually true—in fact, it may be completely wrong. Whatever is learned in college may or may not stay with us, not because what was learned is true or untrue but largely because we are or are not able to successfully apply it to situations we encounter and achieve our goals there.

Third, pragmatists believe that we are selective in what we notice in every situation. We notice—take note of—those aspects that are useful to our goals in the situation. *Objects that we notice are defined by us according to their usefulness.* A hammer is something I sometimes use to pound nails, pull out nails, lend, sell, search for, draw, throw away, or show off. It has a myriad of uses depending on what I need it for to achieve my goals. Objects probably do exist out there in the environment, but we humans notice them according to a context at the time. We perceive and define according to usefulness.

Fourth, pragmatists focus on human action when they study the human being. It is not personality, past events, a trait or quality that is central, but what actors are doing in their situation. To understand human beings we need to understand their action, the causes of their action, the consequences of their action, the perception of our own action, and the perception of other people's action. The human is seen as an actor rather than a person, a thinking actor rather than a responder, a decision making actor rather than a formed organism. The chapters throughout this book attempt to focus on what people *do* in their worlds rather than on what makes up their personality or what makes up the qualities of their society. What social scientists actually see in situations is action, movement, people doing things, action toward their environment. Here is where we must begin our study: what are people doing and what goes into what they do?

Notice what has been introduced so far in this chapter: (1) We began with five ideas that are central to the whole perspective: Social interaction, thinking, definition of the situation, cause in the present, and the human being as an active participant in the environment. (2) We identified certain ideas in pragmatism that made up Mead's basic perspective, and we emphasized that, according to pragmatism, humans never see reality as it is; humans learn and remember what is useful to them; humans see and define objects in their environment according to the use they have for those objects; and it is important to focus on human action rather than the person or society to understand the human being.

Mead and Darwin

Mead was inspired and influenced by the work of Charles Darwin. Darwin's work, of course, helped to revolutionize the study of life through its contribution to the theory of evolution. For most scientists—natural and social—Darwin's work has had a tremendous impact. He was respected by Mead and influenced the direction that symbolic interactionism takes in studying the human being.

Darwin was a naturalist. He believed that we must try to understand the world we live in without appealing to supernatural explanation. God may, of course, exist, but nature should be understood on its own terms, as subject to natural laws. *So too, Mead argued, should we regard the human being in naturalistic terms.* Even if we are free, even if we are unique in nature, even if we possess qualities different from those of other animals—still, human beings must be understood in natural rather than in supernatural terms. Instead of examining the human in spiritual, metaphysical terms, possessing qualities such as soul, we need to identify the natural qualities that characterize what we are. Instead of claiming freedom for humans simply by assuming it, we need to examine those natural qualities that make freedom a possibility. Mead's whole approach to truth, self, mind, symbols, and other quite difficult and abstract concepts is meant to be naturalistic: it tries to understand them as part of the qualities developed by the human being as part of the natural world, as part of our heritage in the animal kingdom. Freedom, then, if it is important and unique, needs to be examined as something that develops in nature as we become active in relation to our environment, rather than accepted by faith alone.

Mead, by regarding the human in naturalistic terms, borrowed heavily from Darwin's theory of evolution, a theory that focused on the development of the various species of animals. Mead, as did Darwin, saw human development as part of this evolutionary process. Humans are animals, social animals, evolved from other forms, and they are like all other animals in some ways, but because of their development, certain qualities make them unique. Mead, more than Darwin, tried to identify those unique qualities and concluded that they are not to be understood as single isolated qualities but as a unique combination of several qualities that together form a qualitative difference between the human species and other animals. This uniqueness is related to physical traits such as a highly developed brain, a helplessness in childhood that makes it essential to rely heavily on society and socialization, and highly developed vocal chords and facial muscles that make it possible to create many subtle and sophisticated sounds. *Such proposed qualities, entirely evolved and combined, make humans able to develop a language system, use that language system in a myriad of ways, including an ability to reason.*

Mead went further, however. To Darwin, evolution for animals is a passive process. Nature plays itself out on various living things, and whatever survives depends on the natural forces acting on the organism. Changes in the environment and changes in heredity together influence the changes in the animal kingdom. Mead accepted this idea, but only until the human formed. Once language and the ability to reason arose in nature, the resulting being was able to turn back on nature itself actively directing how the natural forces act. The language-using human was no longer passive, simply shaped by nature, but could learn about it, understand it, act on it. In contrast to other animals, humans developed a way to adjust to their environment rather than be controlled by changes in their environment. We are able to understand the forces in nature, and we can build, invent, discover, shape whatever tries to control us. Our ability to direct our environment according to our goals allows for tremendous ability to work it for our purposes, but it also forces us to make intelligent and moral decisions about what we do.

Finally, Darwin influenced Mead in his thinking about what the universe actually is. Darwin helped shape people's thinking that the universe is dynamic rather than static. Instead of thinking of everything in the universe as being the same as it was millions of years ago, Darwin emphasized that everything has changed and that there is a constant dynamic process rather than a static one that describes nature. Mead was interested in the human being and society, so the impact of Darwin was that Mead came to see everything about the human being as process rather than as stable and fixed. Thus, instead of the individual being a consistent, structured personality, the individual is a dynamic changing actor, never becoming anything but always in the state of becoming, unfolding, acting. Instead of being socialized, the actor is always in the process of being socialized. Society is not thought to be a static entity out there, influencing us, but a developing process, characterized by ongoing continuous social interaction. Mind, to Mead, is action, and whatever self we have is a process, not a static entity. We converse with ourselves, we make decisions along a continuous stream of action. Truth for us always changes; our symbols change; our rules change; our use for our environment changes. What we are today is different from what we were yesterday or even one moment ago. Our interpretation of our past changes, as do our views of the future. People are not thought to be brainwashed and conditioned so much as actively involved in testing and reassessing their "truths" as they act.

Thus, Darwin's ideas and the theory of evolution combined with the ideas of pragmatism to form the basis for Mead's ideas. Darwin influenced Mead to look for human qualities in natural terms, to understand the development of our most important qualities as having arisen from our physical evolution, but, Mead added, once developed, those qualities combined to make humans active participants in their environment and in their own evolution. Finally, Darwin influenced Mead to see humans as part of a changing universe rather than a static one, and Mead applied this idea to all human qualities. Some scholars have even pointed out that Mead was uncomfortable with the word *society*, since it seemed so static a term, and preferred more active terms to describe the stability and continuities within interactions.

Mead and Behaviorism

There is one more influence on Mead worth discussing. It is the school in psychology called behaviorism. Mead was a behaviorist, but he also broke sharply with behaviorism on some very basic issues.

Mead was a behaviorist because, as a pragmatist, he agreed that humans must be understood in terms of *what they do* rather than who they are. The behaviorist argues that the best way to understand all animals, including humans, is by carefully observing their behavior. Concepts such as personality, attitudes, and society have little place in behaviorism.

However, Mead also sharply distanced himself from behaviorism. He believed that behavior is *not simply physical*, as other behaviorists argued. He believed that behavior included action that is not directly seen, action that takes place within the actor, action we might call thinking, or minded action. John B. Watson, a psychologist who became one of the important founders of behaviorism in the United States (and who was a student of Mead's and Dewey's at the University of Chicago), rejected pragmatism in favor of a behaviorism that discounted all behavior except that which can be directly observed, physical movement. Therefore, although both Mead and Watson were behaviorists, they were very different in their approach to the human.

Mead believed that without an understanding of mind, symbols, and self, human behavior cannot be understood for what it actually is. To measure physical behavior alone without trying to understand thinking was to ignore the central qualities of the human being; it was to ignore our uniqueness as a species; it was to treat humans identically with all other things in nature, as simply physical organisms. Mead called himself a "social behaviorist" and taught that in human social behavior there is always an interpretation to be included in what we do and in how we perceive what others do. He taught that for scientists to understand human overt action they must always take into account human action as involving understanding, definition, interpretation, meaning.

Pragmatism, Darwin, and behaviorism—each has a place in Mead's work. They are his roots, and out of those Mead developed a unique perspective, one that regards the human being as an active being, a thinking, creative, self-directing, defining dynamic actor, one whose ability to use symbols, define, and alter the environment results in a unique being in nature.

A CONTRAST WITH OTHER PERSPECTIVES: WARRINER

Thus far we have examined the general outline of symbolic interactionism by looking at its key ideas and by highlighting some of the influences on George Herbert Mead's thinking. To go further in this analysis, I must introduce the ideas of two more people—Charles K. Warriner and Tamotsu Shibutani— both of whom expertly contrast symbolic interactionism with more traditional social-scientific perspectives.

Warriner (1970, 1–13) explains that the issue of humans' having an active or a passive nature has traditionally been a very emotional issue in society and that society's idea system, its ideology, simply makes assumptions about human freedom and those assumptions are applied to many of the key social issues. Because of these ideological assumptions, the question of human freedom has rarely been tackled from an objective perspective. Yet the real relation between the individual and society is probably "the most fundamental, the most frequently recurring" question we have ever dealt with, and the answers have had the "most extended implication" for our history. Do humans create society, or are we simply created by it? Do humans have an important role to play in the direction of their society, or is society the shaper?

Traditional social science, in its attempt to take its lead from natural science, built the human within the walls of society and incorporated the biological perspective. Warriner calls the traditional social science perspective a "stable-man" view, with the human having a "permanent nature," "inborn or learned." The human is born, is shaped, and, as an adult, is directed. According to stable-man views, human action is caused by human nature or nurture, the individual always acting according to earlier influences. The cause of human behavior is found in earlier influences, and stability is assumed within the human personality. This stable-man point of view, Warriner argues, is tied to a "physicalist," "deterministic and mechanistic," "nonmentalist" view of the world that has dominated science and philosophy.

In reaction, Warriner describes another view that he calls "the emergent-human view," which in fact is the symbolic interactionist view we are describing here. It is different from the stable-man view, emphasizing "immediate situational factors" as cause, "examining the social and 'spiritual' characteristics" of human beings, and accepting "indeterminacy and probability" in dealing with causes of human action. This theory regards the human as an

> actor rather than as a being, treats [the human being's] acts as symbolic in character rather than primarily physical, and views interaction as the basic social and psychological process from which personalities and societies emerge, through which they are expressed, and by which they are maintained as continuities (p. 9).

Human beings are now to be understood as social, interactional, and symbolic by their very nature. Those who see only the physical, who measure only that which is directly observable, miss the whole essence of the human being. Our uniqueness is in:

> the symboling process, in the capacity of [the human being] to see things not as they are but as they have been or might be in the future, in the capacity of [the human being] to use sound and marks on paper as conventional signs and thus to communicate with others, in the capacity of [the human being] through these functions to create worlds that never existed in physical reality (pp. 9–10).

Warriner captures well the spirit of the perspective being described in this book. His views are illustrated in Figure 3–1

SHIBUTANI: REFERENCE GROUPS AS PERSPECTIVES

Tamotsu Shibutani (1955) in "Reference Groups As Perspectives" also highlights the differences between the symbolic interactionist approach to the human being and traditional social science. Human beings, he points out, use

Warriner's "Stable Human View" (traditional social science)

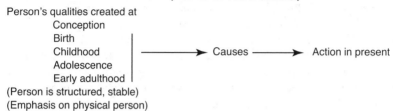

Warriner's "Emergent-Human View" (symbolic interactionist view)

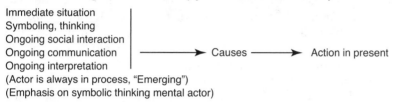

FIGURE 3–1

perspectives when they look at reality as it is. Perspectives filter what we see. Shibutani describes perspectives in much the same way they were described in Chapter 1 of this book. *They are points of view the actor uses to make sense out of his or her world.*

> A perspective is an ordered view of one's world—what is taken for granted about the attributes of various objects, events, and human nature. It is an order of things remembered and expected as well as things actually perceived, an organized conception of what is plausible and what is possible; it constitutes the matrix through which one perceives his [or her] environment (p. 564).

It is necessary for us to have perspectives in order to put objects in place as we look at reality. A perspective is an "outline scheme defining and guiding experience." Shibutani likens a group's perspective to culture (as Robert Redfield [1941, 132] defines it), consisting of the "conventional understandings, manifest in act and artifact, that characterize societies." Culture is a social creation, influences what we do and make, and characterizes every society. Culture is a product of communication and acts as a guide for individuals who take part in that ongoing communication.

Shibutani links perspectives to reference groups. *A reference group is the society whose perspective the individual uses.* It is the group within which the individual communicates and whose perspective is applied to situations. Shibutani defines reference groups as simply those groups whose perspectives the individual borrows to see reality. Each individual has several reference groups. They can be groups the individual belongs to ("membership groups"), but social categories such as social class, ethnic group, community, or society may also act as reference groups. Reference groups can even be future groups; for instance, philanthropists may give for "posterity," or environmentalists may take on the perspective of unborn generations. Reference groups can be societies or groups from our distant past, as evidenced by many people's interest in the ancient Greeks or the American revolutionaries or the early Christians.

What Shibutani is telling us is that *what we see as reality is really a result of perspectives we take on through social interaction, and the groups whose perspective we use are called our reference groups.* Another term for reference group is *society*, and another is *social world.* A reference group is an individual's society, and its significance is not membership but the fact that its culture—or perspective— is used by the actor. Each individual uses many such societies, each one held together through communication, each one linked to the individual through communication. In a sense, sociologists form a society as they interact, and those who use its perspective use the society of sociology as a reference group. The United States constitutes a society, and it, too, is held together through ongoing communication through television, newspapers, economic and political activities, advertising, travel, and geographic mobility. African Americans also constitute a society within the United States to the extent that they interact on a continuous basis and develop a shared perspective that matters to people.

Shibutani also uses the term *social world* to define reference group. It is a less formal and structured concept and emphasizes the role of communication in forming and maintaining our reference groups. We live in modern mass societies, each one made up of several smaller social worlds. He writes:

> One of the characteristics of life in modern mass societies is simultaneous participation in a variety of social worlds. Because of the ease with which the individual may expose [himself or herself] to a number of communication channels, [he or she] may lead a segmentalized life, participating successively in a number of unrelated activities. Furthermore, the particular combination of social worlds differs from person to person (p. 567).

If we are to understand what humans do, according to Shibutani, we must understand each individual's unique perspectives, for they are the basis of what the person takes for granted and how the person defines situations. "But in mass societies we must learn in addition the social world in which [the individual] is participating in a given act" (p. 567).

In Shibutani's description, what causes what we do? It is not our personalities developed in the past. It is not attitudes that are inside of us. It is not society itself or culture. In fact, it is not even our perspective. Instead, as soon as we focus on *perspective* we must recognize the importance of *definition*—a perspective is only something we borrow in order to help us define reality. Our interaction in a particular social world may lead us to take on a particular perspective, but that perspective becomes a tool in the hands of an active defining actor. The perspective is our guide to reality. And what is the stability or permanence in all of this? It is not our interaction, nor is it culture or perspective. It is neither our definition of reality nor our action in the world that results from our definition. Instead, *everything changes*: humans, and everything that happens, is *dynamic and ongoing*, including action, interaction, perspectives, societies, definition, symbolic communication, mind, and self.

ATTITUDES VERSUS PERSPECTIVES

Perspectives are different from attitudes. When we use the term *perspective* to describe the human being, we enter the world of definition; when we use the term *attitude* we enter the world of response. That is why symbolic interactionism is an examination of perspectives and reference groups, whereas other psychological social psychologists are more likely to examine attitudes and social influence. The distinction is a subtle one, but very important.

To focus on attitude is to focus on the individual, because an attitude is part of the individual. It is similar to a trait that is developed socially but carried around from situation to situation. An attitude is an internal response to an object or to a class of objects. The external environment acts as a stimulus: the person first responds internally; the person responds externally after having that internal response. When we have an attitude toward other people who are, say, women or African Americans or poets, and an individual in one of those categories enters our presence, our attitude is thought to be activated, leading us to act in a certain direction. The attitude is a predisposition; it predisposes us to act in a certain way. The actor is not thought to be in charge of his or her own action: *the actor does not use the attitude,* but instead the attitude directs the actor. To focus on the term *attitude* to describe the human being is to describe a passive being and to ignore the importance of active definition of the situation.

A perspective, on the other hand, is not a response to a stimulus but something *used* as a guide to definition and action. It is not an internal trait but something belonging to, arising in, shared in, and changing in social interaction. The actor uses it; it does not cause a response. Because the individual interacts with many others and exists in many social worlds, he or she will have many perspectives, and, therefore, any given object does not become a simple stimulus; instead it can be defined in a number of ways depending on the actor's goals in the situation. A person I see in a situation may be Chinese, a teacher, a male, an artist, a scholar, a liberal, and a member of the upper class, but whatever I focus on and how I decide to act will depend on how I define him or her in the situation; and my definition, in turn, will be influenced by the perspective I use to define the situation. Any one of the individual's characteristics may or may not be important to me. Although I may be prejudiced against artists (an attitude), that prejudice may not be an important influence on my action because I am seeing the individual as a teacher because of the perspective I am using.

An attitude is usually defined as a quality of the individual, so it is thought to be fairly fixed and stable over time. An attitude is generally seen to be tied to other qualities of the person, including other attitudes. The image of the human being described is one of a consistent, whole organism, responding to stimuli in situations according to this attitude brought to the situation. "He has an attitude toward women that causes him to treat them as property whenever he encounters them. That is the way he is." Perspectives, on the other hand, are conceptualized as dynamic and changing, guides to interpretation and then to action, undergoing change during interaction, and not necessarily consistent within the actor. Action can therefore never be perfectly predictable: Even if we know the actor's perspectives carried into a situation, we do not know beforehand which one will be chosen by the actor, nor can we predict how it will change in that situation. And even if we know the perspective that will be used, we still cannot know exactly how the individual will use it to define the situation. Finally, we must also recognize that whatever perspectives the actor brings to a situation may be put aside in favor of one that arises in the actual situation. The selection of juries that favor our side in a courtroom will depend on knowing what groups they interact with on an ongoing basis and, therefore, which perspectives they might use to define the trial, but it is central to recognize that the perspective that emerges from the interaction of the jurors may become the most important one by far. Knowing the attitude an individual may have upon being chosen to serve, according to symbolic interactionism, will give us much less information as to how the jury member will vote than knowing how the person's perspective may change during the trial.

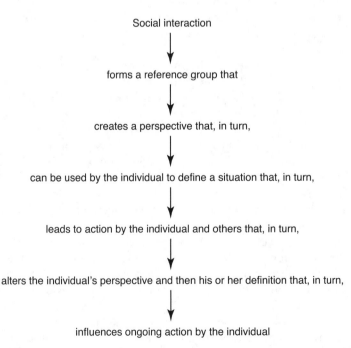

Social interaction

↓

forms a reference group that

↓

creates a perspective that, in turn,

↓

can be used by the individual to define a situation that, in turn,

↓

leads to action by the individual and others that, in turn,

↓

alters the individual's perspective and then his or her definition that, in turn,

↓

influences ongoing action by the individual

FIGURE 3–2

The point of this discussion is that it highlights the fact that when social scientists use the concept "perspective" they conceptualize a very different type of actor than when they use the concept "attitude." The human being interacts, uses perspectives, therefore defines situations, acts according to what goes on in the present situation, and is active not passive. The actor is perceived to be constantly changing actions as he or she goes along. Figure 3–2 shows this view.

The human being, in these terms, is more complex, contradictory, situational, and dynamic and less predictable and passive than in almost all other social-scientific perspectives.

Summary

This chapter introduced the perspective of symbolic interactionism, giving an overview of the central ideas of this perspective and contrasting it with some other perspectives. It described the basic assumptions of symbolic interactionism so you have a context within which to place the following chapters, and, at the same time, it highlighted the uniqueness of these assumptions.

1. In its understanding of the human being, symbolic interactionism focuses on interaction rather than on personality, society, or the influence of others. Interaction includes social interaction and interaction with oneself. It emphasizes that human beings define their environment rather than simply respond to it, that a focus on interaction and definition focuses our attention on the present situation as the cause of what we do. Humans are seen as forever dynamic and active rather than as static and passive.

2. Symbolic interactionism is heavily influenced by the work of George Herbert Mead, a philosopher and psychologist who worked at the University of Chicago during the early twentieth century. Mead's work was heavily influenced by pragmatism, Charles Darwin, and behaviorism.

3. Pragmatism is very important to symbolic interactionism primarily in its approach to how humans relate to their environment. It teaches that we always intervene in determining what is real, that knowledge is believed and remembered because it is useful to us, that objects are defined in our environment according to their use to us, and that humans must be understood primarily by what they do in their situations.

4. Darwin influenced Mead to understand human uniqueness in naturalistic terms and to recognize that humans should be understood in dynamic terms—that the species, society, and the individual are constantly undergoing change. Mead went further than Darwin in understanding humans by emphasizing our ability to be active in nature, even active participants in our own evolution.

5. Mead was a behaviorist in believing that we must always focus on human behavior in understanding the human being, but he was also critical of other behaviorists for not recognizing the importance of human uniqueness,

which includes our ability to engage in mind behavior as well as physical overt behavior.

6. Charles Warriner contrasts symbolic interactionism with other natural and social-scientific perspectives. The human is "emergent," always changing as he or she deals with situations. We are not simply products of our past or of society's past. What we do in a particular situation depends on our definition of that particular situation and makes it important to recognize that we must be understood as primarily social, symbolic, and mental, rather than as simply physical.

7. Tamotsu Shibutani shows the central importance of perspective in understanding how we act in situations. We use perspectives to define our world, and these are always social, dynamic, and guiding, rather than determining, agents. Attitudes are not central to symbolic interactionism because they imply a much more passive being, carrying qualities into situations that lead to a response. The word *perspective* implies definition rather than response.

Symbolic interactionism, therefore, is an important and unique perspective that regards the human being as active in the environment; an organism that interacts with others and with self; a dynamic being; a being that defines immediate situations according to perspectives developed and altered in ongoing social interactions. The assumptions of symbolic interactionism contrast significantly with those of traditional social science. As we go through the rest of the chapters, keep reminding yourself that the relationship with the environment is central: to the symbolic interactionist we do not simply respond to our environment, but we define, act toward it, and use it. We are not simply shaped, conditioned, controlled by that environment (including other humans), but we act toward it according to our ongoing definitions arising from perspectives that are themselves dynamic.

CHAPTER FOUR

The Meaning
of the Symbol

We walked down the path to the well-house, attracted by the fragrance of the honeysuckle with which it was covered. Someone was drawing water and my teacher placed my hand under the spout. As the cool stream gushed over one hand she spelled into the other the word water, first slowly, then rapidly. I stood still, my whole attention fixed upon the motions of her fingers. Suddenly I felt a misty consciousness as of something forgotten—a thrill of returning thought; and somehow the mystery of language was revealed to me. I knew then that "w-a-t-e-r" meant the wonderful cool something that was flowing over my hand. That living word awakened my soul, gave it light, hope, joy, set it free! There were barriers still, it is true, but barriers that could in time be swept away.

I left the well-house eager to learn. Everything had a name, and each name gave birth to a new thought. As we returned to the house every object which I touched seemed to quiver with life. That was because I saw everything with the strange, new sight that had come to me....

I learned a great many new words that day. I do not remember what they all were; but I do know that *mother, father, sister, teacher* were among them—words that were to make the world blossom for me, "like Aaron's rod, with flowers." It would have been difficult to find a happier child than I was as I lay in my crib at the close of that eventful day and lived over the joys it had brought me, and for the first time longed for a new day to come.*

We take for granted the fact that we use language. Rarely do we think about what life would be like without language. Only when we consciously attempt to examine language objectively do we realize how central it is to what the human being is. Indeed, when we teach other primates our language, we begin to recognize how they change once they can use even a few words.

Helen Keller, both blind and deaf, was not able to use language for a good part of her childhood, because she was unaware of words, unaware that humans can understand a reality outside the immediate physical environment, to a reality uniquely human—a social-symbolic reality that opens up for

---

*From *The Story of My Life* by Helen Keller, pp. 36–37. Doubleday, 1954.

human beings behavioral possibilities that other organisms do not have. Keller was dramatically changed once she understood and came to use language. She no longer simply responded to stimuli; she gradually was able to make decisions, control her own behavior, create original thoughts, and a great number of abilities.

The symbolic interactionist perspective takes the use of symbols—especially words—the central concept of the whole perspective. What, after all, is our essence? How should we begin to understand who we are as a species? Are we violent, selfish, peaceful, competitive, cooperative, or loving? Or is it much more fruitful to tie what we become to our symbolic abilities? It is through society and its socialization of the individual that the individual comes to develop symbols. And it is the abilities that arise from our symbols that develop the kind of society within humans exist.

We now turn our attention to two important terms before we examine the meaning of the "symbol." These are "reality" and "social objects."

THE NATURE OF REALITY

To begin with, we must consider further the nature of "reality" for human beings. Because, as we have pointed out, the human sees the world through perspectives, developed socially, reality is *social*, and what we see "out there" (and within ourselves) is developed in interaction with others. We interpret the world according to social definitions. It is important to emphasize, however, that social scientists (including symbolic interactionists) operate from the assumption that a physical objective reality does indeed exist independent of our social definition, that our social definitions do develop, at least in part, in relation to something "real" or physical. Although there are some who question even this assumption, most of us would indeed agree to some *objective reality's* existing out there. Symbolic interactionists sometimes call this objective reality the "situation as it exists."

The important point is that we do not respond to this reality directly. Instead, we *define* the situation "as it exists" out there, and that definition is highly influenced by our social life. We are not like billiard balls responding directly to the impact of other billiard balls, nor are we like rats responding to physical stimuli. Someone may push us physically, and we must respond physically in the sense that our bodies give way to the push, but we also immediately *interpret* that act and decide on a line of action. At first our physical bodies respond to other physical bodies, but immediately we socially define that reality, putting that action into a working context (e.g., Why did he push? Did he mean to be aggressive? Is he bigger than I am? Is he dangerous?), and we define the act accordingly.

Humans therefore exist in a physical objective reality and in a social reality. Something actually exists; we come to learn what it is through social interaction.

However, there is a third reality that is created out of our social reality. Human beings through what they learn are able to think about that reality. Within their internal conversation will words they create a reality that is uniquely their own. Whatever they are taught, they are able to fool around with it as they talk to themselves. No two people think exactly alike; no two people will see the same reality even if they are taught by the same teacher. Each of us privately interprets the reality that we are shown by others.

Importance of a Socially Defined Reality

Howard Becker (1953), in an interesting and comprehensive study of marijuana users, done before marijuana became such a popular part of many social worlds in the United States, illustrates the central importance of a social definition of reality, even the reality that we *feel* inside our own bodies. His point: To identify the effects of marijuana as good and pleasurable is a matter of socialization; it is, in a real sense, a result of social interaction, a social reality. In conclusion, Becker writes:

> This analysis of the genesis of marijuana use shows that the individuals who come in contact with a given object may respond to it at first in a great variety of ways. If a stable form of new behavior toward the object is to emerge, a transformation of meanings must occur, in which the person develops a new conception of the nature of the object. This happens in a series of communicative acts in which others point out new aspects of his experience to him, present him with new interpretations of events, and help him achieve a new conceptual organization of his world, without which the new behavior is not possible. Persons who do not achieve the proper kind of conceptualization are unable to engage in the given behavior and turn off in the direction of some other relationships to the object or activity (p. 242).

The importance of a socially defined reality is one of the central ideas in sociology today, and it does not need to be documented extensively here. However, before we go on I would like to mention a study done by Mark Zborowski (1952). He studied people's reaction to pain, and he points out that pain, although it is "a physiological phenomenon acquires specific social and cultural significance" (p. 17). His research examined patients' definitions of their own pain in order to better understand how their group life influenced how they saw and felt it. Pain, he concluded, is defined differently, given a different meaning and reaction, at least in part because of people's ethnic group membership, from which they get a perspective. There is no reason to believe that some ethnic groups actually experience more physical pain than others, yet some groups complain more than others, some groups focus on the pain itself and are thankful for immediate relief, and others tend to interpret pain as representing something more serious; they are not relieved just with painkillers but need assurance about their future health. It seems that for human beings something as immediate and physical as pain is defined by perspectives the individual borrows from his or her reference groups.

The importance of socially defined reality to the human is even more obvious when we look beyond our own bodies. Every day we encounter countless physical objects. To make sense out of them, the human actor must isolate, identify, and catalog them. How do we do that? To a great extent it is done by social interaction; we come to identify and classify our world according to what we learn from one another in interaction.

OBJECTS AS "SOCIAL OBJECTS"

Objects may exist in physical form, but for the human being, they are pointed out, isolated, cataloged, interpreted, and given meaning through social interaction. In the symbolic interactionist perspective, we say that objects for the human being are really *social objects.* This concept is very important in the symbolic interactionist perspective, for, as we shall see, it will become an integral part of every chapter in this book.

First, we begin with objects "as they are." Again, although objects may exist in physical form, human beings see objects not "in the raw," but only through a perspective of some kind. We learn what things are and what they are good for. Children want to know "What's that?" The newcomer to football wants to know "What are they doing now? What is a 'down'? What is a 'huddle'?" And a student at college for the first time wants to know "What is a G.P.A.? What is a graduate assistant? What is sociology?" We ask. We watch. We are told. But, in the end, we learn from one another what things are in the world. This is why objects are called *social* objects by the symbolic interactionist.

Objects in nature are, of course, acted on by both human and nonhuman organisms. Bernard Meltzer (1972, pp. 22–23) describes Mead's thesis that all organisms must single out certain things around them because only certain things are important to their survival. Other objects become largely irrelevant. (A tree, grass, a human, and acorns are all different things to a cow, a squirrel, a beaver, and a cat.) Objects in the physical world act as stimuli for nonhuman animals, leading to specific responses. The same object (e.g., grass) will lead to different responses depending on which species is involved. For the human being, however, all objects in nature are not fixed stimuli but *social objects* constantly changing as they are defined and redefined in interaction. "Objects consist of whatever people indicate or refer to" (Blumer, 1969, p. 68). Objects are given importance by us not through fixed biological patterns (as is the case in most other animals) but according to what others around us decide to give importance to. And each object changes for the human, not because *it* changes, but because people change their definition. The meaning, says Herbert Blumer, "is not intrinsic to the object" (p. 68).

But how do we define these social objects? We give them *names*, but, more important, we learn what they are good for, how they are *used*. Social objects are defined according to their *use* for people involved in a situation. Meaning "arises from how the person is initially prepared to act toward it" (Blumer, 1969, pp. 68–69). A chair becomes "something to sit in." A desk is "something to write on." A flower is "something to smell." A podium is "something to speak from." In each of these cases, however, the object changes as its use for us changes, as we change the meaning it has for us. Chairs are also something to stand on, to store things on, to draw, to put side by side in order to sleep on, and so forth. A desk is something to sit on or to stand on, to collate papers on, to represent our prestige to others with, to hide something in, and so forth. A flower is also something to give to a loved one or to someone in the hospital, something to send to a person in mourning, something to decorate our yard, something to draw, something to extract medicine from, something to use to attract bees. A podium is also something to represent our authority, something to store notes in, something for children to play with. Objects change for us precisely because our use for them changes. Blumer supplies some excellent examples: "A tree is not the same object to a lumberman, a botanist, or a poet; a star is a different object to a modern astronomer than it was to a sheepherder of antiquity; communism is a different object to a Soviet patriot than it is to a Wall Street broker" (p. 69). Blumer wrote this in 1969. By 1990, communism meant something different to the Soviet patriot. Most physical objects have almost an infinite number of possible uses; thus, they have almost an infinite number of social meanings, and each physical object constitutes, therefore, a multitude of social objects.

This view of objects is one that goes back to pragmatism, which was briefly discussed in Chapter 3. Between objects out there and the individual's overt action is a perspective—a definition, a meaning—socially derived.

Because we live in a world of social objects we are now able to "understand" our environment. We are able to describe it to others and to ourselves. We are able to take what we learn in one situation and apply it to a very different situation. If we understand our environment we can take that knowledge and use it to figure out new situations. No longer do we sense our environment; we represent it in our heads and are able to discuss it with ourselves and with others.

Our understanding of objects has to do with our use of them. We understand that an object—say a pencil—has many uses, and when the occasion arises, we are in the position to use it appropriately. We are able to apply what we know to our actions. Understanding is not habit but is instead *applying knowledge* we have to objects. Mead, Blumer, and other symbolic interactionists maintain that we define objects according to "a line of action" we are about to take toward them. When I see a horse out there, I see something I am about to ride, mount, pet, run from, eat, sell, buy, or use to teach my children that animals are their friends. To say we see according to a line of action we are about to take toward something is the same as saying we organize our perception of objects according to the use they have for us.

A social object, then, is *any object in a situation that an actor uses in that situation. That use has arisen socially. That use is understood and can be applied to a variety of situations.* Other objects are ignored. However, as action unfolds, the individual may change his or her use, notice new objects, ignore objects used initially, and so on. The actor *acts* toward objects, socially defined, of use to him or her in a particular situation.

Social objects include anything. Consider the following examples.

1. Physical natural objects—a tree, a flower, a rock, or dirt—can become social objects in a situation.
2. Human-made objects—a radio, a fork, a piece of paper, a computer terminal—can become social objects in a situation.
3. Animals are sometimes used as social objects by the individual.
4. Other people are social objects. Both individually and in groups, we define other people as important to the situations we are in. We develop lines of action toward them, and we "use" them (not necessarily selfishly). You are someone I ask for a date one day, ask to marry, marry, live with, get angry with, share my cares with, and so on.
5. Our "past" is a social object, as is the "future." We *use* these to work through situations.
6. Our "self" is a social object (as we shall emphasize in Chapter 6).
7. Symbols are social objects. We create and use symbols to communicate and represent something to others and to ourselves.
8. Ideas and perspectives can be social objects.
9. Emotions can be social objects. As with everything else, we can define, use, manipulate, and understand emotions in ourselves and in others.

Anything can become a social object for the human actor. Whatever we use is a social object to us in a given situation. Our use defines it, and almost always that use has arisen socially. "It" changes as our use for it changes. This view alters the nature of the world humans act in. Instead of objects "turning us on," *we define them; we use them* to achieve our goals in a situation; and *we change them* according to our changing goals. We understand the world we live in, and we are able to apply that understanding to situations we enter and use the objects there according to our understanding.

THE MEANING OF SYMBOLS

1. Symbols Are Social Objects

This chapter is supposed to be about symbols. But what are symbols, and why did we first try to understand the meaning of social objects? The answer is that symbols are in fact social objects. Not all social objects are symbols, but all symbols are social objects. This means that symbols constitute a class of social objects that have certain special qualities that I will try to describe.

First, if symbols are social objects then (1) they are created socially, (2) they are objects intentionally used in many different situations and in many different ways, and (3) they are understood by the users.

Social objects—and therefore symbols—are socially established and understood. This means that symbols are defined in interaction, not established in nature. People make them, people discuss them, people agree on what they shall stand for. Symbols are *conventional*, a socially established use for the purpose of representation. Conventional means that the symbol is arbitrarily and purposely developed to refer to something. The fact that holding two fingers in the air means peace, is conventional and arbitrary, as is a hand closed over our head or placed over the heart, or a black mark on our forehead. Because symbols are arbitrary representations used only because people create them to be, they can be used at will and in a large number of situations, they can be changed at any time, and meaning is not physical or immediate, but abstract.

"Hey George." "Let X stand for Y." "Let 'man' stand for 'the human race.'" "Let the number 2 stand for one + one." "Let the Lexus stand for affluence." This is the essence of symbols. And this is the key to understanding the human being.

Instinctive communication in other animals is not socially created; instinctive communication needs no understanding and does not allow the tremendous variety of use. After all, it is only because we learn from one another and agree to agree that the word "butter" will be used to represent that stuff we eat, cook with, buy, and so on; that "butterfingers" will be used to represent someone who cannot catch a ball; "buttering up" will be used to represent what some people do when they want something from others. It is only because we learn from another and agree to agree that a "wink" will be used to represent to you that all is well, a "handshake" will be used to represent that we have an agreement, and a "kiss" will be used to represent that I love you. It is only because we learn from one another and agree to agree that a certain building, a certain flag, and a certain hair style represents something to us. Mead emphasizes that symbols are "significant." He means that they have shared meaning by those who use them. The one who uses them knows what they mean; the one who receives them understands what they mean.

2. Symbols Are "Meaningful"

The fact that symbols are social objects means that they are understood by those who use them. We do not simply respond to them (as the dog may learn to "roll over"), but we are able to describe them to ourselves and to others, and we are able to apply them to thousands of situations where they seem to fit. "Understanding" means an ability to describe something, think about it, apply that knowledge to a multitude of situations, and to dissect and integrate the understanding to other knowledge we possess. When I use a symbol I know what I am doing; I understand what the symbol is supposed to represent. And I also believe that those to whom I am communicating, will also understand. Mead emphasizes that symbols are "meaningful," they are not simply responses but have meaning to those who use them.

3. Symbols Are Used to Represent and Communicate

Symbols are social objects that are used to *represent* (to stand in for, to take the place of, to refer to something), whatever people agree they should represent. Because they represent something, we do not simply respond to our immediate physical environment; we create symbols to stand in for whatever we choose.

Representation is what we use to *communicate*. We use these representations to communicate to other people, sometimes to objects around us, and always to ourselves. Symbols allow us to share understanding, to tell others what we think, what we know, what we are, what we intend, what we feel. It is through symbols that I write letters, teach my class, make love to my wife, express patience with my children, express to others that I am who I think I am. It is through symbols that I can fool others, make them laugh or cry. The word "horse" is used to communicate a certain type of animal. The horse itself may be something I use to communicate to others that I am wealthy, kind, or athletic. A horse is not a symbol, however, if I simply want to ride it—it is then a social object I ride rather than represent and communicate.

Symbols are also used to *communicate to ourselves*, to think with, to converse about ourselves and about objects in our environment. It is through symbols that we are able to rise above our physical world and manipulate objects out there within our own personal world. Specifically, it is word-symbols that allow us to act back to ourselves. Instead of responding to a physical stimulus, we are able to represent that stimulus and fool around within our brains about what we see.

4. Symbols Are Intentionally Used

If symbols are *used* by actors who *understand* their meaning—what they represent—and their purpose is to *communicate* to others and to ourselves, then we are into the issue of "intention." Symbols are used intentionally, not unconsciously, not accidentally, not automatically; symbols are *intentional acts of communication*. One tries to communicate. One communicates on purpose. We are actively using these representations we understand for purposes of sending something to others. And others who also understand these representations label and categorize them with word-symbols to themselves and act back, often for purposes of communication. "What is essential to communication is that the symbol should arouse in one's own self what it arouses in the other individual" (Mead, 1934, p. 149). The actor who uses symbols understands what he or she is doing and uses the symbols for the purpose of giving off meaning that he or she believes will make some sense to the other. A crying infant does not at first use symbols to communicate to parents, although the parents do see and label the act as crying, interpret it, and act accordingly. Crying only becomes symbolic to the infant as the infant intentionally communicates through crying. There is an intentional request for something. Sheldon Stryker (1959) describes this process:

> For the child, the correspondence between sound and meaning will be initially vague, but in the process of interaction over time the correspondence will become more pronounced. So, for example, the child may use the sound "ba" to refer to any approximately round object and, having played this game with daddy, may be led to roll any such object—ball, orange, egg—around the floor.

The response of parent to the rolling of an egg—especially an uncooked one—will soon make clear that an egg is not "ba" and thus is not to be rolled on the floor. In the course of time, child and parent will come to agree on what is and is not a ball, and thus a significant symbol will come into existence. A sound, initially meaningless to the child, comes to mean for the child what it really means for the adult (p. 116).

Each is then in the position to use that symbol on purpose, and the other knows what is being represented.

Bernard Meltzer (1972, pp. 12–13) borrowing from Mead, contrasts symbols with the clucking of a hen or the barking of a dog. He argues that dogs and hens do not understand the meaning of their own act or the acts of the other. A hen clucks and chicks respond. "This does not imply, however, that the hen clucks in order to guide the chicks, i.e., with the intention of guiding them." A dog barks, the bark serves as a cue for a response by a second dog. There seems to be little evidence that each thinks, "What does he mean by that?" or, "How should I bark now?" or, "If I run away now, he will think I am chicken, so I had better fight." Meltzer points out: "Human beings on the other hand…[act] on the basis of the intentions or meanings of gestures. This renders the gesture *symbolic*, i.e., the gesture is a symbol to be interpreted." David L. Miller (1973) contrasts intentional symbolic communication with the dance of bees.

First of all, the dance is not learned; it is committed impulsively. Second there is no evidence that the dancer intends to evoke responses by other bees. Should there be no others present, it will perform the dance anyway; and if others are present but do not "obey the request," the dancer does not perform the dance again, as if to say, "I have told you once, why aren't you on your way?" There is no evidence, in short, that the dancer intends anything by its gesture or that it is in the least aware of the behavioral consequences of its behavior (pp. 86–87).

SOME TYPES OF SYMBOLS

Anything can become a symbol. The more we examine our world, the more it is transformed from a purely physical world to a fully symbolic world.

All *words* that are understood by the communicator are symbols. Probably this is the easiest kind of symbols to recognize, and undoubtedly the most used and the most important.

However, our acts too are almost always symbols when others are around. What we do is meant to represent and communicate to others. We tell one another something in our actions: what we think, feel, see; what our intentions are; what is coming next. For acts to be symbolic we are not including all acts, since many things that we do are not meant to represent and communicate. What many call unintentional "body language" is not symbolic even though it is a way of communicating. If I look at my watch I might only be determining if I need to leave. If you think I am trying to communicate to you

I am in a hurry, I may be communicating but it is not technically a symbolic gesture to me.

Any *physical object* can become a symbol. Colors—blue and red–red, white, and blue–red—can become symbols. Clothes, jewels, hair style, flags, tattoos can become symbols.

For my own understanding I like to identify three types of symbols: words, objects, and acts. However, sometimes this typology does not express the wide variety of symbols that surround us. For example, a letter or a syllable that makes up a word is a symbol, a musical sound is a symbol, any sound can become a symbol, a piece of art is almost always a symbol, a note on a musical staff is a symbol, street signs are symbols, numbers are symbols. Even when people create something that is not meant to communicate to others, it is usually something they are intentionally communicating to themselves.

What is and is not a symbol is complicated. It is easiest to understand what a symbol is from the standpoint of the user. I intentionally use words; I intentionally use objects; I intentionally use acts. I use these to communicate and represent to others. That makes these symbols, even if others do not see or understand them. If these are not understood and intentionally given off it is not a symbol to the communicator, even if others think it is meaningful to the communicator. From the point of view of the receiver the symbol given off by the other may be understood—have meaning—and thus it becomes a symbol to the receiver, even if it is not a symbol to the communicator.

There is obviously a lot of room for misunderstanding in human communication. It is difficult to express what one means. It is often difficult to know if and when someone is intentionally communicating. It is difficult to know exactly what they are communicating; it is probably impossible to know exactly what the meaning of a symbol is from the perspective of the communicator. We get confused if someone is communicating and we cannot tell if it is intentional communication. We get confused because on top of symbolic communication we also communicate with body language that is unintentional, and others interpret our actions without our necessarily knowing it.

Symbolic communication between actors is obviously most successful when both the communicator and the receiver have the same meaning. However, as Hugh Duncan (1968) writes, "perhaps it is the ambiguity of symbols which makes them so useful in human society" (p. 7). It certainly makes communication interesting.

LANGUAGE

Words are special symbols. They are purposely created for a definite purpose: representation. They make up our language system. They have meaning alone and in combination with other words. More than any other symbols, they can be produced at will, and they can represent a reality that other symbols cannot.

It is through language we are able to communicate to ourselves. Indeed, when we say a symbol has meaning, we are actually saying that its representation is associated through word symbols. Thus, all objects and actions that we make into symbols are done so through words. All of this makes words the most important of all symbols we use. Joyce Hertzler (1965) writes:

> The *key and basic symbolism of [human beings] is language.* All the other symbol systems can be interpreted only by means of language ...
>
> It is the instrument by means of which every designation, every interpretation, every conceptualization, and almost every communication of experience is ultimately accomplished.... There are, of course, other forms of conveying messages interpersonally, which express ideas, emotions, intents, or directives: laughter, ... gestures facial expressions and postures especially, writing. But these other signs, signals, expressions, and marks are all other symbolic systems related to words, imply words, are translations, substitutes, adjuncts, or supplements of words.... Bereft of their relation to, and interpretation in terms of, language they would be meaningless. Thus, for example among us the raucous guffaw means "You're a fool!"; the wave of an arm by an acquaintance means "Hello: the green light at the intersection means "Go"; the nod and wink means "Come on"; the beckoning gesture means "Come!" (pp. 29–31).

Language is made up of words, each one having meaning alone and also having meaning when combined with others in a standardized way, according to certain established rules. Roger Brown (1965) refers that the "miracle of language" is that:

> Fewer than one hundred sounds which are individually meaningless are compounded, not in all possible ways, to produce some hundreds of thousands of meaningful morphemes [segments], which have meanings that are arbitrarily assigned, and these morphemes are combined by rule to yield an infinite set of sentences, having meanings that can be derived (p. 248).

Language is a *symbolic system,* defined in social interaction, and used to describe to others and to ourselves what we observe, think, and imagine. Language is made up of words—arbitrary abstract sounds or marks—that identify everything we understand in communication. Language describes all other social objects and all other symbols, all that people point out to one another in social interaction.

Words Are Categories

Words are really categories, used to *refer* to a class of objects that are distinguishable to the human being. To say that words refer to something else is to say that they *represent,* "they take the place of," their referent. And to say that they refer to a "class of objects" means that they rarely simply refer to a single object. Brown uses the example of the word *larger,* a symbol that stands for a difference in size. Not only can it describe the difference between two specific objects (a single cat and a single rat), but it can be applied to all cats and rats, and indeed to all objects. The word can be applied to a host of things once its meaning has been grasped by the person using it. If words did not refer to some general category, humans would need a huge increase in the number of their words, and the real value would be lost. Each concrete object would need a name, and its similarity to and differences from other concrete objects would be lost to us. That specific object named Charles Mole is a "man," a "teacher," an "American," a "father," a "moral person." Each of these terms is a category that tells us what Charles has in common with other objects and what some of his differences are. Without words, Charles Mole would be Charles Mole to us and nothing more (and he would be a physical object, not "Charles Mole"). Our ability to categorize and transfer past experiences to new situations depends on this generalizing capacity; this capacity contrasts our world with the nonsymbolic world of most other organisms, where they must learn specific responses to specific stimuli in order to "know" what to do.

NONSYMBOLIC ANIMALS

Nonhuman animals are not symbolic, as we are here defining "symbols." They do not define social objects in social interaction, do not use symbols or language as we defined above, do not use perspectives to define reality, and do not seem to act in ways that we will identify in Chapter 5. Almost all nonhuman animals have a passive relationship with their environment. Behavior is usually instinctive (biologically programmed) or learned through experience or imitation. There certainly is communication among all animals, but it is what we might call a conversation of nonmeaningful gestures, not symbols that are understood but the act of one organism becomes a cue for the response of the other. "The beginning of the act of one is a stimulus to the other to respond in a certain way, while the beginning of this response becomes again a stimulus to the first to adjust his action to the oncoming response" (Mead, 1934, pp. 144–45).

Nonhuman animals may have highly complex instinctive behavior, their learning through imitation or experience may be extensive, and their communication may be very important, but as far as we know, symbols, social objects, perspectives, and language are not part of their worlds. Humans have taught chimpanzees, orangoutangs, and gorillas human language, and even have taught some the ability to combine some of the words. Even though they may have potential for symbols, they do not produce symbols through social interaction with one another in nature in the sense that humans do. It is also clear that as wondrous these experiments are, the limits of human language use is very limited. Most symbolic interactionists would probably agree with John Hewitt's (1984) position:

> A symbolic capacity, however simple or complex, is one thing; language is quite another. The apes embarked on an evolutionary course different from ours. Our biological nature, unlike theirs, evolved in tandem with our elaboration of a symbolic capacity into a full-blown language. Our speech came to be controlled by the cerebral cortex, while the vocal call systems of other primates remained under the control of the more ancient limbic system. We developed a refined,

biologically based capacity to produce, hear, and reproduce sounds, whereas they did not. Our brains grew larger than theirs. And while we became progressively more dependent on learning and language use in a complex social environment, their development left them still dependent on a call system and with simpler modes of social organization (p. 49).

Evidence is still being sought to determine if symbol use exists in nonhuman animals. The symbolic interactionist, by and large, sees the human as unique in nature, and unique precisely because of symbol use. If, however, it is established that other animals use symbols too, then this fact will in no way detract from the perspective; indeed, our understanding of both the human and other symbol-using animals will be greatly increased. However, if some other animals do indeed use symbols in the sense defined here, it must be established that (1) the symbols are developed socially, through interaction; (2) the symbols are not universally agreed on within the species but are arbitrarily established by and changed through the interaction of users; and (3) a language of sounds or gestures exists that is meaningful and that includes rules allowing for combining the sounds or gestures into meaningful statements. To be symbolic means that the organism not only rotely learns responses to cues (as a dog may do from its master) but also actively creates and manipulates symbols in interaction with others and with self.

How Animals Approach Environment

One of the best ways to understand the nature of the symbol is to contrast it with the nonsymbolic approach to environment that characterizes other animals. Such a contrast is one of the themes in a book by Ernest Becker (1962, pp. 15–22). He makes the point that a symbolic approach to one's environment is a *qualitatively* different one from nonsymbolic approaches. The human is unique in nature, or, borrowing Warriner's term, humans are *emergent* in nature precisely because of the symbol.

Becker describes four basic approaches to environment by animals. In the first type, the organism responds directly to a stimulus. The stimulus controls the action; there is total passivity on the organism's part. The second type is the conditioned response, where the organism is trained to make an association. The organism can learn to respond to a stimulus because it has learned that the stimulus is *associated* with something else of importance. The third approach to environment is the ability of some animals to make relationships in the visual field and to act. The animal is not trained but seems to make the association by itself. Becker describes this approach:

> The best example of it is the chimp who uses a stick to knock down a banana, suspended out of reach. He sees a relationship between two objects in his visual field, and swings the stick to bring down the banana. The crucial difference between this behavior and that of Pavlov's dog is that, for the chimp, the relationship between the banana and stick is something he establishes himself. It results from an alertness to a problem situation. The equation is not built into the

chimp by an experimenter, in step-by-step fashion. There is some masterful autonomy here that is absent in the simple conditioned reflex. It is not easy for an animal to relate itself to two or more things in the environment. A dog, for example, seeing food through a picket fence, will detour to a gate twenty feet down the fence to get to the food on the other side. He has seen a relationship between the open gate and getting the food. But a hen, seeing the same food and the gate as well, does not establish any relationship, and runs helplessly back and forth directly in front of the food, watching it through the pickets (pp. 17–18).

The final type is symbolic action: response "to an arbitrary designation for an object, a designation coined by him or her alone, that stands for the object." As Becker explains:

> The word "house," for example, has no intrinsic qualities within itself that would connect it with an object, since someone else may use "casa" or "maison" or "dom." Unlike Pavlov's dog, [the human being] *creates* the relationship between stimuli. ... Symbolic behavior depends, of course, upon the ability to create identifiable words [and] sounds that become object representations of infinite degrees of subtlety—from "minnow hook" to "minestrone" (pp. 18–19).

Becker emphasizes that the differences in the four approaches are *qualitative differences*, not just a matter of degree. Each one seems to be central to the kinds of responses possible. Symbol use provides *the most flexible and active approach* precisely because the organism has a mind to deal with the environment, whereas in the other approaches to environment, organisms are tied to simple reflex, to conditioning, or to seeing relationships in the immediate environment only.

Symbols Versus Signs

Symbols are often described by distinguishing them from *signs*. Ernest Becker (1962) points out that the difference is that the organism does not give meaning to signs and does not reflect on them but instead habitually responds to them. Signs may indeed be associated with something else; for example, we might argue that the flap of a beaver's tail is associated with approaching danger. Or, perhaps the flap of the tail can call forth an immediate response without there even being an association. In either case, however, signs lead to an automatic response; they are not arbitrary or conventional, they do not arise in interaction, nor is there any meaning assigned through words. Signs are responded to because they are produced in one's physical presence, and they lead to an unthinking response. They must be sensed, and the receiver has neither choice nor understanding.

Humans do not often respond to signs. We are so highly symbolic that, if we are trained to respond to a word or to an object without reflection, in another situation or with another group that same word or object will most likely take on a different meaning and be transformed into a symbol. To the new recruit, the word "attention" may act as a sign. It is associated without reflection with an officer, with danger, with a certain act, and the response is probably made without reflection. The sign acts as a cue that leads to a response. Yet the sign "attention" is transformed when the officer leaves the room and the soldiers may play at "attention," making fun of the whole matter. We are so thoroughly symbolic that our most habitual behavior is transformed as we move from situation to situation, from group to group, from context to context. We act in our worlds according to interpretations of objects in a context rather than through specific responses to specific stimuli, cues, or signs.

Even "signs" in nature become profoundly complex and symbolic and do not exist for us at all in any pure sense. Most other animals, it seems, respond only to signs, cues, and stimuli.

This symbolic nature of ours is profoundly significant to what humans are capable of. It is basic to almost everything we are. Even if other animals do use symbols as described here, none will be found to depend on them as humans do, and probably none will be found whose central qualities are traceable to symbol use. The contrast with the rest of the animal kingdom, be it comfortable for you or uncomfortable, should not be disregarded as unimportant. Kenneth Burke (1966) illustrates this contrast through the interesting example of a wren. He reports how the mother wren was able to get all the baby wrens out of the nest except for one. Nothing seemed to work. "Then came the moment of genius. One of the parent wrens came to the nest with a morsel of food. But instead of simply giving it to the noisy youngster, the parent bird held it at a distance" (pp. 4–5). Slowly the baby was teased out of the nest. The parent pushed, and by obtaining the needed leverage on the baby, whose balance was shaky, was able to push it out. Pure genius, Burke announces. But, on the other hand, the wren is not now able to write a dissertation on "The Uses of Leverage," nor can this technique be shared throughout the wren kingdom so that others too can try it. Three important points to note, according to Burke, are

1. The ability to describe this method in words would make it possible for all other birds to take over the same "act" of genius, although they themselves might never have hit upon it.

2. The likelihood is that even this one wren will never use this method again, for the ability to conceptualize implies a kind of *attention* without which this innovation could probably not advance beyond the condition of a mere accident to the condition of an invention.

3. On the happier side, there is the thought that at least, through lack of such ability, birds are spared our many susceptibilities to the ways of demagogic spellbinders. They cannot be filled with fantastic hatreds for alien populations they know about mainly by mere hearsay or with all sorts of unsettling new expectations, most of which could not possibly turn out as promised (pp. 4–5).

Summary

Human beings learn about and come to understand their environment through interaction with others. Thus, reality is largely social for them. This fact does not deny the existence of a reality "out there," nor does it ignore the fact that human beings also come to unique understandings through inter-action with themselves.

Human beings exist in a world of social objects. They understand and use their environment; they come to understand their environment through interaction with others and with self; and the environment is always changing for them as their goals change.

One class of social objects is symbols, which are social objects used inten-tionally to communicate and represent something. They are understood by the actor who communicates, and they are normally interpreted by the others. Symbols include words and many objects, and almost all acts around others contain a symbolic element. Words are the most important symbols, making human thinking possible. Although other animals communicate, they do not seem to use symbols, and their whole approach to their environment differs greatly from the human being's because they do not use symbols.

Symbols are the basis for almost everything that characterizes the human being in nature. In order to appreciate this fact, we will examine their importance in Chapter 5.

CHAPTER FIVE

The Importance of the Symbol

Communication is a wonder. Dogs growl and they urinate. Birds sing, insects dance or give off odors, baboons gesture, babies cry. Sometimes communication is simple; in some animals it is very complex. Often we wonder how some animals do it, and sometimes it seems that their communication is like human communication. Animals that are domesticated communicate with humans. Humans communicate to horses, dogs, cats. Bears communicate with humans; humans with bears. Petting is one way we extend kindness to animals, sometimes with or without words or sounds.

It is, however, important to distinguish exactly how communication is actually taking place. Some communication is instinctive; some is learned. Some is intentional; some unintentional. Some are physical gestures; some are sounds. Some are simple and repetitive; some are complex and diverse. Some are simple stimulus and response; some are highly abstract. All species of animals have different physical qualities that allow them to communicate in one way or another. Communication will differ considerably throughout the animal kingdom. Every day we find new and interesting ways that animals communicate.

Like the communication of other animals, humans often use unintentional body language. We give off physical cues to others that exhibit, for example, boldness, anger, excitement, lying, or fear. However, on top of this, humans develop and depend on what we have called "symbols": a myriad of intentional, understood words, acts, and objects designed through social interaction, symbols that become complex categories and allow for high levels of abstraction, able to combine in almost an infinite number of ways, able to apply understandings in a number of different situations. Special tongues, highly developed brains made possible by forehead and jaws, facial muscles, vocal chords that are able to create multiple and subtle sounds, and lifelong socialization, make our ability to communicate extraordinarily complex. Some mammals—gorillas, chimpanzees, dolphins, for example—come close, but they are either distinctly different or highly limited because of their physical qualities.

This ability creates the essence of the human being. It is not only very complex symbolic communication that is made possible, but how we see reality is altered, our type of society becomes unique, and our qualities as individual human beings we take for granted are developed. This is not to refuse to identify similarities with other animals, or to state that we know exactly how other animals always communicate, nor does it assume superiority or supernaturally created qualities. This does not mean we have a right to ignore, disrespect, or refuse to respect other animals, or that morality and rights only apply to other humans. It does mean, however, that, like every other species in the animal kingdom, we have developed a unique system of communication, and what has developed allows us to do a whole variety of other actions that make us human.

It is difficult to imagine a world without symbols because the human world is so overwhelmingly symbolic at its very core. Very few cases of nonsymbol-using individuals appear in human history, and the few that do are described in incomplete studies, making generalizations difficult. Symbol use by the human begins at a very early age, first through understanding other's symbols, then through intentional symbolic expression.

This chapter is going to focus on the importance of symbol use. For the human being, symbols create our *reality*, make complex *society* possible, and contribute a number of *important qualities* that together make the human unique in nature.

SYMBOLS AND SOCIAL REALITY

The basic theme of Chapters 1 through 4 is that humans do not see reality as it is, but always they interpret what exists. We use perspectives. Each social science is a perspective on human beings. Pragmatism teaches us that we define objects according to their use, and that we remember whatever we can use. In each case reality, as it is, is not open to us.

It is the symbol that translates the world from a physical sensed reality to a reality that can be understood, interpreted, dissected, integrated, tested. Between reality and what we see and do stands the symbol. Once we learn symbols we are in the position of understanding our environment rather than simply responding to it, and once that happens what we come to see and act on is colored by our symbols. Herbert Blumer (1969) expresses this simple principle in this way: "Meaning...arises out of social interaction that one has with one's fellows" (p. 2), and this meaning involves a symbolic understanding. We label objects in our environment with symbols; we discuss them, we develop ideas about what they are and how they are to be used; and we carry these ideas in our heads from situation to situation. Joyce Hertzler (1965) writes that the human being operates "in a world of ideas. But it is within and by means of the linguistic framework that the ideationally established world exists and operates.... Language is the means and mode of [our] whole mental existence" (p. 42).

This interaction that gives rise to our reality is symbolic—it is through symbolic interaction with one another that we give the world meaning and develop the reality toward which we act.

Kenneth Burke (1966) writes that our reality in the world at this split moment is nothing other than what we have learned from a "cluster of symbols about the past combined with whatever things we know mainly through maps, magazines, newspapers, and the like about the present" (p. 5). Whatever we experience *now* is seen through the symbols we use to see, and our ability to tie the present to a bigger picture depends on symbols. Burke warns us: "To meditate on this fact until one sees its full implications is much like peering over the edge of things into an ultimate abyss." Few of us ever appreciate the extent to which symbols influence how we see reality. Yet, as we meditate about the role of symbols we might come to appreciate Mead's words: "A person learns a new language ... and gets a new soul. ... [Each of us] becomes in that sense a different individual" (1934, p. 283). To the symbolic interactionist, symbols in fact become the reality we see. Symbols transform reality as it really is to one perceived through the lens of socially created symbols.

SYMBOLS AND HUMAN SOCIAL LIFE

Symbols are the building blocks of human society. Human beings are social, as are many other animals. However, throughout our lives we learn to be social, to interact, and to understand one another, and we learn the roles, rules, values, and ideas that others want us to learn. We are socialized into a particular society. However, none of this socialization occurs out of instinct. We become social beings because we have to in order to survive, and we learn this fact right from the start as we interact with others. The way we live our lives around others in society is not something we are born with, nor is it something we simply learn through imitation. Instead:

> *human society is based on symbols. The second contribution that symbols make to what human beings are is that symbols create and maintain the societies within which we exist. They are used to socialize us; they make our culture possible; they are the basis for ongoing communication and cooperation; and they make possible our ability to pass down knowledge from one generation to the next.*

Let us examine each of these aspects of human society in turn.

First of all, *it is through symbols that individuals are socialized*—coming to share the rules, ideas, and values of the group as well as coming to learn their roles in relation to everyone else. We do not know how to act in society through instinct; we do not learn how to act in relation to others simply through imitation or experience. Each individual learns how to act in society through symbols and thus becomes part of society through symbols:

> And it is not from the language of the classroom, still less that of courts of law, of moral tracts or of textbooks of sociology, that the child learns about the culture [he or she] was born into. The striking fact is that it is the most ordinary everyday uses of language, with parents, brothers and sisters, neighborhood children, in the home, in the street and the park, in the shops and the trains and the

buses, that serve to transmit, to the child, the essential qualities of society and the nature of social being (Halliday, 1978, p. 9).

Symbols are also central to society because society's culture depends on them. Recall Tamotsu Shibutani's (1955) "Reference Groups As Perspectives" (Chapter 3): it is, he writes, through symbolic communication that we come to share culture, and it is through this communication and resulting culture that social worlds (groups, societies) are able to continue. Culture, a central quality of every human society, is learned through symbols, and it is itself symbolic. We share ideas, rules, goals, values (all symbolic), and these allow us to continue to interact cooperatively with others.

We seem to grasp almost intuitively the central importance of symbols for our group life. We set up rules (symbolic) to be taught (usually through written or spoken *words*) to newcomers entering an already established group. We ensure that the ideas we have developed are somehow shared and that what takes place is fully understood (has the right meaning) to the newcomer. That process takes place during college-orientation week, when students learn new rules, abbreviations, course names, teacher names, buildings, and requirements for graduation. It takes place in the poker club, which must, during breaks in the action, teach the rules, the meanings, the taboos, the appropriate language, and the proper betting to the newcomer. Both the college and the poker club know that without some shared reality their very existence may be at stake. And if we look at the group situation from the standpoint of the newcomer, he or she wants to understand the *meanings* attached to all the various acts—to learn immediately the shared reality in order to operate within the group.

Human society depends on ongoing symbolic communication. Communication means sharing, and sharing is one very important way that society is held together. Very complex forms of cooperation occur because human beings are able to discuss with one another how to resolve the problems that they face. Indeed, as Ralph Ross (1962) emphasizes, the words *community* and *communication* show an immediate similarity:

> They emphasize commonness, togetherness. People gather or live together for certain purposes, and they *share* meanings and attitudes; the first presupposes the second, for without communication there is no community. Community depends on shared experience and emotion, the communication enters into and clarifies the sharing. Forms of communication like art and religion and language are themselves shared by a community, and each of them contains and conveys ideas, attitudes, perspectives, and evaluations which are deeply rooted in the history of the community (p. 156–57).

Symbolic communication not only brings us together, nor is it simply important for our sharing a view of reality that makes society possible. *Symbolic communication is also the basis for human cooperation.* It is not simple training or instinct that makes it possible for us to work together in achieving our own goals or the goals established in communication. It is, instead, the fact that

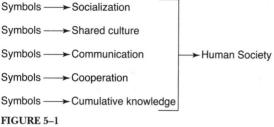

FIGURE 5–1

human beings, as they act together, must inform one another about what is being done, how to solve problems together, how to change what they are doing, or whether to continue what they are already doing. We correct one another, encourage one another, disagree with one another, and direct one another, and we are able to work together. The basis for human cooperation is *ongoing symbolic communication,* the constant attempts by actors to tell others about their own action and what they expect others to do in order to coordinate action.

But there is much more. Groups have histories, and a long history means a very large corpus of knowledge. *It is by means of symbols that the past is recorded— knowledge and wisdom are not lost but are accumulated.* We can reflect and build on them; each interaction need not start from scratch. What one generation learns does not die when it dies. Hertzler (1965) states that language is "the major vehicle whereby we transmit—that is, impart or send and receive—our factualized experience ... to others across space and time ... from one individual, one area, one generation, one era, one cultural group to another" (pp. 50–51). Complex ongoing societies depend heavily on this function of symbols.

Symbols, therefore, are important to the human being because they are the basis for both social reality and society. Social reality is created in symbolic interaction and we come to see reality through symbols we take on. Society depends on symbols for socialization, culture, communication, cooperation, and the cumulation of knowledge (Figure 5–1).

SYMBOLS AND THE INDIVIDUAL

What exactly is the human being? What is our essence? Mead emphasizes that our real essence is traced to our use of symbols. This essence goes beyond the reality we see and the society within which we live. It goes to the heart of our qualities as individual human beings. Whatever else we may be born with, it is only when we take on symbols that we are able to act like other human beings.

There are many qualities that the individual possesses that arise only because of our use of symbols. We are transformed from a being who is weak, helpless, unintelligent, and simple to one whose complexity, flexibility, and intelligence bring about a uniqueness in nature.

Symbols transform the individual human being in at least nine ways, and we will briefly examine these in turn at this time.

Naming, Memory, Categorizing

Through calling something a *name* we have identified it, *marked it out*, and *distinguished it*, and we are able to *store it for later application*. We can recognize similar objects and call them by that name. Naming an object allows us to apply the name to another situation without the object's immediate physical presence. We can identify individual objects that we have never seen before because we have learned their names—that is, what they "are." The name can be stored in memory and can be purposely recalled in a multitude of situations. It might be possible that memory can exist without language (e.g., other animals may be able to recall pictures), but language allows for a much more complex, efficient memory system, one that can be more easily activated, whose parts can be more easily interpreted, transferred, combined, and isolated. As Hertzler (1965) puts it: "The words of language, functioning as categories of experienced reality, not only facilitate more precise analysis, but also aid in the comparison of one portion of experiential data with other portions" (p. 41).

Related to the naming function, of course, is *categorizing*. Language is used *to discriminate, to generalize, to make ever so subtle distinctions* in one's environment. The world is literally divided up by means of the language we use:

> Language has to interpret the whole of our experience, reducing the indefinitely varied phenomena of the world around us, and also of the world inside us, the processes of our own consciousness, to a manageable number of classes of phenomena: types of processes, events and actions, classes of objects, people and institutions, and the like. (Halliday, 1978, p. 21)

A category named is gradually understood, described by qualities we discover it has, and is distinguished from other categories in increasingly subtle ways, each understanding allowing us to capture why things happen in the universe, how various categories are related to other categories, and how to alter and use objects in our environment that we have come to understand rather than simply respond to as individual sensed objects. "A tree. What's a tree?" It is a plant rather than an animal, a living thing rather than something without life, a part of the natural rather than a supernatural universe, a physical object that can be sensed, a thing of beauty, something that prevents erosion and attracts squirrels. Understanding this category called "trees" with symbols that are themselves understood categories allows humans to achieve an understanding not available to nonsymbol users.

Perception

Language guides us through what our senses experience. It constitutes the individual's *perspectives*, and thus it serves the function of alerting the individual to some parts of the environment and not to others. "A language, once formed, has a self-contained organization somewhat like mathematics, and it previsages possible experience in accordance with accepted formal limitations. What we see is influenced by language, by the 'preexisting linguistic categories' we possess" (Shibutani, 1961, p. 122). Symbols are the individual's eyes to the world. As emphasized throughout this chapter, the human being does not sense reality as it physically exists but uses the lens of symbols, and this lens alters every aspect of our being.

Thinking

Hertzler calls language "our means of thinking." To the symbolic interactionist, thinking is conceptualized as symbolic interaction with one's self. Thinking is talking to oneself; it is an activity, a constant, ongoing process. Almost every moment, the individual is thinking in this sense, according to Blumer (1969, p. 16), constantly modifying reality through an "interpretive process." When we act alone we are almost always engaged in self-communication; when we are with others to whom we try to communicate, we also engage in self-communication with symbols, since symbols by definition must simultaneously give off meaning to ourselves as we communicate to others. Thinking is so central to all we do that it, like language itself, is taken for granted unless pointed out to us. If thinking is more than responding to pictures inside our heads, if it is an active process, if it is dissecting, applying, integrating, figuring out what is around us, then it is possible only with a tool such as symbols, which allows us to manipulate representations within our head.

Deliberation and Problem Solving

Deliberation is a type of thinking, but it is more "deliberate" and conscious self-communication than the constant, ongoing thinking just described. It occurs most often when a problem is presented, when the situation requires analysis before action. It involves an attempt to consciously manipulate one's situation. The individual views self as an object in the situation, holds back action, analyzes, engages in lengthy discussion with self as action unfolds. In one sense, there is no difference between deliberation and the thinking described in the preceding paragraph, for the difference is really a matter of the degree of consciousness and the degree of holding back overt action until the situation is fully understood. Deliberation is a matter of degree. It is thinking that holds back action, thinking that allows for careful decision making, thinking that allows for the rehearsal of action before it is performed. Thinking occurs all the time; deliberation occurs when thinking is more conscious and controlling.

Mead emphasizes the problem-solving nature of careful deliberation. The greater the problem to overcome, the more likely we must stop, hold back action, and figure out our situation. Small problems are minor interruptions, involving little deliberation; larger problems are major interruptions necessitating more deliberation.

Life can be thought of as a multitude of problems confronting the individual, each one calling for handling and solving, and each one demanding at least some thinking. Each time we interact with someone else, small problems are presented to us: how to understand the other, how to make ourselves understood, how to influence the other, how to avoid or get to know the other, how to work together or successfully dominate or successfully resist domination. Usually these problems are thought out very quickly without much deliberation. Deliberation occurs when we find ourselves in a situation that involves considering alternative plans of action, predicting consequences, rehearsing how to act, and recalling past situations that may be applicable. We must figure out the situation rather than quickly handling the situation. Thinking is constant; deliberation occurs often; very serious deliberation occurs occasionally. It is an evolving process. We may act and then look back and analyze that act and then deliberate before we continue. We may do one act at one moment and change our strategies later on. All thinking and deliberation are integral parts of human action and depend entirely on our ability to manipulate symbols.

Transcendence of Space and Time

Problem solving and reflection involve transcending the immediate physical situation. We are able to examine the past and future as we act in the present. We are able to examine the universe beyond the immediate physical environment. We overcome space and time through representations of future, past, and other realities beyond the immediate. This process involves more than pictures that flash in our heads; this is the ability to describe, manipulate, and apply worlds outside the immediate situation. We are able "to inhabit simultaneously the past (through legend, traditions, and formal records), the present and the future (by means of declared ideals, projections, anticipations, plans and programs)" (Hertzler, 1965, pp. 53–54).

Language allows individuals to understand worlds they have never seen; it allows them to see the future and to integrate past, present, and future. For example: I "know" ancient Greece without having been there, and I have a strong notion of what the United States will become in twenty years. I also believe that the United States' unjust treatment of minorities *today* is a result of a painful *history* of racism, and I also see today's policies as having some impact on a more just society *tomorrow*. The individual is guided in social situations by recalling the past and by looking to the future, immediate and distant. When an individual acts, others outside the immediate situation may be the most important influences; the struggles of societies the individual has never had any contact with may be his or her most important inspiration, and what is going on "in the next room" outside the immediate field of vision and hearing may be perceived to be most influential on the individual's future. Language allows the individual to break out of the present and immediate stimulus environment and adds immeasurably to the factors that influence action.

Transcendence of One's Own Person

Not only do symbols allow individuals to leave the immediate space-and-time environment, but symbols also allow them to leave their own bodies and get outside of themselves to imagine the world from the perspectives of others. This very important human quality, which symbolic interactionists refer to as "taking the role of the other," allows us to understand others, to clearly communicate with them, to influence them, to sympathize with them, to love them. It allows for human beings' understanding of one another's ideas, because the more we are able to see things from the perspective of the people with whom we communicate, the more we are able to truly "see" what other people are saying. It is through language that we come to understand other people, their perspectives, their perceptions, their feelings, and their behavior. There is a significant difference between responding to a command and trying to see a communication from the standpoint of the other. This ability to take the role of the other, itself dependent on our symbolic nature, is so central to human social life that its nature and its importance are the subject of Chapter 8.

Abstract Reality

Language also allows the human being to imagine and perceive a reality beyond the concrete. Only through language can we establish objects such as God, love, freedom, truth, good and evil, afterlife, and a host of other abstract objects that are so much an integral part of our existence. A reality beyond physical reality is open only through words and the manipulation of words into ideas. The concrete world of our senses is transformed by language into a reality not possible to nonsymbol users. Hertzler (1965) puts it nicely:

> By means of conceptualization, [the human] is able to develop and live in the abstract world of intellectual experience—the world of ethical, aesthetic, evaluational, teleological, spiritual, and supernatural considerations ... "goodness" as an ethical aspect, or "beauty" as an aesthetic characteristic, are not inherent in the event or the object, they are nonexistent, except in so far as we "perceive" and "conceive" them in terms of words. With language, we can wrestle with such perplexing questions as "truth" and "error," "right" and "wrong," "existential" and "transcendental." Words can stand for such abstractions as electricity, force, justice, time, space, future, deity—ideas which cannot possibly be represented by any visual picture (p. 55).

Because human beings are symbol users and are able to create an abstract world, human beings can imagine goals, ideals, values, and morals that themselves become important motivating factors in human behavior. To die for "my country," to work for "freedom," to try to end "poverty" show a kind of motivation impossible to any except symbol users. This means that the human potential is limited only by human imagination. As long as we believe, for example, that "love" and "goodness" and "equality" are worth working for, we can constantly try to guide our behavior toward those ends. And if we believe that "materialism" or "destruction of others" or "power over others" is important, it becomes a guide to behavior. But symbols by their very nature open up a wide range of behavior possibilities. In a sense, no action is "unnatural" to us, because symbols allow for virtually any possibility.

Creativity

The symbolic interactionist emphasizes the central importance of language in creating the active rather than the passive person. It is through thinking with symbols that each individual is able to create his or her own world beyond the physical, develop highly individual interpretations of reality, and act uniquely toward that reality. Language arises from society, yet it is the tool that the human can use to think about and challenge that society. The key is not so much the symbol as it is the *symboling*, the *manipulation of symbols* by active persons, defining and redefining their social situations. Give the child an understanding of certain *words*, and it is impossible to control fully how those words will be combined and recombined. This is the magic of language. To teach "love your country" and to teach "hate other countries," is to create the possibility that students will decide to hate their country and love other countries. To teach a child what "little" means, what "big" means, and what "in a little while" means is to invite from him or her: "No, I'll go to bed *in a big while.*" Every sentence is, in a sense, a creative act. To manipulate the words we learn from interaction is to become an individual—creative, active, and shaping, not passive and conforming.

Although not all creativity depends on symbols, much of it does: we create our own reality. And some of us produce great creations in literature, science, music, and art through playing with the understanding we have learned through symbols.

Self-Direction

Language allows the human being to exercise self-direction. Our communication with ourselves is a form of giving orders: Cooperate! Rebel! Listen! Get away! Run! Walk! Turn right! Work harder! Sleep! Think! Any control that we have over ourselves (and the symbolic interactionists claim it is considerable) comes through symbolic interaction with ourselves, through telling ourselves what is going on, what alternatives there are, and what line of action to take. The decision to conform and cooperate as well as the decision to rebel are a matter of the individual's deciding through symbolic interaction with self what to do. To continue what we do, to hold back action, to control what we present to others, to discover new ideas, essays, art works, pieces of music, or buildings is ultimately dependent upon use of symbols. Indeed, every act we do has an element of creativity, a unique, individualistic, personal, self-directed aspect to some extent, unlike what we have been taught by others.

THE IMPORTANCE OF SYMBOLS: A SUMMARY

The importance of the symbol for the individual can best be summarized by combining all of these contributions to the individual into a single central point: the human being, because of the symbol, does not respond passively to a reality that imposes itself but actively creates and re-creates the world acted in. Humans name, remember, categorize, perceive, think, deliberate,

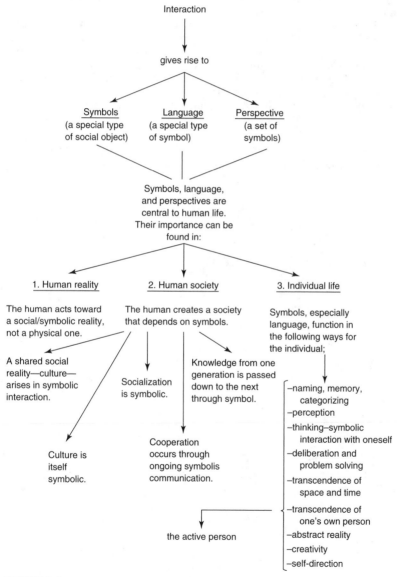

FIGURE 5–2

problem solve, transcend space and time, transcend themselves, create abstractions, create new ideas, and direct themselves—all through the symbol. There is probably no better summary of the central importance that symbolic interactionists give to symbols than that of S. Morris Eames (1977):

> [H]umans can construct symbols and languages, they can speak and write, and by these means they can preserve their past experiences, construct new meanings, and entertain goals and ideas. Humans can make plans and by proper selection of the means to the ends carry them through. They can write poetry and novels, compose music and painting, and otherwise engage in aesthetic experiences. They can construct explanatory hypotheses about the world and all that is in it, of electrons, protons, and neutrons, and solar systems far away. They can dream dreams, concoct fantasies, erect heavens above the earth which entice their activities to far-off destinies, and they can imagine hells which stimulate fears of everlasting torture. The emergent functions of symbolic behavior make it possible for humans to transcend parts of their immediate undergoing and experiencing and to know that death and all that it entails is a part of organic life (pp. 40–41).

Symbols make possible human reality, they create human society, and they are central to what it means to be human (see Figure 5–2).

CHAPTER SIX

The Nature of the Self

In the film "Awakenings" a doctor (Dr. Malcolm Sayer played by Robin Williams) attempts an experiment on people who, because of brain damage arising from illness, were nonresponsive to the world around them for thirty years. Through the use of a drug (L-Dopa) they awoke from their "sleep," and suddenly started to act like other adults. They saw the world around them anew; they wanted to do things they never had an opportunity to do; they wanted to know exactly what happened for the past thirty years. Most felt that they had been cheated; they began to understand what happened to them. Suddenly, people who could hardly talk or walk or do simple things as others, became conscious, active, hopeful beings.

But their "cure" was temporary. Soon they changed back to their former state. The experiment ended up failing them.

The movie was based on a book written by Dr. Oliver Sacks, who was the real doctor described in the book. The question I was plagued by was not really answered by the film. I wanted to know what these people thought during the thirty years they were unable to respond effectively toward other people and toward their physical environment. The film seemed to indicate that some of them were not conscious during these years; they did not know that they were being deprived. Yet, for others there were indications that some knew that their lives were passing without any physical ability to act like other humans. The book seems to suggest that there was a range of differences in the patients.

From a symbolic interactionist perspective, the real question was: did these people exist without a "self" during these years? Suddenly I realized this question highlighted an extremely important human quality that I understood, but until I saw that movie, I did not appreciate.

Imagine if these people did not see and understand themselves. It seemed they did not think of themselves as persons, as boys or girls, men or women, as sick, as disadvantaged, as Americans, as beings in the universe? If so, they would not realize that time was passing them by. They would not know that their potential was severely limited by disease. They would not know they were missing anything. They would not be seeing themselves in time and place. They would not ask themselves what is happening; they would not ask themselves what they could become; they would not seek meaning, happiness, goodness, love.

Almost all other people know what is going on as they live. They are conscious, constantly looking back on themselves, seeing their own successes and their own weaknesses. They see where they exist in the universe, in time and in space. They understand who they are.

To a great extent, I think most of the patients of *Awakenings* did not know what was happening to them over the thirty years. I am not certain of this. And, I believe, after they returned to their earlier state of illness they probably forgot their moments of consciousness.

These are very profound issues. I ponder them because they highlight for me what it means for human beings to possess a "self." To see yourself in time and space, to see yourself as part of the environment, to talk to yourself about yourself, to constantly evaluate yourself as you act, to realize that you yourself are living, you were born and had a past, that you have a future, that you will die, to recognize that you are the object of others, and that others too see themselves as objects, makes the self the tremendously important quality that makes us human. Choosing good over evil, understanding consequences of our own actions, pursuing happiness and freedom for our self, controlling our own actions—all of these important human qualities arise because humans possess a self.

This chapter attempts to continue to examine the essence of the human being from the perspective of symbolic interactionism. Not only do we possess symbols, we also possess a self. And like symbols self is socially created. Indeed, both symbols and self are interrelated; one arises with the other; one makes the other possible; and together they are basic to what humans do and are in the universe.

SELF AS A SOCIAL OBJECT

There are many views of self in philosophy and social science, and few are either clear or consistent. The term *self* is used in so many different ways in our everyday speech that it is often hard to pin down what we mean by it.

In the symbolic interactionist perspective, *self* has a very specific meaning, not perfect but very usable. As Morris Rosenberg (1979, pp. 6–8) points out, this meaning is different from many other meanings that are popular today. For example, it does not have the same meaning as Freud's "ego." It does not mean the "real" person or the "productive person" or "the total person." It is not the same as personality, or identity, or the actor.

For the symbolic interactionist *the self is an object of the actor's own action.* The individual acts toward others; the individual also acts toward himself or herself. It is not the self that acts; it is the actor that acts, and the actor is able to act back on self as well as on the environment that exists outside. The self is part of the actor's environment that he or she acts toward. It is part of the situation the actor acts toward. It is, like all else, used by the actor as a *social object*, one of the many objects in the situation that the actor finds useful in achieving his or her goals. Every one of us is then an actor (one who acts), and we are the objects of our own actions; that is, we have a self. *The self is the internal environment toward which we act.*

When we say that the self is a social object, we mean, first of all, that *it is an object*, and that *it, like other social objects, arises in our social interaction*. This means that the individual comes to see himself or herself as an object in the environment through interaction with others; other people point out to the actor that he or she exists as an object. Others label and define the self to the actor, and they help the actor understand himself or herself in the environment. "You are Andrew." "You are a boy." "You are a big boy." "You are Mom's favorite person." "You exist in the world just like other objects in the natural universe." Each actor becomes an object to himself or herself because of the actions of others toward him or her. "In the beginning [the actor] is quite unable to make a distinction between [himself or herself] and the rest of the world" (McCall and Simmons, 1966, p. 207). Eventually this distinction is learned in social interaction. Thus, our social life not only makes possible our symbolic abilities, but it also makes possible the development of self and all that goes with our ability to act toward ourselves in every situation we enter.

Mead (1934) emphasizes the social origin of the self in *Mind, Self and Society*. He asks: How can the human being get outside and experience himself or herself as an object? It is through

> the process of social conduct or activity in which the given person or individual is implicated. ... The individual experiences [himself or herself] as such, not directly, but only indirectly, from the particular standpoints of other individual members of the same social group. [We become objects to ourselves] just as other individuals are objects to [us] ... it is impossible to conceive of a self arising outside of social experience (pp. 138–40).

Because the self is a social object, it constantly changes for the actor because it continues to be defined and redefined in social interaction. Its social nature means that it is process rather than a stable entity. How I view myself, how I define myself, how I act toward myself throughout life highly depend on the social definitions I encounter every day of my life. Peter Berger (1963) calls this view of the self radical in the sense that the self "is no longer a solid, given entity that moves from one situation to another. It is rather a process, continuously created and recreated in every social situation that one enters. ... man is not *also* a social being, but he is social in every respect of his being that is open to empirical investigation" (p. 106). The self is therefore not what the psychologist means by "personality," nor is it a true transcendental authentic person. It is simply a continuously changing object, one that we see and use in one way in one situation and in quite another way in another situation, and these actions toward ourselves are influenced by the social interaction that takes place on a continuing basis with other people. Sheldon Stryker (1959) makes this point nicely:

> [T]he human organism as an object takes on meaning through the behavior of those who respond to that organism. We come to know what we are through others' responses to us. Others supply us with a name, and they provide the meaning attached to that symbol. They categorize us in particular ways—as an infant, as a boy, et cetera. On the basis of such categorization, they expect particular behaviors from us; on the basis of these expectations, they act toward us. The manner in which they act toward us defines our "self," we come to categorize ourselves as they categorize us, and we act in ways appropriate to their expectations ... the child moves into the social world [and] comes into contact with a variety of persons in a variety of self-relevant situations. [The child takes on] ... a variety of perspectives from which to view and evaluate [his or her] own behavior, and [he or she] can act with reference to self as well as with reference to others. In short, the socialization process as described makes possible the appearance of objectivity (p. 116).

Stryker concludes his description of the self with the word *objectivity*. Socialization makes possible the fact that the individual is able to get outside of himself or herself and look back at the self objectively, as an object like all the objects defined in interaction. Mead makes a very big point of this ability to get outside of oneself, to take the perspective of the other, and as we shall see in the description of the development of the self in children, it is through "taking the role of the other" that the self emerges.

SELF AS SOCIAL: FOUR SOCIAL STAGES FOR SELF-DEVELOPMENT

At first the individual does not have a self. However, the individual is born into a world that acts on him or her. Most of those actions are the acts of other people, and those acts almost always make use of symbols. At first, we do not understand symbols and simply imitate the acts of others, but very quickly we understand who we are through the use of symbols, and, over time, all the individuals who are important in our self-understanding—significant others—are combined by the actor into a group or society that becomes what Mead calls our "generalized other." As we become adults, there is first a consistency in how we see ourselves because of this generalized other, but over time, we come to interact with many different others, and the one generalized other becomes a number of reference groups, each one having a different impact on how we see and act toward ourselves.

This description emphasizes the central role of our interaction with others in the development of our self, and it emphasizes the self as process. The first three stages are drawn from the work of Mead, and the last is suggested by Tamotsu Shibutani in the article discussed in Chapter 3 called "Reference Groups As Perspectives." Briefly, the emergence of self arises in the following four stages.

The Preparatory Stage

The earliest stage of the self is referred to as the *preparatory stage*, with an almost primitive self emerging, a presymbolic stage of self. Mead probably did not explicitly name this stage, but he implied it in various writings (Meltzer, 1972, p. 15). The child acts as the adult does. The child imitates the other's acts toward other objects and toward himself or herself as object. The parent may push the chair and so may the child. The parent may point to the child as object, the child may also point to self. The parent may say, "Dad," and the child may imitate "da." But the interaction, so long as it is only imitation, lacks meaning, lacks a symbolic understanding. The person as object can really emerge only when objects take on some meaning—that is, when objects are defined with words. When Andrew realizes that he is Andrew, separate and distinct from others, someone represented with a name and described with word qualities, then a symbolic self emerges. That is why Mead refers to this first stage as preparatory; it is purely imitation, and social objects, including the self, are not yet defined and understood with words that have meaning to the child.

The Play Stage

The second stage, referred to by Mead as the *play stage*, comes early in the individual's development, during the acquisition of language. For most children, language comes very early and meaning arises early, really making the preparatory stage insignificant in terms of length of time. The child, learning language, is now able to label and define objects with words that have shared meaning, so objects originally acted toward because of imitation now are acted toward according to the meaning shared in interaction with others. The self is pointed out and labeled by the significant others. "Hi, Andrew!" (Hey, Andrew stands for this object: *me, myself.*) "Good boy!" (Hey, *I* am good.) "Are you sleeping?" (Am *I* sleeping?) "Go play!" (She is telling *me* to play.) As others point us out to ourselves, we see ourselves. We become social objects to ourselves. Others point us out; they give us names. The "creation of self as social object is an identification of that object. ... Identification involves naming. Once an object is named and identified a line of action can be taken toward it" (Denzin, 1972, p. 306). Our names, as well as various pronouns and adjectives, are used to identify "me" in relation to others. *Susan, girl, baby, good, you, she, smart, pretty, slow, funny, bad, wise, American, New Yorker:* that's *me!*

During this play stage, the child assumes the perspective of certain *individuals*, whom Mead refers to as "significant others," those people who take on importance to the individual, those whom the individual desires to impress; they might be those he or she respects, those he or she wants acceptance from, those he or she fears, or those with whom he or she identifies. Significant others are usually role models, who "provide the patterns of behavior and conduct on which [the actor] patterns [himself or herself]. It is through interaction with these role models that the child develops the ability to regulate [his or her] own behavior" (Elkin and Handel, 1972, p. 50). For the child, role models are most likely parents but can also be other relatives, television heroes, or friends. As the child grows older, the significant other possibilities increase greatly and can be a whole number of individuals, including Socrates, Jesus, mom, son, the boss, the president of the United States, Madonna, and Bart Simpson. Whoever our significant others are at any point in our lives, they are important precisely because their views of social objects are important to us, including, and especially, our view of ourselves as social objects. The concept of significant others recognizes that "not all the persons with whom one interacts have identical or even compatible perspectives, and that, therefore, in order for action to proceed, the individual must give greater weight or priority to the perspective of certain others ... others occupy high rank on an 'importance' continuum for a given individual" (Stryker, 1959, p. 115). To the small child, significant others are responsible for the emergence of the self; the child comes to view self as an object because of significant others. In a sense, I fail to see myself without my awareness that these significant others see me.

The reason Mead calls this second stage the *play* stage is that the child assumes the perspective of only one significant other at a time. In this stage, individuals are incapable of seeing themselves from the perspective of many persons simultaneously. The child segregates the significant others, and the view of self is a segmented one. The self is a multitude of social objects, each one defined in interaction with a single other. Play refers to the fact that *group* rules are unnecessary, that the child and a single other are necessary for controls at any single point in time. The child needs to guide self, needs to see self, needs to judge self from the view of only one individual at a time in order to be successful at play. Play is an individual affair, subject to the rules of single individuals. Mead's play stage is a time when the child takes the roles of significant others—father, Superman, mother, teacher—and acts toward self as if he or she were those individuals. In taking the roles of these others the child acts toward objects in the world as they act, and that includes acting toward self as they do. This stage is the real beginning of the self as social object.

The Game Stage

The third stage is the *game stage*. The "game" represents organization and the necessity of assuming the perspectives of several others simultaneously. Cooperation and group life demand knowing one's position in relation to a complex set of others, not just single others. They demand taking on a group culture or perspective. This stage is, to Mead, the adult self, a self that incorporates all one's significant others into one "generalized other." The self becomes more a unitary nonsegmented self, changing in interaction but not radically changing each time another significant other is encountered. The child puts together the significant others in his or her world into a whole, a "generalized other," "them," "society." The self matures as our understanding of *society* matures: it is the other side of the coin. Interaction with others brings us face to face with *their* rules, *their* perspectives, and it also brings us *their* perspective of self, and the self becomes an object defined not only by the individual (play stage) but also by *them* (game stage). Mead used baseball to illustrate this point. (Please note that he wrote this in 1925 before most people recognized that baseball is not only a man's game.)

> The play antedates the game. For in a game there is a regulated procedure, and rules. The child must not only take the role of the other, as he does in the play, but he must assume the various roles of all the participants in the game, and govern his action accordingly. If he plays first base, it is as the one to whom the ball will be thrown from the field or from the catcher. Their organized reactions to him he has embedded in his own playing of the different positions, and this organized reaction becomes what I have called the "generalized other" that accompanies and controls his conduct. And it is this generalized other in his experience which provides him with a self (Mead, 1925, p. 269).

The development of a generalized other by the individual is really the internalization of society as the individual has come to know it; society's rules and perspectives become the child's, and society's definition of self becomes the individual's. "In one sense socialization can be summed up by saying that what was once outside the individual comes to be inside him" (Elkin and Handel, 1972, p. 53). Meltzer (1972, pp. 16–17) points out how important this quality is for consistency of actions by the individual as he or she goes from situation to situation: we do not simply use those in our immediate situation as important guides to action, but we also use what we have learned from others in many situations as to how we should act.

The Reference Group Stage

Mead does not always make it clear if the individual has just one generalized other or several. It seems that what begins as one increasingly becomes several. Tamotsu Shibutani (1955) makes this development explicit, emphasizing what amounts to a fourth stage of self, the *reference group stage*, a stage that seems especially characteristic in an industrial urban "mass society."

The individual interacts with many different groups and thus comes to have several reference groups (social worlds or societies), and he or she shares a perspective in each, including a perspective used to define self, with each of them. If he or she is to continue to interact successfully with each reference group, then that perspective must, at least temporarily, become the individual's generalized other, used to see and direct the self while in that group. Thus, in this final stage, those who matter to us become a complex mixture of generalized others, with separate social worlds or reference groups whose particular views of self become important in one situation and then cease to become important in another.

This notion is highly consistent with the definition of social objects discussed in Chapter 4: social objects are defined in interaction and change in the process of interaction and as the people with whom we interact change. The self as a social object has these identical qualities. In interaction with students, I define myself one way; with my family, another; with sociologists, another; and with male friends, another. Think of your life: your self changes as you interact with friends, family, salespeople, strangers at a party. In each case, our view of self is somewhat different, and it is always undergoing change. William James (1915) boldly writes that a human being "*has as many social selves as there are individuals who recognize [him or her]* and carry an image of [him or her] in their mind." James tells us that each self is tied to a group whose opinion matters to us. "We do not show ourselves to our children as to our club-companions, to our customers, as to the laborers we employ, to our own masters and employers, as to our intimate friends." Sometimes, our selves are split apart; often they are highly consistent (pp. 179–80).

SELVES AS EVER-CHANGING SOCIAL OBJECTS

Let us try to bring some central ideas together here. The small child, before the language-play stage, has the beginnings of self. Then the child with language begins to assume the perspectives of significant others, then of one generalized other, and finally of several reference groups, in each case entering into a new stage of the self. The self rests on interactions with other people. To some extent we have several distinct selves, but because our interactions overlap, because our significant others and reference groups probably form a relatively consistent whole, our self is not as segmented as might have been implied in this discussion.

Let us look at some examples of the social nature of the self as well as its complexity. A president of the United States may use various individuals, groups, and categories of people in defining self, including, for example, "the Republican party," "the American people," "the corporate rich," "the 1776 revolutionaries," a small group of loyal advisers, Thomas Jefferson, his or her spouse, their children, the United Nations, the World Bank, or those who died in the Vietnam War. Whoever's perspective is assumed in the definition of the president's self will be critical to how the president acts. If Ivan matters and Ivan defines the president as one who cares about human beings, then in the presence of Ivan (or even away from Ivan) the president will define his or her self as "one who cares" and will behave accordingly. The social nature of the self is much more complex, but this example will help us better understand self-definition and its consequences later in this chapter. Or take the example of Felix the freshman, mom, dad, girlfriend, Ernest Hemingway, the world of hard rock, the college community he is entering, the college football team he plays on, the artists he hangs around with, the Catholic Church, the business world he wants to join—each will influence how Felix defines himself and how he acts. If it is the business world that constitutes his reference group in a situation, then he will tend to act in relation to the college authorities as a cooperative, loyal, hardworking student.

It should be emphasized that the individual may or may not use people in his or her presence as significant others or reference groups. If people in the present situation are not important, then their perspective is not important and their definition of self is also not important. They are not significant others or reference groups. Thus, the poor teacher is often the one whose reference group does not include the students, and the "moral" person may be the one who rejects the standards of those who are *immediately* around him or her doing things people (significant others, reference groups) elsewhere consider immoral.

SELF AS OBJECT

We have stated that the self is an object, a social object. It is a thing, like other things pointed out and shared in interaction. As Herbert Blumer (1962, p. 181) emphasizes, the importance of the self as object cannot be understated: viewing the self as object means that the individual can *act* toward himself or herself as he or she acts toward all other people. In a sense the individual has an additional person to act toward in the situation. Because we sometimes judge other people, so we can also judge our self. Because we can talk to others, so we can also talk to our self. Because we can point things out to our self about other people, so we can actually point things out to our self about our self. We can direct others, so we can direct our self. The actor acts. When he or she achieves selfhood, action now includes action toward self. Blumer (1962) writes that the possession of self is the "key feature of Mead's analysis" of the human being: "This idea should not be cast aside as esoteric or glossed over as something that is obvious and hence not worthy of attention." Mead means that we act toward our self as objects in the same way we act toward others. Blumer reminds us that we get angry with ourselves, we tell ourselves what we do, and we set goals for ourselves and compromise with ourselves. "That the human being acts toward [himself or herself] in these and countless other ways is a matter of easy empirical observation. To recognize that the human being can act toward [himself or herself] is no mystical conjuration" (p. 181).

One way to appreciate the meaning of self as object is to consider emotions. Many other animals emotionally respond to their environment. Adrenalin flows, clenched teeth are bared, a growl is expressed. What, then, distinguishes human emotion from that of other animals? It all has to do with self. It is the fact that we can look back on what we do. We can see, recognize, and understand what is taking place within us: I am angry. I am sad. I am jealous. I am in love. I am afraid. This is what is meant when we say the human actor is able to see himself or herself as object. We see what we are and what we do—we even are able to look back on how we feel.

To better appreciate the importance of the self we need to examine more closely the various actions that the individual takes toward it, or the way we use it in situations. There are three general categories of action that we need to consider:

1. *Self-communication.* We talk to ourselves. That is, our self is an object we talk to.
2. *Self-perception.* We see ourselves in situations. That is, our self is an object we take note of, or notice. Because we can recognize and understand our relationship with other objects in the situation, we are able to understand and assess our own actions in the situation, and we are able to develop a self-concept, self-judgment, and identity.
3. *Self-control.* We tell ourselves what to do in situations. That is, our self is an object we use in order to control our own actions. To claim that humans direct or control their own actions means that humans have an ability to act back on and direct themselves in situations.

1. ACTION TOWARD SELF: SELF-COMMUNICATION

The human being is an actor who is able to communicate to himself or herself. In short, the actor talks to himself or herself. The individual is both a subject (a communicator) and an object of that action (has a self to whom he or she communicates). Talking to self with symbols is what the symbolic interactionist means by thinking. Self therefore makes possible thinking, the ability to point things out to ourselves, to interpret a situation, to communicate with ourselves in all of the diverse ways we are able to communicate with all other humans. "The possession of a self," Blumer (1966) concludes, "provides the human being with a mechanism of self-interaction with which to meet the world—a mechanism that is used in forming and guiding his conduct" (p. 535). Mead (1934) points out that "the essence of the self ... is cognitive: it lies in the internalized conversation of gestures which constitutes thinking, or in terms of which thought or reflection proceeds" (p. 173). To think is to speak to one's self, to continuously point things out, to sometimes reflect, to carry on conversation toward that social object called self in identically the same manner as one speaks to others, except that, in most cases, conversation with one's self is silent.

Without self-communication, the human would not be able to communicate symbolically with others, for it is only because the human can simultaneously give off meaning to other people and understand (through communication with self) what he or she communicates that effective symbolic communication with others can take place. "From Mead's point of view ... only humans can self-consciously and purposively represent to themselves that which they wish to represent to others: this, for Mead, is what it means to have a self and what it means to be human" (Elkin and Handel, 1972, p. 50).

All other action we take toward the self depends on this first action. Self-communication makes it possible to see ourselves, to establish and form a self-concept and identity, and to direct and control ourselves as we act. The use of the symbol to talk to our self becomes the most important action we engage in toward our self. The self, remember, is not the source of that communication, but the object. It is the actor who talks to self.

2. ACTION TOWARD SELF: SELF-PERCEPTION

When we communicate back toward the self, what are we able to say? We are able to communicate about all the objects in the situation that are useful for us: other people, tools, and the clock, for example. We are also able to indicate to the self information about the self in the situation. *The fact is that self-hood means that the actor is able to see himself or herself in the situation and is able to consider that object as he or she acts.* We see ourselves in relation to the situation; we think about ourselves; we judge ourselves; we identify ourselves.

Self-Perception: Assessment of Our Own Action

Self-perception is no small matter. The self allows the human to look at his or her own action in the situation. The actor can understand the others in the situation and the influence they are trying to have on him or her. The actor can appraise his or her own actions as they unfold in the situation. We understand our situations in relation to ourselves. C. Addison Hickman and Manford H. Kuhn (1956) point out that the self "anchors" us in each situation, because, unlike other objects, the self is present in all situations. The self serves as the basis from which a person "makes judgments and subsequent plans of action toward the many other objects that appear in each situation" (p. 43). We imaginatively see ourselves in relation to others, and we determine appropriate actions. For example, when I engage in a conversation with others, I must see my own self in relation to their acts in order to get my thoughts understood. As I hold my loved one close to me, I try to assess not only her activity but also my own activity—for example, whether my action in relation to her is appropriate, tender, manipulative, or immoral. How I assess myself in these acts and in all others will be important guides for my ongoing action. It goes without saying that this activity is ongoing and gives the human actor a social intelligence that is not open to animals without selves. It allows the actor to understand his or her own action, overcoming the simple responses other animals seem to give off in situations.

Self-perception over time develops some stability. We develop knowledge about who we are and what we do. We carry that understanding to situations we enter. We are able to distinguish who we are in relation to objects and people around us. We come to expect how others will act toward us and how we should act toward them because of what we know from previous interaction.

We become increasingly familiar with our own actions. Three important consistencies emerge from self-perception over time: self-concept, self-judgment, and identity.

Self-Perception: The Development of Self-Concept

The term *self-concept* is sometimes used to describe the fairly stable picture we have of ourselves. Morris Rosenberg (1979) describes the self-concept as the "totality of the individual's thoughts and feelings with reference to himself [or herself] as an object" (p. ix). It is *what we see* when we look back on ourselves. It is our "picture" of ourselves. Of course, this picture will change over time in every situation: it is a process, not a fixed entity. Yet, to some extent, the picture is stable over time and across situations. It is sometimes useful to call this consistency "self-concept" and describe it as somewhat different from the particular "self-image" we have in a certain situation. Our self-concept is enduring and built up over time: when others surprise us or act toward us in ways that are unusual to us, the self-concept continues without a great deal of change because of its stability. On the other hand, a serious confrontation with someone may have much more of an effect on us than that stable self-concept, and, if that confrontation continues to be important in our life, it may have a significant influence on our self concept.

This self-concept is a "shifting, adjustive process" that influences what we do in every situation. It is an "average tone of self-feeling." It is more than the isolated "groups of persons" that we care about; it is instead a general view of our self (James, 1915, p. 294).

Self-Perception: Self-Judgment

Our view of ourselves involves judgments about ourselves. We give ourselves credit; we blame ourselves; we like what we do and are; we reject what we do and are. Here is the issue we sometimes call "self-esteem." We not only see ourselves as objects in situations but we also appraise ourselves. The self is something we judge, evaluate, like or reject, love or hate. We may feel good as we look at ourselves; we may feel bad. Good boy! Stupid! Insensitive! Klutz! Beautiful! Wow! Ugh! We judge ourselves, and those judgments involve feelings we have toward ourselves. Charles Cooley (1970) emphasizes this aspect of the self in his description of "looking-glass" self: he states:

> As we see our face, figure, and dress in the glass, and are interested in them because they are ours, and pleased or otherwise with them according as they do or do not answer to what we should like them to be; so in imagination we perceive in another's mind some thought of our appearance, manners, aims, deeds, character, friends, and so on, and are variously affected by it. A self-idea of this sort seems to have three principal elements: the imagination of our appearance to the other person; the imagination of [his or her] ... judgment of that appearance; and some sort of self-feeling, such as pride or mortification (p. 184).

"He sees that I am talking a lot. He likes that about me. I like me, too." "She sees me walking toward her slowly and deliberately. She thinks I'm cool. Yes, I'm cool!" "I must appear to them to be skillful at this game. They hate me for it, for I threaten them. Maybe I shouldn't be so showy. I don't like this aspect of me!" What we think of ourselves and what we feel about ourselves, like all else about the self, result from social interaction: what I end up liking or not liking about myself is, to a great extent, the result of the acts of others toward me and of my acts toward them.

Shibutani (1961) clearly describes the interrelationship of our self-judgment to social interaction. He points out that "Through role-taking a proud [person] is able to visualize [himself or herself] as an object toward which others have feelings of respect, admiration, or even awe." If we are addressed with deference, we come "to take for granted" that we deserve this. If we are constantly mistrusted or ridiculed, we are influenced to reject ourselves; if ignored we may think of our self as a "worthless object." And "once such estimates have crystallized, they become more independent of the responses of other people" (pp. 434–35). And, Shibutani reminds us, it is not all people with whom we interact whose perspective we assume in judgment of self, but our significant others and reference groups:

> Standards differ from one reference group to another. In the social worlds that make up American society there are an amazing variety of attributes of which people are proud or ashamed: their speaking voices, the straightness of their teeth, their ancestry, their muscular strength, their ability to fight, the number of books they have read, the number of prominent people they know, their honesty, their ability to manipulate other people, the accessories on their automobiles, or their acquaintance with exotic foods (p. 436).

People see themselves from the standpoints of their groups. Appropriate action in relation to these groups becomes "a source of pride" (Shibutani, 1961, p. 436).

Yet this causal relationship is not a simple one. On the one hand, it is not merely the judgments of others that affect our self-judgment; rather it is our perception of other people's judgments that becomes important. They may actually like us, but we define their acts as negative toward us. They may think of us as stupid, yet we may think they are kidding when they say we are stupid. On the other hand, even if others consistently see us in a certain way, and even if we correctly interpret that perception, we still do not necessarily accept it, because we also interact with ourselves, and whatever others say or do we are able to define self in a way that is useful to us. We can, for example, reject the judgments of others as unfair, inaccurate, or close-minded. ("They really do not know me.") ("After all, who are they anyway? Who cares what they think of me?") Or others might continuously tell me that I am thin, intelligent, smart, ambitious, but because I do not like what I am I find it useful to label them polite, kind, and easily taken in. There are several studies that show that self-judgment and the appraisals of others do not match perfectly (Gecas, 1982, p. 6). We select from whatever others may think of us; we interpret, ignore, exaggerate, alter whatever fits what we think about ourselves. We may even select our significant others in order to enhance or reaffirm our self-judgment, thus making self-judgment a factor in influencing what others think of us (Rosenberg, 1979).

The importance of self-judgment, of course, is in the consequences it has for the individual's behavior. John Kinch (1963, pp. 482–83) relates the following story about the importance of self-judgment for action. The story also underlines the central importance of interaction and its relationship to self:

> A group of graduate students in a seminar in social psychology became interested in the notions implied in the interactionist approach. One evening after the seminar five of the male members of the group were discussing some of the implications of the theory and came to the realization that it might be possible to invent a situation where the "others" systematically manipulated their responses to another person, thereby changing that person's self-concept and in turn his behavior. They thought of an experiment to test the notions they were dealing with. They chose as their subject (victim) the one girl in the seminar. The subject can be described as, at best, a very plain girl who seemed to fit the stereotype (usually erroneous) that many have of graduate student females. The boys' plan was to begin in concert to respond to the girl as if she were the best-looking girl on campus. They agreed to work into it naturally so that she would not be aware of what they were up to. They drew lots to see who would be the first to date her. The loser, under the pressure of the others, asked her to go out. Although he found the situation quite unpleasant, he was a good actor and by continually saying to himself "she's beautiful, she's beautiful ..." he got through the evening. According to the agreement it was now the second man's turn and so it went. The dates were reinforced by the similar responses in all contacts the men had with the girl. In a matter of a few short weeks the results began to show. At first it was simply a matter of more care in her appearance; her hair was combed more often and her dresses were more neatly pressed, but before long she had been to the beauty parlor to have her hair styled, and was spending her hard-earned money on the latest fashions in women's campus wear. By the time the fourth man was taking his turn dating the young lady, the job that had once been undesirable was now quite a pleasant task. And when the last man in the conspiracy asked her out, he was informed that she was pretty well booked up for some time in the future. It seems there were more desirable males around than those "plain" graduate students (pp. 482–83).

This story makes clear that judgment of self is a complicated interacting process, one in which other individuals influence self but also in which the individual, in interaction with self, actively defines and judges self. Thus, although this woman may have at first highly depended on others for self-judgment, she was able to break away and become increasingly independent in relation to self. The story highlights the role of power in human relationships, and it reveals some of the selfish motivations and harmful effects that may result when people in unison "pick on," "scapegoat," or "stereotype" someone. It also highlights the fact that there were far fewer controls on social research in the early 60s than there is now. No "study" such as this would probably get past the ethical research standards committees in place today.

Erving Goffman (1959, pp. 14–60) describes the situation in which the individual's judgment of self is almost completely in the hands of other people who have very great control over the physical and social environment the individual is in. He calls these instances total institutions, institutions that are apart from the wider society, isolated, where for a length of time the individual's life is in an enclosed, regimented space. Prisons, mental hospitals, the army, and some religious orders are examples. Goffman describes the process by which the total institutions systematically (but not always intentionally) manipulate the individual's world so that the individual comes to redefine self— to reject or question the conceptions of self brought in from the outside, which resulted from interactions in various social worlds. One is, in a real sense, redefined at first through "a series of abasements, degradations, humiliations, and profanations of self." Isolation itself, as well as the dispossession of property and loss of one's name, contributes to the pattern. Individuals may be stripped of privacy and also of the ability to present themselves to others in the way they choose. For example, clothes, cosmetics, haircuts are all restricted. A host of other acts that the individual is forced to perform, such as the constant use of "sir," asking permission, and figuratively bowing to those in authority, all operate to bring about a "mortification of self." New self-judgments slowly replace the old ones. Gradually, any positive self-judgments depend on the authorities and on the actions they wish to support. To obey passively becomes action rewarded with praise and approval, so a positive self-judgment, as it becomes more and more dependent on authorities, is tied to obedience. This whole process depends on (1) isolation from significant others and reference groups outside the institution, (2) total control of the individual's environment by a few powerful individuals, and (3) constant interaction within a social world whose perspective is assumed, including perspective on self.

This model, although extreme and unusual for most of our lives, still serves to sensitize us to a multitude of situations in which people do have power and do indeed manipulate self-judgments. Parents, teachers, and peers may do this to the child. Sometimes the judgments of these others are highly consistent and lead the individual to reject self totally or to love self fully. More often, significant others and reference groups are inconsistent, and the judgment of self is to some extent a continuously changing process. Many religious cults resemble the total institution, and some societies do on occasion: isolation of the individual, control over the environment, limited interaction with outsiders, rejection of self-judgments developed elsewhere, and assumption of the group's perspective. Most of us, however, are not controlled by anything resembling a total institution. Instead, we live in a highly complex world, where many significant others and reference groups contribute to the actor's possible self-judgments, but where the individual also actively forms them.

One more point. Self-judgment makes possible moral choice. Individuals are able to assess and monitor themselves. They can praise themselves for good behavior and censure themselves when they are bad. Self-control involves threatening and punishing self as well as congratulating and rewarding self:

> Unlike the animals in the researcher's laboratory, people exert considerable control over the rewarding and punishing resources available to them. They congratulate themselves for their own characteristics and actions; they praise or abuse their own achievements; and they self-administer social and material rewards and punishments from the enormous array freely available to them. (Mischel and Mischel, 1977, p. 34)

Self-Perception: Identity

As we look back on ourselves and see who in the world we are, we develop an *identity*.

Identity is the name we call ourselves. It is socially recognized and validated. It is usually the name we announce to others that tells them who we are as we are acting.

We have names for all social objects; naming allows us to identify and classify our world. So too do we attribute names to other people, and they, in turn, name us. Naming objects allows us to understand our environment, and it allows us to understand ourselves in the environment. Gregory Stone (1962, p. 93) describes identity as the perceived social location of the individual: where one is "situated" in relation to others, who one tells the self one is, and, in his or her actions, the name one tries to communicate to others.

Identities then are part of what we mean by self. Self is the object we act toward. *Identity is the naming of that self, the name we call ourselves.* As are all objects, identities are "socially bestowed, socially maintained, and socially transformed" (Berger, 1963, p. 98). Thus, defining who the self is, as are all other actions the actor takes toward his or her self, is carried out in interaction with others. As others label me, so I come to label myself. The names given us become our names, our social addresses, our definitions of who we are in relation to those with whom we interact. The identities are labels used, not by all others, but by the reference groups and significant others of the individual. And these identities become central to us over time as our interactions reconfirm them over and over.

"Identities are meanings a person attributes to the self," wrote Paul Burke (1980). They are relational, social, and placed in a context of interaction, and they "are a source of motivation" (p. 18). "I am a man! That is important to me! Like many other men I must develop male friendships that mean having fun without sexual involvement, and like other men I must date, court, and have sexual contact with women!" Needless to say, such a male identity will matter in an individual's interaction and relationships. Indeed, as Harold Garfinkel (1967, p. 116) notes, sexual classification is especially important to all societies for dividing people and placing them into "natural" categories of male and female. The individual sense of "the real me" begins with sex identity; it is central to who we think we are. Spencer E. Cahill (1980) concisely describes how children take on this identity:

> From the very first day of life the child is responded to by caregivers in terms of his or her sex. Caregivers' sexually differential responsiveness is associated with their use of sex designating terms. By the second year of life the child has incorporated these complexities of responses to his or her self and their association with sex-specific verbal labels into his or her self-conception. The child then attempts to actively confirm his or her gender identity and is influenced in these attempts by the responses of others. Through initiation, playing at gender specific roles, selection of dress and objects of play, and increased interactional experience the child becomes increasingly competent in the subtleties of gender expression. During this same period the child learns the importance of anatomical features to the confirmation of gender identity. Of course, the content of this process is dependent on cultural definitions and common sense understanding of sex and gender (p. 133).

The central importance of identity to the individual is the subject of a great deal of theoretical and empirical work at the State University of Iowa. Much of this work has been done or inspired by Kuhn, who developed the Twenty Statements Test (TST), which simply asks the individual to answer the question *Who am I?* with twenty statements. The answers to the question tell the researcher the central identities or self-definitions of the person (boy, Christian, Smith, student, and so forth). As one would expect, as the person identifies his or her self, there is almost always a simultaneous identification of reference groups. The instructions for the TST are as follows:

> There are twenty numbered blanks on the page below. Please write twenty answers to the simple question "Who am I?" in the blanks. Just give twenty different answers to this question. Answer as if you were giving the answers to yourself, not to somebody else. Write the answers in the order that they occur to you. Don't worry about logic or "importance." Go along fairly fast, for time is limited (Kuhn and McPartland, 1954, p. 70).

Probably "identity" would be more correct than "self" because the answers to the questions are *core names* with which the individual labels self. As Stone (1962, p. 93) emphasizes, identities are *social locations*, and individuals will usually answer a question such as "Who am I?" by identifying themselves in groups or in social categories. "I am a woman" is a valid social category in that it refers to the fact that women constitute an important reference group, that in the individual's relations with others *she sees this* as an important identity, and that *she believes others* also regard it as such. Several hypotheses can be made on the basis of the order in which subjects list their identities, the degree to which the order changes over time, or the relationship between identities and such things as age, sex, social class, and marital status.

There are different types of identities. Some are central to the individual; others are not very important and are easily changed. It is important to make this distinction. Stone, for example, distinguished three types: basic (such as age and sex), general (such as priest or father), and independent (such as part-time employee). These go from the very basic, central, difficult-to-change identities to the nonpervasive and easy to change. In a more recent attempt to distinguish types of identities, Stryker (1980, pp. 60–62) used the terms "identity salience" and "identity commitment." *Salience* refers to the level of importance a given identity has to many situations. Some identities are important only occasionally; others are important to the individual all the time. We must recognize that all individuals have a hierarchy of salience, with some identities being at the top and others at the bottom. My identities as sociologist, teacher, father, and husband are very salient; homeowner, golfer, union member, and author are less so. Stryker also describes *commitment*, the degree to which a certain identity matters to the individual in relation to certain other people. When I am around family, my identity as a family member is very important to me; when I am around students, I have strong commitment to the identity of professor. Some identities—sociologist, for example—have high salience to me, and among many people with whom I interact I give these identities high commitment. Other identities—tennis player, for example—have low salience but high commitment when I am with my friends on the tennis court. There are yet other identities—full professor, for example—that are not salient and that I do not give much commitment to.

Ralph Turner (1968) makes the same type of distinction. However, he refers to core identities as "role-person merger" or "real selves." By real self Turner means that the individual believes that a given identity reflects who he or she really is: the person and the role are seen to be one and the same. Who am I? I am a man, I am a moral being, I am a Confucianist, I am a breadwinner. This is who I *really* am! Of course, Turner points out, this is not who people really are, but who they think they are.

Identity is important. It is what individuals think they are and what they want to present to others who they are in word and action. Identity arises in social interaction; it is reaffirmed in social interaction; and it is changed in social interaction. It also arises as we act back on ourselves and label who we are in the world. Not all identities matter. However, some may matter almost all the time.

3. ACTION TOWARD SELF: SELF-CONTROL

We act toward ourselves through our symbols: we talk to ourselves. As we talk to ourselves we also come to see ourselves as objects in situations. Perception of self includes assessing our own action, developing a self concept, judging ourselves, and creating our identities.

However, acting back on ourselves also means that we are able to control our own actions. What we do is not simply a matter of training and response; it is the ability to gather knowledge about ourselves and the world outside us in order to guide whatever we do. The self becomes *an object that we are able to direct, influence, control.* The self allows us to act toward our environment according to our own goals, decisions, definitions, choices. Objects that exist out there can be manipulated by us internally, and the same goes for our self as object. I am able to direct Martha, I can tell Daniel what to do, and I can try to influence Friska, the freshman, but I can also do all this toward myself. That the individual has a self is important precisely because the individual has this ability. That is what we usually mean by "self-control" (the actor is able to control himself or herself) and "self-direction" (the actor is able to point to himself or herself and direct what is to be done). The actor does not passively respond to commands but is able to hold back, consider options, hesitate, act aggressively or calmly, guide action according to a set of morals learned in other times and other places, change streams of action, and so on.

Language is sometimes confusing, so I should for a moment point out that "directing your self" does not mean here that the self actually acts. It means simply that actors, because they have developed a self, are able to control their own overt actions because they are able to act back on themselves.

Self-control, or self-direction, allows us to cooperate and perhaps to exercise some freedom. Because we act toward self we are able to align our action with the actions of others and therefore to do our part in any cooperative venture. We see what others are doing, and we determine our line of action in relation to them. A basketball team is a number of actors who exercise self-control throughout the game, and, if successful, each forms his or her action as he or she goes along and takes the others' actions into account.

Also, at any time, self-direction and self-control mean we are able to say, "I must determine what the truth is for myself," or "Stop! Don't you do that with those guys! You know better!" Individuality, freedom, and nonconformity as well as cooperation depend on this ability to exercise control over ourselves. Action is organized by the human being for a purpose: it is "elicited and directed without the presence of immediate rewards, external agents of control, or controlling conditions" (Wells and Marwell, 1976, p. 43). Without a self that we are able to act back on, there is only direction and control by forces that control us. All conflict with others, all planning, all problem solving, all symbolic interaction with others and with self, moral action, assumes the existence of self-control.

Our self-direction, or self-control, like all else, depends on other people. Our self is pointed out by others, and our self-control is in large part guided by others. We direct/control our action according to those whose perspectives we assume in the situation we encounter, those who are in the situation, and those outside of it. We are thus not "free" to direct and control self in any complete sense, but we are guided by the perspectives of others. The guides to our behavior, the guides we use to determine "right" action, appropriate action, rational action, depend on the perspectives of significant others and reference groups. When Mead points out that the self and society are two sides of the same coin, he is referring to the idea that society's perspective becomes the individual's, the rules of society become the standards by which the individual controls his or her own action. According to Mead "the principal outcome of socialization that makes self-regulation possible is the development of the *self*" (Elkin and Handel, 1972, p. 50). Human conscience in this sense is the assumption of a social world's perspective, and use of conscience is acceptance of this perspective as a guide for one's actions. The individual uses perspectives not to *determine* response but to converse with self, guide self, control self, and direct self. Each situation we enter is different, and each, to some extent, demands active participation by the individual in relation to self.

Self-direction is neither completely social, nor is it completely determined by the actor. As in all else human, it is interaction with others and with self that matters. Although the acts of others play an important role in how we direct ourselves, because we are able to act back on ourselves, part of what we do is independent of the acts of others. We plan our own actions; we figure out what to do in situations; we work in relation to our goals or values or to morals we believe in. Although the self must be understood as socially created and socially anchored, it is equally important to recognize that once the self is developed, the actor has the ability to act on his or her own to a great extent. The power "out there" is tempered by the fact that the actor comes to exercise self-control. To possess a self means that the actor is able to direct self in situations, and if freedom means anything, this is what it seems to mean. *We may be free or we may not, but without self, freedom is unthinkable.* As Tom Goff (1980) describes it:

> [The human being's] relationship to nature is a *self*-conscious, reflexive relationship. ... [This fact] is understood as the basis of the ability to inhibit overt and immediate reaction to stimuli, to think or act implicitly, or in mind, before responding overtly and intentionally to the environment. [Human beings] thereby acquire a control over their own activity and their environment which is denied to other species (pp. 56–57).

And Blumer (1966) emphasizes the same point: "With the mechanism of self-interaction the human being ceases to be a responding organism whose behavior is a product of what plays upon [him or her] from the outside, the inside, or both" (p. 536). Instead, the actor interprets, defines, and organizes his or her own action on more than that which confronts him or her.

It seems truly paradoxical that the origin of the free actor—selfhood—should be a *social* creation.

CENTRAL IDEAS ABOUT THE SELF

The self is highly complex and very important. Let us review some of the key ideas discussed so far.

1. The self is social. It arises in interaction, and it changes or remains stable because of interaction.
2. The self arises in childhood through symbolic interaction with significant others (play stage). The child develops a mature self with the

development of a generalized other (game stage). With adulthood come reference groups, each influencing a different view of the self and making the self somewhat different in each situation (reference group stage).
3. The meaning of the self is that the individual becomes an object to his or her own action. The actor is able to look back on self in situations and is able to imagine himself or herself in the situation. This process involves social interaction with others, and it depends to a large extent on seeing and acting toward self according to our definition of the acts of others toward us.
4. Much of our action with other people is symbolic communication; all of our action toward the self is symbolic communication. The basis for all actions toward self is that we talk to ourselves. This is what is meant here by *thinking*.
5. As we communicate toward self we are able to see ourselves in the situation, to recognize who we are in relation to others and vice versa, as well as to evaluate our own action in the situation. We are able to develop a self concept, judge our own selves and establish an identity.
6. Self means that the individual is able to be active in relation to the world, for self makes possible self-control, or self-direction. The ability of the individual to influence the direction of his or her action makes possible both individuality and cooperative action. It allows the individual to agree to cooperate or to refuse to conform.

THE "I" AND THE "ME"

Thus, all humans act toward their environment, and all are able to act toward themselves. We are all actors; and we all have a self. Mead's great insight is that we are both subjects (actors) and objects (selves).

For many symbolic interactionists the self should be understood as two aspects of the human being: the "I" and the "me." The "I" is the self as subject; the "me" is the self as object. I have chosen not to make a big issue out of the "I and the me" even though it sometimes seems interesting and even logical to students and colleagues. I have chosen instead to describe the self as an "object," the "me" we act toward. I have called the one who acts the "actor," because it makes much more sense to me. Herbert Blumer, in all of his work, reminds us that the real importance of the self is overwhelmingly the "me." I agree.

For some symbolic interactionists, the "I" is thought to be the beginning of the act; the "me" completes the act. For others the "I" is that part of the self that is untouched by human hands; it is the side of us that is sometimes impulsive, spontaneous, or creative. For still others, the "I" is the side of us that allows us to be free actors. And, often, scholars and students will boldly announce that the self is really a conversation between "I and the me." Sometimes we do act spontaneously; sometimes we act without conversing with ourselves; sometimes we act impulsively; sometimes we act in ways that even surprise us. However, it is important that we recognize the "me" as that which makes us all able to control our own own action, it is the "me" that makes possible thinking, it is the discussion with our self as object that allows us to make decisions and choices as we act; it is the "me" that is the identity we establish in our world. The magic of human action remains the ability of the actor to back on himself or herself. This is the "me."

Although Mead does indeed discuss the "I" as part of the self his discussion is vague and contradictory. Therefore, I choose to call the self only the "me," the one who does the acting the "actor," and I recognize that sometimes human beings when they act can be impulsive, spontaneous, or creative mixed with the conversation they have toward themselves.

Humans also possess "mind" and this too is part of human essence. To Mead (1934), the mind is the "twin emergent of the self." The "self" is an object; the action we take toward that object he calls "mind." In fact, if we include symbols, we have a triple emergent. Symbols, self, and mind arise together and are extricably interlinked. The actor acts back on self; the actor engages in action toward the self we call mind; the actor acts toward self through the use of symbols.

Mind will be the subject of Chapter 7.

CHAPTER SEVEN

The Human Mind

Stop a moment. What are you doing as you read this page? Whatever it is, it is accompanied by a silent conversation with yourself, what we might call thinking, what symbolic interactionists call *mind*.

If you try to understand this word or sentence or paragraph or page or chapter or book, mind is involved. If you are daydreaming your conversation within your head is far away from this page, focused on places or times far away, sometimes real, sometimes imaginary, mind is involved. If you are angry because people around you are bothering you or you realize you are thirsty, mind is active. If someone around you is attractive and you would like to find a way to start a conversation, you are talking to yourself, and when you begin to talk to the others you are also talking to yourself. Careful planning is what mind is; but mind is also a constant stream of thinking in every situation we enter.

Mind, to the symbolic interactionist, is a certain kind of action. It is not brain, which is a physical organ. It is not unconscious, since it is intentional. It is not occasionally active, but always active when we are awake. Two qualities make mind possible: symbols and self. *Mind is defined as all symbolic covert action toward oneself.* When we talk to ourselves with symbols, we are engaged in mind action. Indeed, it is really better to call what we do "mind action" rather than mind, in order to better understand what is going on within the human being.

When social scientists emphasize that people are conditioned, caused, shaped, moved, controlled, and driven by such forces as their past, social structures, roles, culture, social institutions, and other people, they are supporting the notion that people lack the tools within themselves necessary to act back on their world, to determine their own action, to direct themselves through some decision making on their part, some free choice in what to do.

As soon as we recognize that almost all action is accompanied by a constant stream of consciousness, a mind, the human becomes less passive, moved much less by deterministic forces. We are able to turn back on our environment and shape its direction rather than simply respond to it.

THE MEANING OF MIND: SYMBOLIC INTERACTION TOWARD SELF

Mead describes mind extensively in his book *Mind, Self and Society*. There are important links between these concepts. Just as society, self, and symbols are interdependent, so is mind. Mind is described by Mead as what we might call *thinking*, the ongoing covert action (action not open to observation by others), talking to oneself, the conversation toward oneself concerning the environment and one's own action in that environment. Mead (1982) writes that mind is best described as "activity, and the different phases of consciousness are parts of this activity." Mind is not an object like the self or symbols; it is the *action the actor takes toward himself or herself.*

The distinctions here are far from perfect, but still important to make. Recall that the *actor* is the one who acts. Actors act toward their outside environment. They "do things." They do things with their bodies toward that environment. They manipulate objects in their environment to achieve their goals. The action that actors take toward the outside environment we call *overt action* (action that is "open"). However, actors also act toward themselves; this we might call action that is *covert* (action that is "covered" because it occurs inside each actor; it is internal). *All this covert action is called "mind." Mind is all the action that the actor takes toward himself or herself. It is all thinking, all active manipulation of symbols by the actor in conversation within his or her head and toward self.*

Then what is the *self*? Remember, the self is the *object* that the actor talks to when he or she engages in covert action. The actor acts; the actor acts toward the outside environment; when the actor acts toward the self he or she is engaging in mind action. In almost every situation, the actor is simultaneously engaged in both overt and covert (or mind) action. Our overt action is caused by our covert action; our own overt action is considered by us when we engage in covert action back toward our self.

Herbert Blumer's (1962) insight that we engage in mind action all of the time seems obviously true to me. The mind, he states, is "anything the individual indicates to [himself or herself]...from the time that [he or she] awakens until [he or she] falls asleep; it is a continual flow of self indications—notations of the things which [he or she] deals and [that he or she] takes into account" (p. 181–82). We do not, then, sometimes think; we are constantly thinking in every situation we encounter in our waking moments. As we hold conversation with others, we hold conversation with ourselves: that is mind activity. As we walk into situations, we determine what is important for us in those situations; we define the situations. That is mind activity. The manipulation of symbols is not the same as simple recall of pictures. We may be sometimes stimulated in a situation and that automatically recalls a picture, and the picture may lead us to respond without mind, but this is not action that involves intentionally combining and recombining symbols. A picture in our head can be responded to; mind allows us to manipulate and evaluate that picture.

Mind, then, should not be confused with brain. The two are not the same. Most animals may have brains, but that is not to say that they have minds. Brains with the capacity to store and manipulate large numbers of symbols are necessary for minds, but "brains, *per se*, do not make mind" (Troyer, 1946, p. 200). It is the manipulation of symbols, made possible through the learning of those symbols and the development of self, that makes mind. And these tools, you will recall, are developed in interaction with others. William Troyer puts the case clearly and to the point: "It is society—social interaction—using brains, which makes mind" (p. 200). Give the human the self and the words to communicate with the self, and the active person emerges, manipulating words, thinking, and creating.

MIND ACTION: MAKING INDICATIONS TOWARD SELF

Mind is action made possible by the fact that humans have both symbols and self. It is ongoing conversation. It is, as Mead (1938) emphasizes, actors' "making indications" toward themselves: "He [or she] talks to himself [or herself]. This talking is significant. [He or she] is indicating what is of importance in the situation ... indicating those elements that call out the necessary [action]" (p. 384).

Simply put, mind action means that the actor is able to pull things out of the environment that he or she has words for, and use them as he or she considers what to do in the situation. We isolate, label, and develop plans of action toward objects around us. We do not simply respond to these objects but define and discuss these objects internally. We notice certain objects and ignore others, and those we notice we perceive and define according to our specific goals in that specific situation. Mind means we are actively telling ourselves what exists around us, and, because we understand these things, we are able to determine how we are going to use them.

Initially, we may notice certain objects, but then we leave these aside and move on to other objects. Our goals may change or other actors in the situation may inform us of something, and we indicate to ourselves different objects or new definitions of objects already indicated to ourselves. I may walk down the street and note the cold weather. I notice the wind on my thighs and realize I have not worn my long underwear today. I note a subtle change in the weather and wonder if there is a storm approaching. I walk toward a snow-covered car I pray will start. If I am religious, my prayer may not simply be a hope, but I will even take note of a God I think may be listening to me. On another occasion, I may walk down this same street, noticing the tickets on the cars and worrying about my car, which may have a ticket on it. Or I may take note of the different styles of clothing people are wearing this year. Or I might be walking down the same street noting the faces of everyone because I am looking for someone in particular: my friend in need of help or the no-good guy who stole my wallet, or the person who looks like a good experimental subject, someone who would make a good model or the one who might protect me from a gang, or the one who might make a good date. The point is that people point things out to themselves as they walk down the street, or run or talk or play. Things that are out there are noticed and defined in our heads through minded activity. The world is transformed into a world of definitions because of mind. Blumer (1966) emphasizes this idea throughout his work. We pull things out of our world, define them, and give them meaning according to the use they have for us at the time, and we act. We act, therefore, as we manipulate these things in our heads:

> To indicate something is to stand over against it and to put oneself in the position of acting toward it instead of automatically responding to it. In the face of something which one indicates, one can withhold action toward it, inspect it, judge it, ascertain its meaning, determine its possibilities, and direct one's action with regard to it. With the mechanism of self-interaction the human being ceases to be a responding organism whose behavior is a product of what plays upon [him or her] from the outside, the inside, or both (p. 536).

Blumer (1969) contends that "by virtue of engaging in self-interaction the human being stands in a markedly different relation to [his or her] environment than is presupposed by the conventional view" (pp. 14–15).

MIND ACTION: THE ABILITY TO CONTROL OVERT ACTION

Mind stands in marked contrast to a simple response to a stimulus. If we respond to something, we mean that "we can't help it." Mind, on the other hand, means we take some control away from the stimulus. This is what Blumer means in the previous paragraph when he writes that we have a "markedly different relation" to our environment.

Because of mind, we tell ourselves how to act toward the environment around us. We are able to apply what we know to the situation, to make plans of what to do, and to alter our plans and definitions as we and others act in the situation.

To point things out to ourselves means that our own acts make sense to us. We understand what we are doing, the failure or success of what we are doing, the reactions to what we are doing by others. Through all of this we are changed from responders to planners, from beings "who can't help what we do" to beings who understand what they are doing, understand what they did, and understand what they are going to do before they do it. We are able to rehearse our actions before we actually act out in the environment. We are able to predict the reactions of others to what we do before we do it. Mead calls mind the ability to approach objects in our environment according to what we plan to do with them in the future. There is, he writes, an organization of parts of our own "nervous system that are going to be responsible for acts, an organization which represents not only that which is immediately taking place, but also the later stages that are to take place." Mead (1934) gives the example of the hammer. "If one is approaching a hammer, [he or she] is muscularly all ready to seize the handle of the hammer. The late stages of the act are present in the early stages." The actor is in control of the ongoing act. The actor controls the process. How we will use an object in the near future influences "the steps in our early manipulation of it" (p. 11).

This control over action that mind allows means that, at any point, we can speed up action or delay it. Mind means we are able to hold back, to put off acting in the immediate situation so we can achieve goals that can be achieved only by planning. Trial and error gives way to problem solving; the immediate sensed present gives way to pointing out to ourselves events from our past and future; stimulus response gives way to understanding and holding back what we are able to do. Just as symbols and self make the active human being— maybe even some free choice—possible, so does this ability to engage in mind action. Blumer (1981) highlights the significance of this ability:

> The organism is not just there—in a relation of merely responding to the thing—it points it out to itself and consequently, it can do something. By indicating the thing to itself, the organism can stop and figure out what it will do before it acts toward the thing. To indicate something to oneself is to put oneself in the position of being able to talk to oneself about the thing. This cannot be done by the organism which doesn't have the means of pointing out the thing to itself (pp. 115–16).

Maurice Natanson (1973) makes this same case nicely: "The human animal has the unique capacity of isolating his or her responses to environmental stimuli and controlling those responses in the very act of these both to [himself or herself] and to [others]" (p. 7). William Troyer (1946) reminds us that mind is what Mead means by "choice and conscious control" (p. 199). "Mind makes it possible," according to Bernard Meltzer (1972), "to control and organize" action, and thus to do "considerably more than respond to the environment" (p. 20).

The ability to direct oneself, to hold back what one does, to rehearse action is all mind activity, and this activity is one that changes our relationship to the environment into an active manipulating one.

MIND ACTION: THE ABILITY TO PROBLEM SOLVE

The ability to represent the environment that exists outside of us with words we can manipulate internally enables us to figure out how to act in our situations. We can plan, rehearse, and try to overcome whatever stands in the way of our achieving the goals we have in a particular situation. To create goals and then define a situation in relation to those goals means that what we do is constantly being evaluated by us and altered in relation to our successes and failures. We change what we do because it no longer works for us.

Mead (1938) emphasizes that mind action is most likely to arise when problems arise for us:

> Consciousness is involved where there is a problem, where one is deliberately adjusting one's self to the world, trying to get out of difficulty or pain. One is aware of experience and is trying to readjust the situation so that conduct can go ahead. There is, therefore, no consciousness in a world that is just there (p. 657).

Mead is telling us something very important about mind. It is focused on goals, and when something stands in the way of our achieving those goals smoothly, we must stop and carefully discuss the situation and what we are doing there. Although he does not clearly say so, Mead at least implies that to some extent each situation poses a problem that must be resolved if goals are to be achieved. We need to think about it to some extent. It is, in the end, a matter of degree: the more our action is interrupted because something stands in the way of our achieving our goals, the more important our mind action becomes, and the more deliberate and conscious it becomes, the more planning, rehearsal of action, and making deliberate choices are required. Pure overt action without any mind activity is unusual simply because each situation is unique, poses at least a minor problem to be resolved, and therefore demands some covert action.

This does not make us all careful, clear, rational, and successful thinkers. Mind simply means that we engage in action toward ourselves as we act in situations, and we act according to our decisions we make because we come to believe that our action is going to achieve our goals. All of us fall short in our attempts; some of us fall short much of the time; a few of us fall short almost all the time. How we come to define our situation, how we interpret the acts of others and our own acts, how we develop strategy, how we arrive at decisions, whether or not we are willing to change as we go along—all of this and much more—means that mind does not automatically make us brilliant or compassionate or successful or rational. Mind means only that our overt actions are accompanied by covert action that defines the situation, not necessarily with precision. Mind allows us to understand; mind also allows us to misunderstand.

The story of Robinson Crusoe as described by Van Meter Ames (1973) highlights the role of mind in the affairs of the human being. Robinson Crusoe sailed on many voyages before his ill-fated one. Without question, every one of those voyages involved mind action on his part. As he worked from day to day, his stream of mind action accompanied what he did on his ship. Usually he did tasks he had faced before, and so little deliberate mind action was needed. Undoubtedly, serious problems arose every day that involved deliberation, and occasionally a brand-new situation arose that involved much. Even hearing commands from officers and conversing with other sailors involved mind action. But one day he found himself thrust into a very dangerous and life-threatening situation, one that involved him in having to take stock of the situation quickly but carefully and having to assess himself in relation to a brand-new future. Everything changed for him as he discussed the situation with himself. Here Van Meter Ames (1973) describes Defoe's story in a symbolic interactionist context.

Robinson Crusoe was in the act of sailing for Guinea when this act was interrupted by shipwreck. Other voyages and adventures of his had preceded, but the story associated with his name begins with his being wrecked off an unknown island. There the ongoing act of the voyage was halted when he was plunged into the sea. Now it was no longer a question of going to Guinea but of reaching a rock he could hold on to until a huge wave subsided. Then he made a dash for shore and clambered up a cliff. On the next page, as Defoe relates:

After I had solaced my mind with the comfortable part of my condition, I began to look around me to see what kind of place I was in, and what was next to be done. ... I was wet, had no clothes to shift me, nor anything either to eat or drink. ... I had nothing about me but a knife, a tobacco-pipe, and a little tobacco in a box. ... All the remedy that offered to my thoughts at that time was, to get up into a thick bushy tree.

Things appear, with their limitation and promise, as he looks about. Taking in the surroundings, with himself as an organism in their midst, an object among objects, he sees things loom up on account of the antecedent act which had been thwarted. What Defoe tells is pure Mead. Mead is generalizing and analyzing what Defoe or any storyteller knows: that the appearance of things of interest must follow upon the blocking of activity. ... Only then does the individual appear to himself as an object caught in the midst of things, scanning them for hints of how to get going again. Robinson Crusoe was previously too immersed in a smooth ongoing [act] to confront himself as something separate. He appears to himself, along with other objects, when he has to sort them out in search of cues for getting under way again. The situation takes on a structure momentarily lifted out of passage, by the fact that alternative options of different courses appear in the guise of different objects, before any one or one set of them is chosen for pursuit. Surveying land and sea, Robinson Crusoe brings distant points into his own breathing moment, suppressing the time it would take to get to them and touch them. The hills and trees, the rocks in the sea and the wreck beyond, are all magically present in his present, as if the completion and consummation of arriving at each of them were all achieved simultaneously. (pp. 46–47).

We all enter brand-new situations that call for a careful examination of objects in the situation. Someone insults us or surprises us and suddenly we need to figure out what to do next. We lose our keys or the car won't start, we cannot find our purse, or we realize we forgot an appointment. What happens? We carefully consider what to do next; objects around us take on new meaning; a new plan of action is hatched and followed.

When our identity is threatened—"You are a stupid person," "You are a child," "You are boring"—our situations become problematic and thus must be thought out and acted on appropriately. If we desire money or honor or love or sex and we are unable to get it in a situation, we will perceive that situation as a problem with which we must deal. When we see that someone is taking advantage of us, or when we are late for an important appointment, or when we have little time to study for an important test, or when we want someone to think well of us, or when we want to tell our roommate to cut out the chatter so we can get some sleep, we are faced with problems to be solved in order to continue our flow of action without hassle. We may carefully and deliberately look around for useful objects to help us in the problem situation. Problem solving is the key point in Mead's approach to mind. Meltzer (1972) reminds us that mind action inhibits action, holds action back in order to first appraise the future consequences of what we are about to do.

> It consists of presenting to oneself, tentatively and in advance of overt behavior, the different possibilities or alternatives of future action with reference to a given situation. The future is, thus, present in terms of images of prospective lines of action from which the individual can make a selection. ... The individual *constructs* [his or her] act, rather than responding in predetermined ways. ... When the act of an animal is checked, it may engage in overt trial and error or random activity. In the case of blocked human acts ... consequences can be imaginatively "tried out" in advance. ... What this involves is the ability to indicate elements of the field or situation, abstract them from the situation, and recombine them so that procedures can be considered in advance of their execution (p. 20).

The human pursues interests, values, and goals, and in these pursuits problems arise that must be resolved. Here lies the essence of minded activity to Mead (1936): "It is this process of talking over a problematic situation with one's self, just as one might talk with another, that is exactly what we term 'mental.' And it goes on within the organism" (p. 385).

MIND ACTION IS PART OF ALL SOCIAL INTERACTION

When humans act in a social situation, other people become objects for them that they point out to self. To interact with others involves taking account of others, to make indications about them to ourselves, to define and redefine what they are doing in relation to us, and to evaluate what we are doing in relation to them. All of this activity is mind, and thus it is important to recognize that human interaction is not stimulus response or fixed and automatic, or simply overt and physical. As is everything else in our action, it is accompanied by ongoing conversation with ourselves.

We engage in mind action when we are alone and when we are around others who somehow make a difference to us at the time. When others act in our presence, we need to interpret and understand those actions if we are to know what to do. In their actions (including their speech, their simple symbolic gestures, and their unintentional body language) we try to understand their thoughts, their intentions, their past actions, their plans, their age, their belief system, their perspectives, and their abilities, and, by indicating these to our self, we consider such things as we act in the situation. Sometimes we are concerned about what they think of us, or perhaps what we think of each other. We may wonder what they had for breakfast or how they look naked or on the toilet, or we may consider what their marriage is like or what their childhood consisted of. We may also consider how to escape the social situation, how to control it, how to appear to conform to others at least until we can get away, or how to disrupt the situation. We might escape the situation in our minds by thinking about last night's party, tonight's book that we're definitely going to get to, tomorrow's Super Bowl, or next year's job. But whenever we are with others, just as whenever we are alone with our own self, we are engaging in a constant conversation with self—not always a conversation that we are fully aware of, but a conversation nevertheless.

It is important to consider not only what others are saying to us but also what we are saying to others. To give off symbols to others is to give them off to ourselves simultaneously. Our communication is an attempt to share something with others. What we share therefore has meaning to us. We are able to "know" the meaning that our words will have to others only because the words have meaning to us. Ames (1973) points out that "this is the main basis of communication among [humans]; that the same utterance or other gesture should affect the organism initiating it as it does another" (p. 50). Mind activity, therefore, includes the ability to understand our symbols when we are using them. Symbolic communication with others assumes conversation with ourselves.

Mind is involved in all social situations because other people are objects that must be defined like everything else. People pose greater problems for us, however, than other objects because we must understand what they are doing, we must make ourselves understood by them, and we must actively interpret their acts in situations in order to revise our own acts. We develop lines of action toward other people, but these lines of action are constantly being revised in the situation because each actor is also acting back and we must adjust accordingly. Rehearsing our acts before we act overtly is especially important in social situations because what we do overtly is seen and defined by others.

Games provide especially good examples of individuals' engaging in mind action, rehearsing overt action, redefining the other person, and altering overt action. In a sense, games are slow-motion human action. In chess, for example, a move by Ivan may be preceded by something like: "I think that the capturing of his queen will be accomplished in three moves if I now move my castle to this position. The American might interpret this as meaning I am after his knight, and if he does, I have him. If he figures out my move, then I will have to alter my plans." Then as he moves, Ivan reexamines the situation, looking especially at John, his opponent. Noting that John moves the pawn, Ivan realizes that John has not fallen for the trap, and Ivan must now revise his line of action. Self-communication, making indications, rehearsing acts, developing and altering lines of action, understanding the meaning of the other—all these activities characterize both Ivan and John in their playing chess, but they also characterize all of us in every social situation we encounter. Or consider the game of football: "I think the action should be right through the center of the line, because they won't be expecting it. Their backs are expecting a pass, and the center is weak. However, if they line up as if they are expecting a run, I will change the play by calling number 88." After the play is run: "We did that well, but they were somewhat ready for us. I wonder now if the time is right to try the same thing again." That is the quarterback, but all the actors on the field, including tackles and guards, the opposition, and the referees, as well as the coaches, the cheerleaders, and the fans, are making indications to self, rehearsing acts, and doing all the other activities called mind.

These formal games are replayed throughout our lives in all social situations: in the classroom, at the party, in the bull session, during the meeting, through traffic, while shopping at the store, and while getting ready to meet someone for dinner. But mind is like all else: we become most conscious of it when it is pointed out to us by others and when we, in turn, point it out to ourselves. In a sense, what the perspective of symbolic interactionism does is to make us more aware of the mind activity that characterizes much of our lives.

Summary

Mind then is not the same as self or symbols, but mind depends on both self and symbols. Mind is defined as the ongoing symbolic action the actor takes toward the self. It is the constant process of making indications to ourselves about objects in our environment and especially their use for aiding us in achieving our goals.

Mind action allows us to control our own overt action, and in that way we are able to take an active role in relation to our environment. Mind action allows us to problem solve in situations, going beyond trial and error and habitual response. Mind action accompanies all human social interaction, since social interaction demands constant understanding, interpretation, and definition of the others in the situation.

There are two emphases concerning mind introduced in this chapter. At first, we emphasized that mind action is a continuous process of the individual's making indications to self all day long. This is Blumer's point. The actor moves from situation to situation, defining goals and social objects, thinking, rehearsing, evaluating. Then we emphasized that mind action takes place around problems in situations: where our goals are not immediately met, we need to figure out what to do. Where action is blocked, we have a problem and we must engage in mind action. This is Mead's emphasis.

Although different, both views are very important for understanding mind action. Mind action becomes most deliberate and conscious when we must stop and figure out how to solve a problem facing us in a situation. Yet Blumer is also correct in suggesting that mind action—often less deliberate and conscious—is necessary throughout our day, in every situation. Each situation is new for us, at least to some extent, and that means that some problem solving is necessary. Each situation has objects we make into social objects around the goals we seek; each involves perceiving self in the situation. Every situation we enter demands some adjustment on our part, presents itself as a "problem" to be resolved. Every situation requires some covert action, some self-indication, some rehearsal of various lines of action. When we speak to others, making ourselves understood may be a minimal problem, but it is still a problem, and we must pay some attention to organizing our presentation. To understand others is usually a minor problem, but it is a problem nevertheless, and we must pay some attention to meaning. Mind activity becomes more deliberate, and we become more conscious of it, when a major problem confronts us, and we must sit down and carefully analyze the situation, considering the consequences of what we are about to do. Mind covert activity should be conceptualized as present in all our situations, as a constant flow of activity, and this activity is organized around situations we encounter, where some definition and adjustment on our part must be accomplished. Sometimes it is rapid and we are barely aware of it; sometimes it is obvious and deliberate; but almost always it accompanies overt action since each situation is unique and demands some definition.

We are, then, symbol users, we possess a self, and we engage in mind activity throughout everything we do. Is this the end of what we are? These qualities are interdependent with one other quality, one that is central to everything else, and one that we have not even touched upon so far. This quality is called *taking the role of the other*, and it is important enough to spend all of Chapter 8 on.

CHAPTER EIGHT

Taking the Role
of the Other

"Imagine!"

Imagine a world without war!

Imagine truly loving someone for the rest of your life!

Imagine how someone must feel who loses a job, a child, a fortune, a skill, a memory, good health, or fame.

Imagine what the words on this page mean to an author struggling with the problem of clarity and a desire to teach a view of reality that makes good sense to him.

Imagine how someone would think and feel if he or she won the lottery. Imagine how you would feel if you won. Imagine what it must be like to create a great piece of art or music, a film, a novel, or a poem, or imagine what it must be like to kill in war, to be killed in war, to see yourself as the enemy of someone else, or to be loved by someone you love.

Imagine what you would think about American society if you were a homosexual. Imagine what you would think if you were the one who comes to America believing that it is your last chance for living a decent life, yet you are confronted by many others who do not believe you have a right to be here.

Imagine the view of the U.S. president as he or she must try to deal with an enemy that wishes our destruction.

Imagine how another is thinking when he or she is caressing you, or giving you a compliment, or laughing at you, or punishing you.

Imagination is truly a magnificent quality. It is an ability central to human life. To imagine means to "create an image" of something. This is an *active process*, not simply a response to a stimuli, not simply seeing an image because it "pops into your head." It involves doing, creating, active building on the actor's part; something is created by the one who imagines; a discussion is involved, a discussion with oneself, what we have called mind action. It is his or her own; it is controlled by the individual. To imagine is to actively see something beyond the immediate and make possible overcoming that immediate while one acts.

Imagination is something we all do; it allows us to get outside our simple egoistic present physical environment. It allows us to jump out from the immediate to see the future, recall the past, pull out knowledge, events, ideas, and people from our past, play around with what we already know, even create and perceive something new that does not exist in our physical environment nor taught to us by others.

IMAGINATION AND TAKING THE ROLE OF THE OTHER

In the movie *Dead Poets Society*, Robin Williams plays a passionate English teacher who tries to bring the class to feel the greatness of poetry as he feels it. His character in one scene asks individuals in the class to read their assignment—their own poem—to the class. One of the students casually tells him: "I didn't do the assignment." Williams smiles and immediately gets into a conversation with the student by firing a number of questions at him, not meant to embarrass or punish, or belittle, but to turn this situation into a very positive one for everyone. He quickly gets the student to consider his own actions, to realize that his refusal to write a poem can become a part of the creative venture, to get the student to confront his own feelings about not doing the assignment, and gradually pull out from the student the beginning of an impressive poem. Everyone seems to gain through the teacher's reaction: he gains because he continues to show passion for poetry and respect for the student's independence; the student gains because he begins to discover his own potential as a poet; the whole class gains because they are able to witness a creative process right in front of them. Many who watched the movie might have said to themselves, "But Williams was wrong! He did not hold the student responsible for his actions. He should have punished him!" For me, however, Williams's character showed greatness as a teacher. I wondered what I would have done in his place. I wondered what I had done in the past as a teacher in a similar situation. I wondered how often we are so busy being defensive about what we do in the classroom that we forget that students are more than objects that need to be trained according to our own egoistic viewpoint. As an *actor*, Williams succeeded because he was able to imagine what his character must be thinking; the *character* imagined what the student and the rest of the class was thinking; the *individuals in the class* were undoubtedly thinking what both were thinking. And all of us in the *audience*, in our own individual way, imagined what all these characters were thinking, and none of us were imagining the situation in exactly the same way.

This example highlights one very important type of imagination: the ability to move outside our own view of the environment and *take on the perspective of someone else.* This allows us to temporarily jump out of our own perception of reality and define a situation as though we were someone else. It might be others in that particular situation; it might be others outside the immediate situation. It might be others from our distant or recent past or others who we are about to meet in the future. It might be real people or imaginary ones. It might be groups of people or individuals. It might be people we know well or people we never meet. It might be people we respect; it might be people we fear.

SYMBOLS, SELF, MIND, AND TAKING THE ROLE OF THE OTHER

The symbolic interactionist calls this quality the "taking the role of the other." It is an act of imagination because one must leave what others have simply taught us and "create an image," in this case how someone else thinks and sees. Taking the role of the other is the same as "taking on the perspective of the other," to see the world from the standpoint of someone else. It involves using *symbols*, because taking on a perspective means we are using someone else's symbolic framework; it is symbolic because, more than simply an unthinking response on our part it involves trying to capture what someone else is thinking, imagining how he or she is "defining the situation." It is an act that is continous as we encounter other people, and it should thus be understood as a central part of our covert *mind action* that takes place as we act overtly in the situation. It involves *self* since covert action is directed toward oneself; it involves self also because the self is an important object in the situation that other actors are defining and acting toward. It also involves self because I try to transcend my own viewpoint and enter into someone else's. It involves self because the self direction results in part from role taking the others.

Indeed, the links between taking the role of the other, the self, symbols, and mind are complex and highly interrelated. It is really impossible to separate these four processes: they arise together, they depend on one another, and they influence one another. It is probably best to simply state that the nature of the human being depends on these four socially created qualities. Together these qualities allow for a very unique animal:

> An animal that depends on symbol use!
> An animal that possesses a self!
> An animal that engages in ongoing mind action!
> An animal that almost always takes the role of the other!

This "human nature" is not biological; it is socially derived. To claim one quality without the others is to miss the essence. To claim that we are simply products of certain DNA is to miss the essence. To claim we are no different from other animals is to miss the essence. To claim that we are simply selfish by nature, or violent, or evil, or prejudiced, or conditioned by our environment, is to miss the essence. And when we claim that other animals sometimes "act like humans" we almost always mean by that they too may have these qualities. The question of essence and uniqueness is not a simple one; it is too easy to reject or claim humans are unique in the animal kingdom. However, symbols, self, mind, and taking the role of the other is one way to begin to examine and understand.

These are the key qualities of what humans are, according to the symbolic interactionist. Our essence cannot simply be found in the microscope; it is to be observed in how we act in the world. If other animals depend on these qualities we should see a similarity of actions. To the extent that other animals do not communicate with symbols as defined, do not have a self as defined, do not engage in mind action as defined, and cannot take the role of the other as defined, to that extent we can see that their essence depends on something else.

Symbols, self, and mind have been the topics in previous chapters. Now we will turn to a brief discussion of the fourth quality: "taking the role of the other."

THE MEANING OF "TAKING THE ROLE OF THE OTHER"

Taking the role of the other is an activity that people do in every social situation and probably in almost every situation where they are awake and alone. It is a process that accompanies all human interaction, all symbolic communication, almost all human cooperation, much of how we learn, and much of how we influence others. The more we understand its meaning, the more we will be able to recognize how central it is to what it means to be human.

"Taking the role of the other" or "role taking" is imagining the world from the perspective of another. As we imagine the other's perspective, so we act; as we place ourselves in the other's role in order to see the world from his or her perspective, so we know when to flee, how to become friends, how to become part of a group, how to act morally, how to win, how to understand, how to share, and how to communicate.

This ability to take the role of the other is a central quality that is difficult to discover in other animals. It is difficult for all organisms—even the human being—to overcome the "egocentric viewpoint and understand things from different points of view. The perspective-taking inherent in self-reflection requires abstraction, the ability to manipulate symbols—words, for example—as though they were concrete objects" (Vallacher, 1980, p. 7).

The angle that others have is always different from our own; it is thus impossible to perfectly grasp the other's viewpoint; it is easy to be inaccurate; and the difficulties it presents often cause misunderstanding, social conflict, and even destroy relationships or bring on a world war. As imperfect taking the role of the other is, however, it is still an essential part of all social interaction, and without it we would be left with communication, cooperation, and relationships based on stimulus–response, imitation, habit, or biology.

My friend Gene, who is an economist and who likes to teach me the nature of human relationships, once told me: "Joel, there is no way that humans can really ever understand anyone else. There is no possible way to ever get into someone else's head." Gene, of course, is correct, but it is also correct that the effort to do this is something that all of us do, and we are required to do if we are human beings.

Gene is right, in part because even if we do take the role of the other and accurately capture the perspective of that other, we still cannot leave our own perspective aside, and our understanding of the other will be colored, in part, by our own perspective. Gene is also right because the other's overt action is really our only clue as to what he or she is thinking, and that always involves some interpretation by us. However, the accuracy of role taking is like all types of accuracy: one of degrees of accuracy. Sometimes we are very accurate; sometimes we are not. Sometimes we are able to successfully put aside much of our own perspective, and see the situation from primarily the other's perspective; more often when we interact we see the other's perspective, but we handle it and judge it from our own, and thus our own is considerably mixed in with the other's. When we meet someone new we might successfully imagine his or her views to be similar to what we already have experienced, or we might make a horrible mistake. We might immediately correct our mistake, or we might refuse. Like all mind action, we do not necessarily think or imagine the situation accurately. Too often when we are mistaken in role taking, social interaction is unnecessarily undermined. War does not simply arise because someone decides to go to war; often, there is a mistake in taking the role of the possible enemy, there is overreaction, and leaders end up going to war unintentionally. Accurate communication and role taking goes a long way in preventing unintentional consequences.

Taking the role of the other is necessary for love, friendship, cooperation, teaching, learning, good parenting, being moral, making peace, and compromising. It is often necessary for destroying enemies, taking advantage of others, controlling others, oppressing others. It is an integral part of crowds, mobs, groups, and society. It is part of all social conflict, attempts to control populations in a democracy or in a dictatorship. It is a necessary part of teaching, selling, supervising, arguing in court, treating patients, successfully working on computers, writing, and usually expressing oneself in art, music, or, or poetry. In short, it is central to success of all kinds that involves other people. To be able to successfully take the role of the other may lead us to compassion, sympathy, or emphathy; however, it can also aid us in successfully exploiting or destroying those who we have come to understand. Those who successfully play on our fears and hatreds depend on this ability; those who con us, rob us, exploit us, or enslave us do; and those who abuse us, lie to us, or cheat us do. The successes of an Adolf Hitler or Joseph Stalin on the one hand, and a Martin Luther King, Jr. or Mother Theresa, on the other, depend on their ability to take the role of the other.

In a very basic sense, the ability to role take amounts to what I would term "social intelligence." It is basic to all interaction with others. If we are highly capable in it, and if we actually use it as we act, then we will be able to understand others, communicate clearly to others what we desire, understand the expectations of others so we are able to conform, rebel, or pick and choose, influence others, gain power, contribute to the welfare of others, or build lasting friendship with others. I cannot think of a more important ability as this one if an actor is going to achieve his or her goals around other people. This is not intelligence uncovered in I.Q. tests; it is not intelligence that necessarily arises in school; it is not intelligence that is always used; but it is intelligence in that it aids all of us in handling situations, achieving goals, and solving problems that we face.

TAKING THE ROLE OF THE OTHER: SIGNIFICANT OTHERS, GENERALIZED OTHER, AND OTHERS IN THE SITUATION

Who is this "other" whose role or perspective we take? Mead calls such people our "significant others" or our "generalized other." We simply take the role of individuals—significant others—who have become important to us. Usually they are role models, individuals we respect, individuals who we regard as knowledgeable, individuals we love, individuals who love us, individuals with whom we interact on a continuous basis. Sometimes our significant others are not respected by us, but we fear them or are hurt by them or are rejected by them—their perspective might still remain important to us, however. Sometimes our significant others are people we have never really interacted with: characters in a book or movie, or those important in the history of our people, our religion, or our nation. Most often our significant others are our friends, family members, teachers, neighbors who we have become to know over time.

Mead's discussion of the generalized other means that each of us creates a more general view, a combination of several significant others who for us make up a group, a community, a society whose perspective we use to view our situation. The child takes on the role of the organized whole, them, the view of the "community, the Law, the rules of the game and so on. Such role taking involves generalizing the attitudes of constituent members of the whole and reacting to one's self from the standpoint of those generalized attitudes" (Natanson, 1973, p. 14). I may consider "my friends" when I am with them or as I decide how to act around my parents; I may consider "my family" when I am with them or as I decide how to act around my friends; and I might consider my ethnic group, neighborhood, or professional group as I decide how to act around them or around my friends and family. I may consider the perspective of "people my age" or "my social class" or "my gender" as I act in school, home, or neighborhood. And, I may even think about "my country" or "my generation" or "my religious group." I like Shibutani's description of a "reference group" as a "generalized other." The two concepts are close. Both Mead and Shibutani describe the process of taking the role of a general other, a group whose perspective we learn and apply to situations we encounter, and which guides what we end up doing in that situation.

However, it is essential to recognize that what we do in situations also depends on taking the role of those who exist in the situation. If my action is going to be relevant for others in one way or another, it is incumbent to take their role and see their action as well as my own action from their point of view. Anselm Strauss (1959, p. 59) succinctly points out that taking the role of others in a situation must assess these others in terms of (1) their general intent, (2) their actions toward themselves, and (3) their actions and feelings toward us and our actions. In any ongoing situation, we must continuously accompany our actions with trying to understand others in the situation. When I lecture in a class, discuss plans with my children, express my disappointment to my wife, ask the doctor what I need to do to retain my health in the future, play a tennis match or a poker game, talk on the telephone, make love, pick someone's pocket, successfully protect my valuables from someone who wants to take them from me, I need to plan and execute action toward these other actors, and thus I must quickly and accurately imagine both my act and theirs from their point of view. The other actor, in acting back toward me, must consider my perspective. This is not only "because we should be considerate or kind," but it is necessary for many selfish and unselfish acts we do.

There are some exceptions, however. Two exceptions that come to mind are extreme selfishness and extreme power. A totally selfish act may, in fact, simply ignore other people and arise only from the viewpoint of the one who acts; understanding the other in this case has no value. The same goes for someone who has great power in a situation. Others may not be seen as people, but simply physical objects to be played with and pushed around; what they might think in the situation may have no relevance to the power holder. Of course, the totally selfish act may ultimately be met with anger and retaliation, and this might become costly in future interaction, and the powerful person who acts without role taking may create a situation where only force and fear characterize the relationship, and recognition of legitimacy by the actor and voluntary obedience is lost. These two exceptions are extreme examples; in most cases, even selfishness and power necessitates some role taking if one is going to be effective.

There is then a great diversity of people whose role we take. We take the role of others who existed in our past (my father who died many years ago) or who might exist in our future (a child yet to be born). We take the role of others who lived centuries ago (Moses, Socrates, Jesus, Mohammed, Newton, George Washington, Beethoven), and we take the role of others who may only be fictional (Don Quixote, Candide, Uncle Tom, or Dick Tracy). We sometimes take the role of a God; or we to try to take the role of someone we consider to be evil (the devil, a sadistic guard in a death camp, a mass murderer). We even take our own perspective used long ago (as a child or an adolescent) or how we might see reality in a distant future (when we retire or are about to die). We ask how we will see our present actions when we wake up the next morning, or we recall and apply to the present situation something we were thinking two days ago. Imagination allows us to exist in a very broad universe of perspectives and apply these perspectives to what we do in situations we encounter. Role taking is therefore not a simple or simpleminded view of the human being. We do not simply need to know what others are thinking in order to be accepted; we usually need to know what others are thinking simply to exist.

It is critical to recognize that taking the role of the other often has an important emotional component. We are not only able to take on the perspective of the other, the way one approaches reality; we are also able to take on the emotions of the other, the way others feel about situations. We might come to feel as they do: we feel their love, sorrow, fear, hatred, ecstasy. We might ignore or manipulate what they feel: we selfishly turn inward to our own lives or we use their situation for our own gain. We might understand their feelings and develop our own feelings about them: disgust, sympathy, jealousy, or hatred. As I walk down the street and someone approaches me for a handout, it is possible to try to feel what that person feels (empathy), know what he or she must feel but decide it is not my problem, or I might develop a feeling of sympathy for his or her situation. Or, you may exhibit anger toward me. I may feel your anger, I may understand but ignore your anger, or I may become distressed by your anger. In each case, it is partly through taking the role of the other that we come to feel and act in such situations.

THE IMPORTANCE OF TAKING THE ROLE OF THE OTHER

Role taking is not the only kind of mind action we engage in, but it is one of the most important; it is not the only kind of intelligence we have, but it is one of the most important; it is not the only aspect necessary for success in every activity, but it is one of the most important; it is not the only quality we use to understand others and to communicate clearly to others, but it is almost always central when we interact, learn, teach, and try to influence; it is not the only quality that allows us to cooperate in some kind of society, but it is one of the most important; it is not the only quality that make us human beings, but it is one of the most important. Perhaps it might be useful to be more systematic in understanding the importance of role taking.

Successful *symbolic communication* assumes the ability to role take. George Herbert Mead, in his description of the *symbol*, describes symbolic communication as an intentional and meaningful act. We know what we are doing as we communicate; we intend our communication to be understood by the one to whom we communicate; as we communicate we imagine our own communication from the perspective of the other. We are understood only because we try to share a message; we are understood if and when the other sees our symbol as we see it.

> The symbol involves two fundamental elements: First, the individual making the significant gesture [the symbol] places [himself or herself] in the position of the individual to whom [his or her] gesture is addressed; second, from the point of the other, the individual then regards the content of [his or her] own gesture (Natanson, 1973, p. 8).

Meaning is obtained through determining what a word or an act represents—to the other. The individual must "complete imaginatively the total act which a gesture stands for" and, to do that, "must put [himself or herself] in the position of the other person" (Meltzer, 1972, p. 14). Herbert Blumer (1969) uses the example of the robber and the victim: when the robber orders the other to "put up your hands," the robber must see the future action from the perspective of the victim. Correspondingly, the victim has to see the command from the standpoint of the robber who gives the command; he or she "has to grasp the intention and forthcoming action of the robber" (p. 10). Both have to act according to accurate role taking or unintentional consequences can occur for either: for example, unintentional murder of the victim or the unintentional failed anonymity of the robber.

A good friend, a good public speaker, a good teacher, a good politician, and a good comedian communicate effectively only by understanding those they communicate to; the other, in turn, is able to understand the communication of the other through accurate role taking. Without role taking, communication lacks understanding, and ends up becoming a response to a physical stimulus.

Mead also emphasizes the importance of role taking to the *development of self.* It is through taking the role of significant others that the self arises, and it through taking the role of a generalized other that the self matures. Mead writes: "The individual experiences [himself or herself] as such, not directly, but only indirectly from the particular standpoints of other individual members of the same social group, or from the generalized standpoint of the social group as a whole to which [he or she] belongs" (1934, p. 138). It is through taking the role of others who act toward us that we come to recognize ourself in the first place, and over time we come *to act toward, evaluate, direct, identify, assess ourself as we act.*

Mead shows the importance of role taking for *human society.* He does not regard imitation or habit or instinct as central to cooperative actions as much as the fact that humans continue to act with one another in mind as they go along. *We act in relation to our understanding of other people's actions and they of our actions, and that involves taking the role of the other. We control our actions in line with our place in the group,* so it is essential to take the role of the group—to use the rules and perspective of the group—as we act. Direction of the self according to the controls of society is what we mean by social control, and this comes through role taking. Mead (1936) describes this link between role taking and social control by emphasizing that in all communities individuals will "admonish" themselves as others would, recognize our rights and duties in relation to the the community, and direct themselves as others act toward them. Role taking becomes the way human beings come to organize themselves, and it "belongs to human society and distinguishes it from social organization which one finds among ants and bees and termites" (p. 377). Cooperation by humans does not depend on simple training in simple individual tasks; it involves, instead, understanding one's place in relation to the others. It involves coordinating action with others. It involves the understanding of one's own acts and the acts of others. "We enter in this way into the attitudes of others, and in that way we make our very complex societies possible (Mead, 1936, p. 375). Shibutani (1961) reminds us that "coordination of action re-quires anti-cipation of the movements of others, and this requires role taking" (p. 141). The football team, the couple that lives together, the committee that makes decisions for the annual dance, the General Motors Corporation—the people in each must role take, understanding and anticipating one another's actions, if any kind of cooperative action is to take place toward a goal. If we do not role take we are doomed to keep bumping into each other, to dupli-cate tasks, to be unable to adjust our own acts to the acts of the other—all of which, of course, make cooperation very difficult, even impossible.

We understand the consequences of our own actions through understanding their effects on others through role taking. Acting morally considers the per-spective and possible actions of the other. Trying to work out any problem in-volving others demands ongoing communication that encourages creativity, mutuality, and constant evaluation of alternatives and outcomes, and all of this assumes taking the role of the other.

Much of our *learning* results primarily from taking the role of the other. We do not simply react to words or acts of others; we also try to get into their heads and try to understand their words from their perspective. "Aha! At last I understand what you are trying to teach me!" Those of us who wish to *influence or teach* others must recognize that this includes understanding "where others are at" so what we do makes good sense to them. Successful learning involves mutual understanding through taking the role of the other between teacher and learner, lecturer and student, film maker and movie watcher, novelist and reader, minister and congregant, political leader and citizen, demagogue and follower, journalist and reader, counselor and patient.

If *love* is made up of qualities such as *giving* to others in order to benefit their lives, *respecting* others as individuals with rights of their own, *under-standing* others, *feeling responsible* for others, and *caring* for others (a list of qual-ities I am borrowing from *The Art of Loving* by Erich Fromm) then each one of these qualities is impossible unless we role take those we supposedly love. In my view, love, compassion, sympathy, empathy all demand taking the role of others.

And when I look at very selfish people who have been able to success-fully achieve their goals in life, I recognize the importance of role taking to them. *Those who abuse* power, abuse children, abuse women, abuse employees, abuse customers are all examples of people who need to understand at least superficially the perspective of those they abuse. Not because they care about their victims but because they seek to successfully abuse them.

I cannot imagine a more important ability than role taking that humans need in order to successfully achieve their goals in relation to other people. Almost everything that involves social interaction involves this quality. Some of us do it very well; some poorly. Some of us do it well in almost every situation; some of us do it occasionally. Some of us do it without caring about the other;

others care. Sometimes we face difficulties in role taking because we meet actors who are very different from what we are used to; sometimes it is easy because we meet actors we have known before or actors very similar to actors we have known. This is a skill that is necessary to cultivate; it is amazing to me that very little seems to be written about how to improve it, or if it is actually a general ability which an actor may be able to apply to many people and situations or if it is a much more specific ability. Perhaps it needs to be nurtured through lots of social interaction with lots of different people in lots of social situations accompanied by a desire on the actor's part to focus attention to the acts and perspectives of others. McCall and Simmons (1966) wrote that it is truly difficult to come to a workable understanding, to "truly communicate and interact in harmony" because good role taking must be accomplished. The ability to role take effectively, they contend, depends on the "amount and breadth of our experiences," as well as whether or not the one with whom we are interacting is known to us either because of ongoing interaction or because of the identity he or she presents. Perhaps we sometimes learn from forgetting to role take and making a grave mistake in our actions; perhaps we learn the importance to be more open-minded in situations we encounter, to listen more intently, and to refuse to get in the trap of simply observing others from our own point of view. Perhaps we need to consider more how others see what we do so we can communicate more effectively. Perhaps we need to seek honest feedback as to how others see us, and we need to learn better to understand what others mean than simply what words come out of their mouths.

This human quality is both central to human action yet too often neglected by those who systematically study human social interaction. Although it raises a number of very important questions, if we think seriously about it, most of us will undoubtedly recognize the many ways role taking enters our lives and the many problems it may create if we do not do it intelligently.

Summary

It is necessary to always remember that taking the role of the other—along with symbols, self, and mind—is the core of what it means to be human.

Taking the role of the other means understanding the perspectives of others as we act—significant others, our reference groups, our generalized other, and/or the perspectives of those we are acting toward.

Taking the role of the other is essential for symbolic communication and for the development of self. It is also one of the most important of all mind activities.

Taking the role of the other is largely responsible for successful teaching, learning, cooperating, acting morally, loving, sympathizing, empathizing, influencing, helping, protecting against exploitation, controlling our own actions, perceiving consequences of actions, leading, and competing successfully. It is also very important for successfully forcing, manipulating, and exploiting others.

Taking the role of the other is one of the most important parts of what we might call "social intelligence."

Taking the role of the other is necessary for continuing the successful operation of any group, organization, and society.

Taking the role of the other is an active process where the actor is able to take control of his or her situation, overcoming simple response to the acts of others, allowing more intelligent decisions in achieving goals.

In the end, by taking the role of the other we do not simply become what others want to make us; instead, we are able to define their intentions, their plans, and their actions, allowing us to determine how we shall act on them.

CHAPTER NINE

Human Action

The great puzzle in human affairs is the question: what causes human behavior? This is ultimately what social science wants to know.

Religious thinkers, philosophers, historians, lawyers, judges, journalists, psychologists, economists, people who are in the business of selling or helping, natural scientists, various political parties, and social movement leaders, also want to know and share with others what they have come to believe about the cause of human behavior.

In fact, almost all of us seek to understand cause—for example, why people divorce, kill, bully, oppress, succeed, find happiness, work hard, give up, break the law, become prejudiced, rise above poverty, fail in business or school, get A's in exams, become religious, always get angry, lie, get all the breaks.

I am presently completely confused as to why people who are so successful in society turn out to risk everything for a sexual encounter. I am stymied as to why so many people have abused children. I continue to push myself to understand the mysteries that have haunted me all my life: exactly why humans make war, or commit suicide, or become happy, intolerant, successful, religious, or are able live a meaningful life, or teach a successful class.

Of course, we all have pet theories that we use to attribute cause—to others and to ourselves. Too often, however, such theories are much too simpleminded, often very ideological, accepted from others who know little, or generalize from our own experience uncritically. Too often it is what authors of fiction or writers of film tell us, or our immediate family or friends that tell us about cause. Attribution of cause is very important; it is very complex; it is, I believe, highly mysterious, and it is something that we unfortunately believe we actually understand.

Personally, I have tried to overcome a lot of statements that others casually throw out at me. Some of these are thoughtful, but all of them are too simple for me; all of these do not fully satisfy my own search for understanding.

S[he] must be crazy.
It is his/her childhood.
S[he] is brainwashed.
It is instinct.
It is human nature.
It is in his/her genes.
Something traumatic has caused what he does now.
People are simply free and responsible for what they do.
It is all heredity.
It is all environment.
Everything comes down to heredity and environment.
Society makes us.
He is a man isn't he?
She is a woman, isn't she?
(S)he was born evil.
(S)he acted impulsively.

Some of these I think are silly. Others are important for what we do sometimes. Every one of these is much too incomplete for almost every action. The reason will be developed throughout this chapter. The bottom line, however, is that every one of these neglects a very important force that enters into almost every action we take: "Humans act according to their definition of the situation." If we want to understand human beings, we need to suspect any attempt to simply identify causes outside or inside the person, or that there is no real cause other than the individual's free will, unless we also bring in the importance of an ongoing thinking actor who defines the situation he or she is acting in.

To understand how the definition is created, symbolic interactionists focus on *social interaction with others* and the *thinking within the actor* as he or she acts overtly. Whatever else might contribute to human behavior, what we are thinking as we act matters a great deal, as does our ongoing interaction with others. "This is what she is thinking!" "This is what people are thinking when they interact with one another!"

It is very surprising how easy it is for people to ignore the definition of the situation as cause. We tend to claim the situation itself as cause; or we claim an attitude developed in the past as cause; or we identify an experience as cause; or someone else's influence over us. However, once our definition of the situation enters into our understanding of cause, all other causes no longer seem inevitable nor are they necessarily seen as the major reason. The human becomes an actor who is in charge, an active, living, choosing, deciding, evaluating, synthesizing, abstracting, dissecting, problem solving being, perhaps free to some extent but always limited by factors that enter into his or her definition. The model of the symbolic interactionist is simply presented in Figure 9–1.

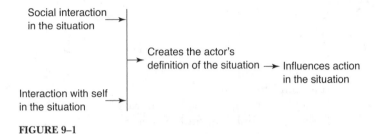

FIGURE 9–1

This chapter will focus on the meaning of overt action and the role of mind, self, and definition as cause.

After focusing on action in Chapter 9, Chapter 10 will add the role of social interaction as cause, and Chapter 11 will add the importance of society. Together these three chapters will introduce cause from the perspective of symbolic interactionism.

THE "STREAM OF ACTION"

The reality of action is that it is continuous, a constant process that is never ending except when we die. It is best described as a *stream of action*. "This stream of action is complex, manifold, multiplex. It is the full reality with many aspects, characteristics, features, dimensions, and interconnections" (Warriner, 1970, p. 15). The actor does not stop acting along this stream. One act leads to another; acts overlap; action flows, with only arbitrary lines separating one "act" from another. The word *stream* describes exactly what is meant by human action.

Streams of water constantly change direction; human action also is to be understood as changing direction. We act, and our stream goes one way, then another. Our lives change direction constantly, sometimes in small ways, occasionally in very significant ways. Barriers in the water change the direction of the stream; different environments do; and changes in the weather might. So too do our directions change as we encounter new situations, as new factors enter our lives. Streams of water change because smaller brooks enter and cause a change in the direction. So too do other people—individuals and groups—enter our stream of action, and as we interact with them our directions are changed, too.

This description of human action as an ongoing stream of action is not all that obvious to a casual observer. Most of us tend to focus attention on single, isolated acts. He stole a pig; she took a bus to the store; he robbed a bank; she just completed her exam; he became a lawyer; he did the dishes tonight; she put the kids to bed. This kind of description seems sensible and accurate, but it does not describe what the actor really does, because it divides this never-ending stream into manageable segments. We watch others and we label their acts; we look at our own action and we label those acts. It is really impossible to capture this never-ending stream, even though that is in fact a more accurate portrayal.

Actually, the comparison with a stream of water is misleading in two ways. For one thing, human beings actually engage in two streams of action simultaneously. Thus far, we have focused on a stream of overt action. However, humans also engage in a continous *stream of covert action.* We are actively and continuously engaged in an ongoing conversation with ourselves about what we are encountering and doing in the situation. The novelist captures this ongoing conversation when he or she describes the "stream of consciousness" of the main character, the internal discussion the character is having about the situation he or she is in. We see the thinking that goes into the decisions and actions, because the novelist recognizes the importance of the steam of covert action. Just as our stream of overt action is continuous and flowing in different directions, so is our stream of covert action. Both are important, and both influence one another. There is absolutely no reason to believe that water "has a mind of its own" or that a continuous stream of consciousness accompanies what a stream of water does. Water exhibits overt action, but it does not engage in covert action.

The second reason the water analogy is misleading is tied to the first. Because humans engage in a covert stream of action along with the overt, they are *active in their stream,* not passive as water is. Water responds to its environment. It flows because of the environmental conditions in which it exists. Humans, however, make active decisions along their stream, deciding what to do as they go along, and therefore they have some control over their directions. We evaluate our own action, we change our minds and establish new goals and redefine objects in new ways. When we interact with others we evaluate their acts, we role take, we interpret their actions and their acts of symbolic communication. Our relationship with the environment is therefore different from a stream of water because we determine our own directions to some extent. We are not simply pushed around by the outside environment acting on us; we are in control of our overt action. We need to see human action as illustrated in Figure 9–2.

FIGURE 9–2

Decision making is therefore ongoing. It has a long history, and in most cases an isolated decision must be seen within this historical context if it is to be understood. We do not simply make a decision and fix our direction in life or even end up doing a certain isolated act. We make many decisions as we go along, and this fact needs to be recognized. To decide something does not simply cause something. We do not simply make one decision to go to college; to go to college takes a number of decisions, and even if we end up going, if we are to remain there, a large number of decisions need to be made that keep us acting in that particular direction. We do not simply decide to marry someone or decide a particular major. In every case, many decisions are made to cause us to go in that direction. A series of decisions will reaffirm, slightly alter or completely change the decisions we made earlier. And this decision making is constantly being influenced by our interaction with others and with self along the way. What others do in relation to us makes a difference in the decisions we make; in defining goals and objects along our stream, we ourselves will also make a difference.

THE ACT

We all divide human action into separate acts because it is useful for us to do so. It helps us understand what is taking place; it gives us a handle on what others are doing as well as on what we ourselves are doing. As we do everything else, we divide up action in a way that makes sense to us at the moment. Any way we divide it is somewhat artificial, but we must divide it to survive. It is important to realize that whatever way we divide action is, of course, limited and incomplete and changes as our purposes change.

From our commonsense point of view, the human is thought to take part in a number of separate acts in a single day; we get up, wash ourselves, get dressed, make breakfast, eat breakfast, leave the house, start the car, drive the car, park it, arrive at the office, and collapse in our office chair for a morning nap. Of course, no one can capture all that an individual does in a single morning. If asked, the actor may combine all these small acts into "I went to work," or at lunch we might wonder, "Did I turn off the stove after breakfast?" We each divide up our stream of action in a number of ways; we isolate individual acts that sometimes take a moment or might even take days. We give those acts names and apply them to situations at the moment. In this sense, then, *acts are social objects* the actor pulls out of the stream of action in order to decide something in the present. Each act, it should be noted, is like all other social objects: it is named; its name is social; and it changes as our use for it changes. Acts that we point out to one another and to ourselves are like the people, plants, physical objects, and symbols that we also point out. A given act, Warriner (1970) writes:

> is recognized by the members of the society as a unit act with a particular meaning. ... The "sawing of a board" by a carpenter has primary significance for

sociological purposes, not because it involves certain muscles and nerves, not because the carpenter has particular motivations, not even because the board gets sawed, but because the act is given a name, conceptually separated from the other parts or aspects of the stream of action. ... "Thumbing one's nose," "punishing the child," "giving a speech," "going to church," "riding a bus," "going to class"...are all ... acts because they are named and are identified by the conventional understandings of the members of the society (pp. 17–18).

Therefore, anything that humans do that is also given a name is an "act." Consistent with the chapter on mind, action includes covert action, so "thinking about a good meal," or "thinking about how to get away from an embarrassing situation," and "telling oneself not to be afraid" are all acts. "Eating a meal," "excusing oneself from a conversation," and "telling a big bully to get lost" are also acts, overt acts.

The way we divide up our stream of action and pull out segments, calling them by name, depends on the perspective we use. Some perspectives, for example, emphasize large units of action (driving a car to California), whereas others emphasize much smaller units (turning the key in the ignition). Our stream looks different from the point of view of a teenager than from that of a middle-aged person, or that of an older person. An hour in our life will appear different to us if we look at it from the perspective of a wounded lover or a jealous lover or someone yearning to be free. Each segment in our stream will take on different degrees of importance—yet the actual stream of action stays the same.

One way we can understand the arbitrary nature of dividing our stream of action into separated acts in order to simplify understanding is to consider the whole notion of "decades." What is a decade? It is a ten-year period in society's ongoing stream of action, pulled out and labeled. It always begins with a year whose last digit is zero and ends with one whose last digit is nine. Think about it: decades are really artificial arbitrary descriptions created for the sake of convenience. Ten numbers actually make up a decade, yet once we see the decade as possessing a theme or a basic character, we tend to add or subtract years before and after that ten-year period. The 1940s can be thought to begin in 1939 and end in 1945 or 1948. We may determine that the 1920s actually ended in 1929. In looking back, we also might determine that centuries are not actually 100 years so much as a useful division for understanding many years. Thus, the twentieth century, we might say, started in 1914, because of World War I, and ended in the early 1990s with the collapse of the Soviet empire. The sixties are often shorthand for people describing 1965–1975. Decades and centuries, like acts, do not have precise beginnings and ends; they are simply useful guides to understand a complex stream of action by dividing that stream into manageable boundaries (Davis, 1984, p. 16).

Just as we divide recent history into decades and distant history into centuries, so too do we constantly divide our own lives and the lives of others into separate acts. In reality, however, there is only a constant stream of action. The reality of action is an ongoing process of decision making and doing things in relation to our environment, the environment outside and inside each of us. The segment we pull out and give significance to becomes an act, a decade, or a century. This is how we remember, and this is how we are better able to understand the ongoing stream of action.

ACTION, GOALS, AND SOCIAL OBJECTS

The symbolic interactionist, like everyone else, divides up the stream of action so that action is meaningful and manageable for understanding. We conveniently divide action into individual acts. Acts are sometimes even said to have a "beginning" and an "end," but such designations are usually used only for analytical purposes. Most symbolic interactionists understand full well the fact that *individual acts are simply social objects pulled out from the ongoing stream of action.*

Action exists in situations. Individuals define situations and act according to those definitions. We define goals, immediate or distant, and we see objects in the situation around those goals. We are planners; we use objects according to our plans. Social objects are those objects useful for achieving goals in a given situation. George McCall and J. L. Simmons (1966) describe the human being as a "thinker, a planner, a schemer," who

> continuously constructs plans of action ... out of bits and pieces of plans left lying around by culture, fitting them together in endless permutations of the larger patterns and motifs that the culture presents as models. The ubiquitous planning is carried on at all levels of awareness, not always verbally but always conceptually (p. 60).

Action in situations unfolds around goals that we have, and as we act goals are achieved, altered, or set aside. We notice objects in the situation that we tie to our goals, and these objects are defined according to our use for the purpose of achieving goals; objects become part of our plan. Objects, of course, include other people, self, past acts, symbols, and so on. We act in a stream of action that does not stop for us during the day but focuses on first one goal and set of objects in a situation, then another goal and set of objects in another situation. My goal is to get to George's house as soon as possible. I see Marsha down the street. I decide to talk briefly to Marsha, or evade her, or kiss her and run along, or shake her hand, or treat her with cool respect, or reject her completely—and I act overtly on the basis of that decision. Action toward the object may change during the course of action; for example, Marsha might tell me she is about to quit her job, and my goal may immediately change to trying to convince Marsha that her plan is not wise. Thus, my definition of Marsha as "someone to greet and get away from as soon as possible" is replaced by a definition of Marsha as "someone to take the time to help." I may eventually achieve my goal in getting to George's house—after helping Marsha solve her problem, giving Mark the brush, running across a beautiful lawn that is graced with a "Please Do Not Walk on the Grass" sign, and waiting for what seems like forever for a train to pass. Once I arrive at George's house my goals will change again, my social objects will be transformed, and, for example, Mark may now become someone that I had better call to explain why I was in so great a hurry. Indeed, now that I am at George's and I see who else is there, my action may be organized around getting out of George's house as soon as possible.

Each act, then, although separated for purposes of analysis, is in fact part of an ongoing stream of action. Each act *has a goal or goals* as well as *social objects*, and each *involves decisions* made by the actor. The human, from the moment of waking in the morning to the moment of falling asleep at night, is engaged in a continuous stream of action toward an innumerable list of social objects that are defined around a great number of goals. He or she changes lines of action, alters direction, redefines goals, and redirects action as objects in the environment act back.

The actor we make love to is someone we feel affection for, try to give happiness to, and gain happiness from. Making love is an act, and once it has been completed, our goals change immediately, objects take on new meaning, and our action changes direction. The beautiful, wonderful person whom we desired to make love to is redefined as one to speak softly to, to share a meal with, to joke with, perhaps to quietly say goodbye to until later in the day or week. As we leave that person's presence, he or she becomes someone to remember with affection, perhaps someone to talk about to parents or friends. But as we leave, we walk toward an elevator, and we act toward the button in order to get downstairs, in order to leave the building, in order to make our appointment at two o'clock. Other social objects have begun to replace our loved one ever so slowly, and our stream of action continues, centered on new goals and objects. As we prepare for bed at night, our thoughts may be directed toward the morning hours, so our action includes setting the alarm, picking out our clothes, perhaps preparing a lunch that we will take to work the next day. We might recall the isolated act of love during the previous day, making that into a social object, and feeling good. As we awaken the next day, the stream of action continues, guiding us from one social object to another. Herbert Blumer (1969) points out: "In this process, given lines of action may be started or stopped, they may be abandoned or postponed, they may be confined to mere planning or to an inner life of reverie, or if initiated, they may be transformed" (p. 16). But the action continues throughout our waking day, directions always changing, sometimes slightly, sometimes greatly.

MEAD'S FOUR STAGES OF THE ACT

To understand *what happened* in our various acts along our stream, Mead goes further by dissecting the act into four stages: impulse, perception, manipulation, and consummation. Although most symbolic interactionists do not see these stages exactly as Mead did, nor do they give them the importance he did, it is widely recognized that the four stages represent a further understanding of human action.

Stage 1: Impulse

The act begins when the organism is in "a state of disequilibrium." There is "discomfort leading to behavior" and an "activation through disruption." *Impulse* is simply a "generalized disposition to act." It does not tell the organism what to do or even what goal to achieve. It does not determine the direction of the act but only that there will be action of some sort. In every situation there is at least slight disequilibrium, discomfort, and disruption, and the organism must act out in the environment. Humans act from a state of slight or great disturbance that does not come only once in a while but characterizes their entire life (description borrowed from Shibutani, 1961, pp. 65–66).

Other symbolic interactionists do not go so far as to give a reason for the beginning of the act: we act, and that's all there is to it. John Dewey (1922) states that the human being "is an active being and that is all to be said on that score" (p. 119). Gregory Stone and Harvey Farberman (1970) announce emphatically: "Man simply acts, period!" (p. 467). In essence, most symbolic interactionists simply *assume* action on the part of the organism and pay little attention to why an act begins, focusing instead on understanding the direction that action takes. Mead's "impulse" is not developed extensively in the literature and is still somewhat vague, yet imbalance or disequilibrium seems as good a reason as any for the beginning of an act.

Perhaps a personal note might be introduced here. Throughout this book it has been emphasized that human beings are goal directed and problem solvers. Each situation is unique and thus is a challenge to the individual. We might simply suggest that an act *begins with a problem to be solved, a goal to be reached, something to be overcome* by the human being in the environment.

Stage 2: Perception

Humans perceive; they look at objects in their situation. Mead calls "perception" the active ongoing process of selecting objects out of the environment, those objects that can be used to achieve the actor's goals. Perception thus makes objects into *social objects* in a situation. "Stimuli, therefore do not initiate activity, they are pivots for redirection" (Shibutani, 1961, p. 68). The individual acts in a world that has meaning for him or her at that moment. Perception and definition in selective and ongoing. To Mead such thinking is the most important part of what we do and the larger part of that thinking is a process of discovering "just what it is that ought to be attacked, what was to be avoided" (Mead, 1936, p. 403).

Mead explains how this second stage is related to the first: our goals in a situation are formed in order to restore our equilibrium; that is, we decide to go to lunch (goal) in order to satisfy our hunger (impulse, problem), or we decide to sing out loud (goal) in order to satisfy our uneasiness (impulse, problem) in the social situation. That is, individuals define goals, and they perceive and define objects in situations in order to reach those goals and overcome problems.

The important point that must not be lost is that human beings define their situation by perceiving, identifying, and understanding objects that can be used related to goals and problems.

Stage 3: Manipulation

In the third stage, manipulation, humans use their environment, act on it, handle it, reassess what it is, and move objects in the environment according to their use. Humans manipulate things and persons by physically handling them, talking to them, breaking them, writing letters to them, or caressing them. We act toward objects overtly (for all to see), after the foundations have been laid in stages 1 and 2 which are covert phases.

Mead emphasizes the importance of human hands—the ability to take physical objects, dissect them, put them together with other objects, change them, use them in a creative way. We become aware of the object; we plan a use for it; we use it; we revise our plan and use it in another way. We handle objects in situations as tools, as means to an end, as objects whose purpose lies in the future. The house is dark; in order to change the fuse, we pick up the flashlight, find the stairs, watch out for things in the way, open doors, find the blown fuse, take it out, put in the good fuse. The lights are on; we go up the stairs, reset the clocks... New goals, problems, definitions, manipulations. Manipulation comes to mean that humans use objects as tools. We are therefore tool users in every situation we enter.

Stage 4: Consummation

This stage, consummation, is the end of the act; the goal is achieved and the equilibrium is restored even though only for a moment. Acts are not always consummated, because we may start another act before ending an act, focusing our attention on something else, shifting our stream of action. After consummation, if it takes place, another sequence of impulse, perception, manipulation, and consummation takes place, and the stream of action continues. I finished lunch, I left her alone, I won a tennis match, I blew my opportunity, I finally read *The Grapes of Wrath.*

Another Look at Mead's Four Stages of the Act

Mead's attempt to dissect an act is interesting, useful, and easy to memorize. However, there is a danger in breaking the act up into stages, because it loses the essence of action, the fact that action is ongoing, it is constant, it really does not end until we die. Much of what we do is not nearly as neat as these four stages. We often change goals before there is any so-called consummation. The reality of action is not that we engage first in covert action then in overt action, but that both are simultaneously going on.

The real importance of describing action is captured much better, in my opinion, by Herbert Blumer (1966), who does not dissect the act into four phases:

> In order to act the individual has to identify what [he or she] wants, establish an objective or goal, map out a prospective line of behavior, note and interpret the actions of others, size up his situation, check [himself or herself] at this or that point, figure out what to do at other points, and frequently spur [himself or herself] on in the face of dragging dispositions or discouraging settings (pp. 536–37).

Blumer reminds us that this does not mean that our action is constructed well. Sometimes the actor constructs action intelligently; at other times, the construction may be done poorly. We need to constantly be aware of others—their actions and their expectations for us, the relevant rules of the group—but we must also continuously examine ourselves as relevant objects in the situation, so we need to assess our own wants, feelings, goals, actions, expectations, recollections, and view of self. As we act, we must take all of this into account and consider options as the action unfolds between others and us (Blumer, 1966, pp. 536–37).

LOCATING THE "CAUSE" OF HUMAN ACTION

Where does this discussion lead us for understanding why humans act as they do? We must always remember that action is a stream, so it is important always to understand the context of what the individual does over time, trying always to assess the direction of his or her action. The study of the history of the stream is critical for understanding.

Instead of seeing action as constituting a stream, we are tempted to examine the cause of an isolated act. Why did you go to Harvard? Why did you major in history? Why did you decide not to study for your physics exam? Why did you break up with Roberta? Each of these isolated acts can be easily analyzed, and causes can be determined. This makes cause much more easy to isolate. Often we will focus on one of three clusters of causes:

1. Free choice. The individual chooses to do it.
2. Personality. The individual did it because it is the way he or she is.
3. Social environment. The individual did it because of society, social forces, culture, groups, or other people.

We can understand such causes. They are relatively easy to isolate, study and comprehend. And we have something to act on. We can punish or reward the person who committed an act out of free choice. We can try to rehabilitate the person whose action was caused by personality traits. We can try to alter a person's social environment if that is what caused the action.

However, the symbolic interactionist tries always to see action caused by a set of decisions along a stream of action. Each decision needs to be understood as arising from the definition of the situation at the time of action, including establishing goals and plans, selecting and defining social objects, considering consequences, and applying relevant knowledge and memories recalled and applied from the past. In turn, the definition of the situation is the result of ongoing action toward the self (thinking), and interaction with others. The act is not necessarily free, nor is it simply the result of personality and social forces. And always the direction that one tends to go along the stream of action must take in the history of decisions (arising from the definitions of situations) that led the individual to the situation he or she encounters.

I took a job at Moorhead State University long ago. I took it because of several decisions I had made at the time: to leave my previous job and community, to move from Minneapolis, and to stop looking for other jobs. Those decisions were each made on the basis of the goals I had defined for myself at the time: to become a college professor, to finish my doctorate, and to settle in a community close to my family. These decisions were made because of social objects relevant to me at the time: a job offer, an attractive community, a past that I no longer wanted to continue, a job in a sociology department that looked both promising and secure, my wife's welfare, my children's welfare, the easy highway from Moorhead to Minneapolis, and a good school system for my children. I recalled situations in my past job that I wanted to escape, and I saw an opportunity for something new and exciting. Throughout the decision-making process, I interacted with my wife, my adviser, my friends at the university, and people from the sociology department who had asked me to come. Many decisions had to be made, and together my stream of action was altered in the direction of university life at Moorhead State. Why did I move? Because of the decisions I made along my stream *at that time*, Which were, in turn, caused by my definition *at that time*, which in turn, was caused by my social interaction and interaction with self *at that time*. And staying at Moorhead for over 30 years, becoming chair of the department, and eventually retiring from teaching each were the result of many decisions I made along my stream of action, and ail of these were made according to my definition of my situation, my ongoing thinking about my life, and my interaction with family, friends, students, faculty, administration, and publishers.

It is misleading to isolate an act (like moving to Moorhead). In fact, the cause of that act can be understood only by placing it in the larger context of a stream of action in which many decisions are made. We might decide on one act and change our actions moments or minutes or hours later. To actually change my job and move took many decisions, all made over time, and at any time the direction. I ended up taking could have been changed dramatically. To decide to get married does not mean that one actually gets married; to decide to major in history does not cause us to be history majors. Instead, many decisions go into these actions, and all of them are influenced by interaction with self and others over time.

The cause of a single act is easier to understand than the cause of the direction of our stream of action. Streams of action are influenced by many instances of social interaction, definition, and decision making. At times our streams are steady; at other times they waver a bit; and at other times they are dramatically changed—always because of social interaction, definition, and decision making.

Let us for a moment summarize what is being said here about the cause of human action:

1. Action is not simply caused by our past, our personality, or social forces working on us. It is largely caused by the decisions we make that arise from our definition of the situation we are in.
2. The definition of a given situation results from interaction with self (thinking) and social interaction.
3. Each act is really part of a larger stream of action that flows in different directions. The direction of our stream of action is due to many decisions we make over time along that stream.

Two final points should be made. When we say that interaction influences our definition of the situation, we mean that, as actors act toward each other, the action of each becomes part of the situation that each actor is defining, and thus each actor becomes a social object to the other. The acts of each are influenced, and the stream of action of each is influenced. It is interesting to note that social interaction really is the intersection of different actors' streams of action, each altering his or her own stream according, in part, to what others do. And, as we shall see later, over time such interaction leads to a shared view of reality—a perspective—and this too enters into definition, decision making, and the direction of action.

Finally, there is the question of freedom. Because the actor is continuously defining the situation in conversation with self, part of the reason for a given act is the free choice that is made in the decision making. We are conceived here as active participants in what we do in a given situation; our action in part springs from decisions made by us through manipulating the situation in our heads and making choices. It is hard to prove that this is in fact an act of freedom; however, if there is any freedom for the actor, this is what must be done. The perspective of symbolic interactionism explains more than most other perspectives the possibility for this free choice in this description of cause.

THE DEFINITION OF THE SITUATION

To better understand cause we will now turn our attention to the concept "definition of the situation," which we have identified up to now as the process that leads to the decisions the actor makes along the stream of action.

William and Dorothy Thomas (1928) wrote: "If [people] define situations as real, they are real *in their consequences*" (p. 572). Their point is simple: humans act in a world they define, and although there may actually be a reality out there, their definition is far more important for what they *do*. In the end, it does not matter if you are a scoundrel or not; what matters is that I see you as a scoundrel and I act toward you as if you were one. And you, in turn, may not be a scoundrel, but you may accept my definition of you as one and then proceed to act that way. If I see a situation as threatening, then I will act accordingly, even if people in that situation did not mean to appear threatening. If I define school as hard or good or silly, then I will act toward school in that manner, no matter if others feel as I do and no matter if it is in reality harder, better, sillier than other schools. Our realities are our definitions of situations. Definitions of the situation may be influenced by others, but in the end, each individual must define the situation (including those others) by engaging in mind activity. We each act in a world that we create through interaction with self influenced in part by interaction with others.

Donald Ball (1972) described the definition of the situation as the "sum total of all recognized information, from the point-of-view of the actor, which is relevant to locating self and others, so that [he or she] can engage in self-determined lines of action and interaction" (p. 63). It is, as we have described throughout this book, the definition of social objects the actor creates within himself or herself that has consequences for overt action in the situation.

Although it is difficult to summarize all the different activities that are included in defining a situation, we might list the following as a start:

1. Establishing goals in the situation
2. Applying a perspective from a significant other or a reference group to the situation
3. Pointing out to self the relevant objects in the situation—this may include other people, natural and human-made objects, ideas, words, and so on
4. Taking the role of the other—both of individuals and of the group as a whole
5. Defining self in the situation, including
   assessing what one is doing in relation to the situation
   assessing what is happening in the situation in relation to the self
   judging self in the situation
   giving self an identity in the situation
   interpreting what one is experiencing emotionally
6. Defining the future, distant and near, and imagining the effects of one's acts before one performs them
7. Applying knowledge and memories from the past to the present situation

It is therefore imperative to understand human action from the definition of the actor. How he or she defines the situation is central to how he or she acts in it. The cause of action is always definition, and the actual definition is not easily understood, measured, predictable: goals, perspective, significant others, reference groups, objects, other people, view of future and past, self, identity, and assessment of what is taking place in the situation are all matters that must be considered if action is to be understood. And to make cause even more difficult to isolate, recall that the definition as well as the situation itself always change: the actor engages in an ongoing stream of action, defining the situation one way at one point, another way later on, and as he or she acts the real situation is altered.

HABITUAL ACTION

Of course, our definition of the situation is not usually a matter of careful deliberation but rather a quick assessment. It is when we are confronted by interruptions in our stream of action, when we are faced with serious problems, that we become more aware and deliberate. However, every situation is at least somewhat new for us—goals and objects must be worked out; others are taken account of—and therefore *some definition is almost always involved.*

Habitual action does not involve definition, but is simply a response to a certain type of situation that we have developed over time. It does not involve covert activity. Habitual action takes us through some situations; we may be able to respond entirely on the basis of past learning, but usually such action is short in duration. Habitual action is sometimes functional, allowing the individual to act without hesitating; it is good when an immediate response is demanded. On the other hand, action that is purely habitual is dysfunctional for most situations because each situation is unique, each involves other people acting, and therefore each demands some adjustment on the part of the actor. Walking to work in the morning may become highly habitual, but often we must tell ourselves to speed up or to slow down or to watch out for a car at this intersection, or we must adjust to an increase in traffic, perhaps by taking a slightly different route. Driving a car may also be a highly habitual act much of the time, but that too is loaded with covert action—giving ourselves direction and acting in response to traffic signals, other cars, pedestrians, and detours.

Indeed, the more habitual our actions, the less prepared we become for alterations in situations that demand some adjustment on our part. Perhaps we can afford habitual action for small, simple acts such as putting the key in the ignition, but when acts are larger than simple motor movements, such as driving a car to California, we must rely less on habitual response and more and more on covert definition and interpretation of the ongoing situation. Purely habitual action would be especially inappropriate to activities that involve other people because the individual must constantly make adjustments to an ever-changing interactive situation. Definition and analysis of self and others are absolutely essential to working out social situations.

Purely habitual action is extremely rare. In most cases, ongoing definition while we act overtly is the rule. In some cases, careful deliberation is necessary.

THE ROLE OF THE PAST IN HUMAN ACTION

Needless to say, action always takes place in the present. We act *now*, and, when we are through, our act becomes part of our past. Past is massive; the present is a split second. (Actually, we might define the "present" longer in time than a split second if it becomes useful to us.)

Throughout this discussion, we have emphasized that our action in the present is determined not by what went before but by the definition of the situation in the present. This emphasis is in sharp contrast to what most psychologists emphasize. My past does not cause my acts in the present; my definition in the present does, and that definition is also not caused by my past but by interaction with self and others *in the present.*

Does the past play any role in what we do? Of course it does, but not so much because it has shaped our personality, but because *we use it in our definition of the present.* What we know and remember from our past is applied to situations we encounter. Significant others, reference groups, perspectives, beliefs, decisions made, situations experienced, and information from our past are recalled and used as social objects to work through the present situation. When I enter Math 210, I use what I already know to make it through that class—experiences in other math classes, experiences with former teachers, strategies I have developed elsewhere to get through classes like this one, knowledge of mathematics, and so on. But it is important to realize that these are items I *use* in Math 210, that I apply to the definition of that particular situation. The past, therefore, does not cause what I do in the present; instead, *I use the past to define the present and to guide my action in the present.* Mead (1934) describes intelligence as "essentially the ability to solve the problems of *present* behavior in terms of its possible *future* consequences as implicated on the basis of *past* experience ... it involves both memory and foresight" (p. 100). The past is used to make sense out of the present.

The past is rich for us, and it provides us with the tools to define the present. The past changes every second because the present is always moving forward, with new experiences being added to it. Further, our past is always changing because our new experiences, the new situations we encounter, and the new perspectives we come to believe in reinterpret the past and cause us to see it as altered. As a society, we are always rewriting our past: African Americans, women, and Native Americans, to name a few groups, are clearly reconstructing our past for us, causing us to see it anew, and seeing it anew is affecting what we do *now*. The past is also constantly changing in our personal biographies: the man who becomes a parent sees his own parents in a new light and understands their anxieties, hopes, and feelings when he was a child. He is redefining his past, as he also does when he looks back twenty years at his high school days, fully remembering some beautiful moments, conveniently forgetting the horrors of adolescence experienced at the time.

Our past is very important for another reason: *The decisions that we made in our past have brought us to the present situation.* We all have histories; our streams of action go back a long way. If our decisions had been different, the situation we are facing at the moment would also be different. Many decisions went into my marriage to Susan; had those decisions not been made in my past, then the situations I define every day that involve Susan would not confront me. Figuring out how to study for a final in a sociology class you are taking right now would not be a problem except for the fact that you made *many decisions* that have brought you to the final exam. The past (including decisions we made in that past) brings us to the present situation; but the definition of the past in the present influences what we do there.

Finally, our past is important because *where we begin our life really matters a great deal in our direction.* We are born poor or rich or neither; we are born in Boise, Idaho, or in Atlanta, Georgia, or somewhere else; we are born into a family that loves us, ignores us, or abuses us. This is the beginning of our stream of action. The situations we encounter in life depend in part on where we begin in life. Therefore, our past enters in by starting us out. Nothing is inevitable after that, but it is foolish to ignore the starting line, for the situations we end up defining are influenced by that.

To fully understand the role of the past in human action, therefore, it is important to understand three points: (1) how the individual applies the past to the present, (2) the history of decision making (including interaction with others and self) that brought the individual to the present situation, and (3) where the actor's stream of action began. This emphasis by the symbolic interactionist is significantly different from the emphases of other social science perspectives, because it does not assume that the past causes action in the present. Rather, it is always the definition of the present that does. *Where I begin my life does not cause what I do now;* it is simply the origin of my stream of action. *My actions in my past do not cause what I do now;* instead, just as they resulted from choices and decisions made at the time, so too does my action now arise from choices and decisions that I make now. *My past experiences do not cause what I do now,* but they become important as social objects I can pull out from memory and use to make my decisions.

THE ROLE OF THE FUTURE IN HUMAN ACTION

The future is a very important part of the individual's definition of the situation. What we do in the present depends in part on our conception of the future. Our acts have consequences, and we try to imagine these as we act. To Mead, the actor sees objects according to how he or she plans to use them in the future. We develop a plan of action toward objects; the "later stages of the act are present in the early stages" (Mead, 1934, p. 11), what we will do later is imagined in the present:

> If one approaches a distant object [one] approaches it with reference to what [one] is going to do when one arrives there. If one is approaching a hammer [one] is muscularly all ready to seize the handle of the hammer. The later stages

of the act are present in the early stages—not simply in the sense that they are all ready to go off, but in the sense that they serve to control the process itself. They determine how we are going to approach the object, and the steps in our early manipulation of it (p. 11).

We are planners. We consider what our present acts will lead to. We are problem solvers. We imagine the consequences of the alternatives we choose. We are social beings. We imagine the effects our acts will have on others:

> The intelligent man as distinguished from the intelligent animal presents to self what is going to happen. The animal may act in such a way as to insure its food tomorrow. A squirrel hides nuts, but we do not hold that the squirrel has a picture of what is going to happen. The young squirrel is born in the summer time and has no directions from other forms, but it will start hiding nuts as well as the older ones. Such action shows that experience could not direct the activity of the specific form. The provident person, however, does definitely pursue a certain course, pictures a certain situation, and directs [his or her] own conduct with reference to it. The squirrel follows certain blind impulses, and the carrying-out of its impulses leads to the same result that the storing of grain does for the provident person. It is this picture, however, of what the future is to be as determining our present conduct that is the characteristic of human intelligence—the future as present in the realms of ideas (Mead, 1934, p. 119).

The future and the past are therefore social objects to the actor. Memory is applied to the present; the imagined consequences of an act are considered. The past and the future change as we change our uses for them in the present.

The focus of symbolic interactionism remains the present. For each actor, "the past and the future do not exist in themselves, but are the past and the future of a particular present. The past is a different past for every particular present; a new present means a new past and a new future" (Tillman, 1970, p. 537). Memory brings "the past into the present," and imagination brings "the future into the present" (p. 541).

ACTION AND MOTIVES

According to the symbolic interactionist, individuals are goal directed. We are constantly determining lines of action toward objects in keeping with our goals. Goals are not static, and therefore lines of action are constantly shifting. Whatever is done at a given moment must be understood as having developed over a period of time, with a number of factors contributing to the direction of action at different points, with goals in mind shifting, objects being redefined, and other people's acts affecting direction. Action is to be explained not by deep-seated stable motives but by shifting goals and definitions of the situation.

The distinction between motives and goals is a subtle but very important one. If we imagine human action as being the result of individual *motives*, there is a tendency to see action as *determined by an internal state*, preceding action, stable over time, having little to do with either the definition of the situation encountered or with interaction in the situation. A motive is a trait that the individual carries to the situation that causes action. The human is conceptualized as possessing a stable internal state that produces action. Action is said to spring from motives. To ask about motives normally assumes a constant underlying cause that drives the direction of an individual's stream of action over time. Although such causes do exist and people often use them to explain behaviors, normally their importance is exaggerated.

Goals are emphasized in symbolic interactionism, and as soon as they are brought into the analysis, a rational process is seen as taking place; the human is conceptualized as defining and redefining situations in relation to those goals. The situation itself, rather than the motives we might bring to it, becomes central to what we do. A goal is something that the human being *defines*, and thus human action is thought to be governed by definition, interaction, and ongoing decision making. Situations are worked out in relation to the goals we define, and because action is ongoing, our goals and definitions are constantly being defined and redefined.

Symbolic interactionists, however, regard motives as important in a different sense. They are important in the same sense that past and future are; *we define them as important in situations, and so we act as though they are important.* Whatever the actual role of motives (and in most cases that role is probably minor), humans *impute* motives; we *explain* one another's actions through *assigning motives.* Motives are the *stated reasons* for an act, the *verbalized cause* of human action that assumes intentions on the part of the actor. "You kept my money because you wanted to cheat me, because you wanted to take advantage of my weakness in order to get rich," or "You treated me to lunch because you need me for your friend," or "You saved that man from drowning because you are a loving person and were doing a courageous thing in light of the danger facing you." Whatever the many complex actual reasons for our action's taking a certain direction, the explanation we find easiest to give involves deep-seated motives. *Motives, however, are oversimplified explanations.* They become important in the sense that what we say or *think* is the reason for our act or the acts of others makes a difference in what we do. Motives are attempts by people to summarize and make some sense out of complex acts. *Motives are labels, summary statements of reasons we give for why an act occurred.* The losing baseball coach cries out: "We lost because you did not try hard enough. You did not want to win this game badly enough. You lack desire." It is difficult to imagine anyone disagreeing with this interpretation; it is also difficult to discover other possible reasons for the loss. Lack of desire is the easiest explanation; it is the only thing that can be easily changed; it is the easiest thing that individuals can control. And, finally, it is something that the coach can always find evidence for. It is indeed a very useful explanation (Fine, 1987, p. 64).

Dennis Brissett and Charles Edgley (1975) describe motives as communications people use "to justify or rationalize" conduct and "enable certain interactions to persist" (p. 6). Max Weber (1947) and C. Wright Mills (1940) describe motives as "verbalized explanations of behavior, and as such are used to explain, rationalize, or condemn one's own acts or the acts of others." Marvin Scott and Stanford Lyman (1968) call motives "accounts," reasons we give for why we do what we do. In all of these discussions of motives, motives become post facto explanations of cause, simplified, easily stated, and almost always meant to attribute cause that seems to make sense. It makes it much easier to separate good people and bad ones. It is a shorthand assumption of cause so we know how to act around others. We often declare our motives so we establish a cause in the minds of others; we criticize or compliment the motives they seem to exhibit.

However true a certain motive is really the cause of an act, it should be cautiously accepted, and in almost all situations it must be placed in a much larger context: what was I thinking at the time? What were they thinking at the time? That is, what was the definition of the situation at the time?

ACTION AND EMOTIONS

The symbolic interactionists have influenced greatly the study of emotions in sociology. Increasingly, sociologists have recognized that emotions are very important in human social action and have been neglected for too long. But, true to style, the role of emotions changes as the symbolic interactionist examines them.

Most people treat emotions the same way as attitudes, motives, and our past: as the source of action. Action is thought to spring from within the individual. The usual conceptualization of emotion is as an internal response that the individual has little or no control over and that leads to an overt response. Although emotions do have an element beyond control and do sometimes lead directly to action, emotions have a far more important role in human action.

On the one hand, emotions are biological: something changes inside the physical actor—rapid heartbeat, flushed face, for example. On the other hand, emotions, as is everything else, are *defined:* we isolate them, give them a name, direct them, *use them.* Just as there is an objective reality "out there" that we learn to identify and define, so there is also an internal reality we define. Physical changes occur within our bodies at various times in our stream of action. Some are fleeting, and some last for a long time. The bodily change may be in heartbeat, pulse, respiration rate, facial flush, perspiration, or motor activity (Kemper, 1978, p. 47). But the human is able to act back on himself or herself, defining, thinking about, feeling guilty or good about that bodily change. Indeed, other animals also have bodily changes we might define as emotional responses, but it is difficult to imagine other animals' defining them, reflecting on them, controlling them, discussing them, or using them as human beings are able to do.

Human beings not only respond to their environment because of an internal emotional response, but they also *feel* those emotional responses. They give meaning to their bodily changes. "I am angry!" "I am in love." "I am jealous!" "I feel good." "I am sad." To human beings, emotions become social objects defined and used in situations. Whatever changes occur inside the individual, the actor must deal with them: label them, control them, hide them, direct them, use them to achieve goals, and even try to alter them. There is a control that the actor exercises over his or her emotions, actions that take place in relation to self. The emotion is not simply a causal response to a stimulus in the situation. The mere existence of physical change may in fact influence an act or even the direction of action over time, but our action toward our own bodily state—what we feel and what we do with that—is usually more important.

There is, admits Norman Denzin (1984a), "nonreflective emotional experience," parts of the body that exist as sensations or states and that do not become part of our stream of consciousness. However, emotions are generally more than this. They are reflective and emotional experiences that become objects to define, to consider, and to use (pp. 71, 112–13). The human actor recognizes that something is happening internally, defines what it is (anger, depression, frustration, happiness), judges it as positive or negative, expresses it, represses it, or manages it; the actor may store it and in the future recall it. In all of these ways—and undoubtedly others—emotions become social objects used by the actor; they involve "reflection, feeling, cognition, and interpretation," some being "purely private, others public or collective" (p. 5).

Humans express their emotions, and in that sense they use emotions in the same way they use all objects. We feel angry; we express that anger. We love someone, and we use that love toward the other in our action. We feel sorrow, and we express it. We feel hatred toward a group of racists, and we use that feeling in our speech and acts toward the group.

Humans also repress their emotions. In this sense, emotions become social objects that we think should not be expressed. Gary Alan Fine (1987, p. 87), for example, in his study of Little League baseball teams, points out the central importance that emotional control has for the boys, the parents, and the coaches. It is important not only to learn how to play baseball but also to repress inappropriate feelings (e.g., laughing at another's pain or getting angry at the other team's winning), to control aggression, to hide fears, to keep from crying. In their study of medical doctors, Robert Coombs and Pauline Powers (1975) found repression of feeling. The doctor "cannot take death and dying too personally." The doctor

> is expected to retain composure, no matter how dramatic or tragic the death scene might be. Rationality and clearness of judgment in moments of grave peril must characterize [his or her] every action. The physician who loses coolness and presence of mind also loses the confidence of patients and staff. Clearly, a doctor sobbing over a favorite patient is no doctor at all (p. 251).

Yet, for those doctors who were interviewed, emotion was felt internally but not expressed. One interviewer in the study reported: "Everybody I've talked to so far is having a horrible time dealing with death and dying; and it isn't just on a professional level, but personally too" (p. 264).

Humans are active in situations, and perhaps nothing makes this clearer than the fact that we also *manage* emotions in situations. We create them; we make ourselves feel. Arlie Hochschild calls this "emotion work." We try to get psyched up for our classes; we try to feel good in order to have fun on a date; we try to feel sympathetic when others are depressed; we try to feel grateful when someone helps us; we try to fight the guilt we feel when we do something wrong. In a study by Hochschild (1983), students were asked to describe an event in which they experienced a deep emotion. Their reports were filled with such phrases as "I psyched myself up; I squashed my anger down; I tried hard not to feel disappointed; I forced myself to have a good time; I mustered up some gratitude; I put a damper on my love for her; I snapped myself out of the depression" (p. 39). All of these people were trying to take charge of their internal state—trying to manage what was taking place inside their body.

Emotions are therefore social objects, used in situations by the active, problem-solving human being. And because they are social objects, they too are learned in interaction with others. We learn to isolate physical changes within us, to label them, to judge them, to manage them, to repress them, to express them, and even to produce them. "They are learned in social relationships, initially in the primary group of the family" (Denzin, 1984a, p. 52). We are taught to be polite in expressing our emotions: "I'm sorry"; "Thank you"; "I feel bad about your misfortune." Emotions "are embodied 'self-feelings' of people," learned from culture (Power, 1985, p. 215).

Emotions, motives, past, future, significant others, reference groups, knowledge, symbols, and self—all of these are social objects, shared in interaction, used in situations by the actor to guide decision making and action.

HUMAN ACTION AND FREE CHOICE

It is significant how symbolic interactionists treat emotions. Most social scientists treat them as shapers of actions, causes of human action. Symbolic interactionists treat emotions as part of what the active human being uses in situations. The actor defines and takes charge of much of his or her emotional life along the stream of action.

So, too, the past, motives, attitudes, and other people are not treated as major causes. Instead, the actor acts on the environment, using it according to his or her goals at the time. Decisions are made in every situation according to very complex and continuous definitions by the actor. The actor is able to hold back, to turn around, to go one way and then another based on his or her own definition of the situation. Mead (1934) states that ideas become "possibilities of overt responses which we test out implicitly in the central nervous system and then reject in favor of those which we do in fact act upon or carry into effect. The process of intelligent conduct is essentially a process of selection from among various alternatives; intelligence is largely a matter of selectivity" (p. 99).

It is very difficult to state that freedom exists in this decision making, but it is exciting to see how human beings are able to overcome being simply products of their inner or outer environment. Always there is conversation toward oneself; always there is control over self by the actor; always there is an ability to reassess and change direction; always there are new and creative goals to organize one's action to; always there is fresh interpretations of the environment that will alter our actions. William Desmonde (1957), interpreting Mead, writes that it is our capacity to readjust our developing acts to what we anticipate the future to be that enables us to achieve freedom. "We are not bound to the past, but we can utilize the past to prepare for the future" (p. 39). "Needless to say," Bernard Meltzer casually points out, "this view contradicts the stimulus–response conception of human behavior" (p. 20).

My own view of freedom is that symbolic interactionism may not actually prove freedom, but for me it comes closest to any other explanation as to how freedom is possible in the natural world. In a way, the best I can do is to propose to the student and to myself that if freedom does exist it is only because humans possess certain qualities described throughout this book. And, in relation to this chapter, freedom is possible only if the actor is able to define the situation he or she acts in. If definition is not a central part of what we do, it is impossible to imagine free action.

Summary

This chapter tied in everything from earlier chapters. Social objects, symbols, self, mind, and taking the role of the other play themselves out in our understanding of action. Human action is highly complex, and this chapter discussed that complexity by emphasizing the following points.

1. Humans engage in a continous stream of action, both overt and covert, influenced by ongoing decisions along that stream, which are influenced in turn by definition, social interaction, and interaction with self. Cause is continuous decision making arising from continuous definition. Action has a history that is directional. Directions in life change because of many decisions, many definitions, many actions we take.

2. In order to understand this stream of action, humans will normally separate it into separate acts. An act is a segment within our stream, given a name, and given significance. An act becomes a social object to us as we isolate and define it according to our goals in the present.

3. Action results from our definition of the situation. Action is directed toward the goals and objects we determine to be important. Seeing action as arising from social interaction, interaction with self, and definition, emphasizes

cause in the present rather than in the past. Decisions are made in the present by the actor. The past is not the cause of an individual's actions; nor are objects in the outside environment.

4. What other perspectives treat as simple causes of action—such as past, motives, emotion, other people, society—symbolic interactionists treat as social objects, part of our definition of the situation. Although all of these may sometimes contribute to action and although habit too may enter in, humans are thought here to be in control through their on-going definition of the situation and through their ongoing organization of their own action toward their own goals.

Human action, of course, often involves other people. Other people become social objects to us, and we become social objects to them. This is the link between human action and human social interaction. Where people organize their action with one another in mind we have an instance of social interaction. This is the important topic we will examine in Chapter 10.

CHAPTER TEN

Social Interaction

It is possible to write a very long essay describing what people are doing in a single greeting. "Hi" "Hello!" "How ya doing?" "Great! How about you?" Such an encounter is done in a few seconds, done many times, on occasion exactly this way, usually similar, sometimes very different. A greeting is much more than simply a few words that are spoken. It involves role taking, mind action, and self. It involves definition of the situation. It is also more than one person acting toward another; it is action that builds back and forth, where each actor must adjust what the other actor is doing. What each actor does depends in part on what the other does. Human social interaction is not like two dogs communicating by barking, nor is it like insects exchanging chemicals, nor is it like birds chirping back and forth. Nor is it a single human trying to wrestle with an onion or a poem or a painting.

Social interaction is a certain kind of encounter between two or more actors. It also involves constant definition and redefinition of the acts of others and one's own acts. The essence of social interaction is that each actor acts in part through adjusting what the other actors do. Streams of action cross among actors, and each is influenced by what takes place.

A moment of interaction can make a great difference to the actors. I became a sociologist in part because I interacted in front of my home with friends who encouraged me to consider it. My wife and I have interacted over thirty-five years of marriage, and each of us had to alter our actions toward one another almost every single day. Sometimes in our interaction a simple question developed into an argument neither one of us intended.

As we interact with the same actors over time—in a marriage, in a family, in friendship, in neighborhoods, in whole communities, in business—a great influence on all actors may gradually alter their stream of action or change their perspectives, views, interests, abilities, goals, and actions toward their own selves.

"Interaction" is increasingly becoming part of the language people use today. Although most of us use this word very casually and rarely analyze it, to symbolic interactionists it is the heart of what people do. Much of the world is changing because social interaction has been revolutionized by cell phones, world travel, outsourcing, and the internet. Many of us recognize that social interaction among world leaders, among artists, among terrorists, among the elderly, among religious groups, among youth are all important keys to understanding what is going on around us. We seem to know more and more that the successes and failures of families, businesses, friendship groups, neighborhoods, communities, societies, and the world are dependent to a great extent on the social interaction that people are involved in. And in our increasingly complex society, social interaction is no longer simple and isolated, but usually it goes in directions that are neither predictable nor even intentional. Parents who want their children to go to religious private schools understand the power of social interaction; individuals who become members of Alcoholics Anonymous and various other therapy groups understand the power of social interaction; world leaders who wish to prevent war understand the power of social interaction; a team knows the power of social interaction; those who have a car accident or become involved in tobacco, illegal drugs, crime, or adultery usually know the power of social interaction. Those of us who must make decisions completely on our own know the difficulties of action without the benefit of social interaction. And many of the great treasures of life—love, friendship, helping, sharing, encouraging, working together, discussing, giving—all involve social interaction. The world is changing and much of it is because of social interaction: political revolutions, worldwide economic cooperation and conflict, rapid industrialization, traditionalism moving toward modernization, education, and much easier access to all the world's knowledge are dominant trends in the world largely because of what is happening in social interaction. The explosive use of television, film, radio, and internet encourage easy social interaction across physical and cultural boundaries that were impossible a few years ago.

Social symbolic interaction is an essential part of what people are. Look around you! Watch people carefully! You might not fully understand what is going on, but you should be able to recognize a process that involves intentional communication, interpretation, role taking, definition, self-direction, and the ongoing adjusting of acts in relation to one another.

One of President Clinton's strategists continuously kept his supporters focused on what really mattered to people: "It's the economic stupid!" Well, here "It's really social interaction stupid!" I personally do not like to call anyone stupid, but for emphasis, I encourage everyone to understand that what goes on in the human world is almost always traceable to social interaction.

THE MEANING OF SOCIAL INTERACTION

Social Interaction Develops Out of Social Action

We need to begin with *social action*.

Social action is the name sociologists usually give to actions that in some way take account of other actors. Action is thought to be social whenever we consider others as we act. Others make a difference to what we do in a situation. In other words, other people are *social objects* to the actor. When I talk to you, listen to you, wink at you, ignore you, impress you, make love to you—in all these ways and many others—I am engaging in social action because you have become a social object to me in the situation. When we try to influence others or convince them of our views, or when we share something with others, help them or hurt them, reject them or encourage them, give support to them or try to destroy them, we become social actors. Herbert Blumer (1953) simply calls this phenomenon "taking others into account as we act" He calls it "the most important feature of human associations." Our own action is directed as we take into account the other. Social action involves holding back our "inclinations, impulses and feelings when the social situation demands it. The presence of others and their actions become events that we use to guide our own action" (p. 194).

Almost always social action is an act of symbolic communication. When the actor controls what he or she does in order to communicate something to others, this is social action and it is symbolic communication.

> In sum, then, whenever we come into contact with another through the mails, over the telephone, in face-to-face talk, or even merely through immediate co-presence, we find ourselves with one central obligation: to render our behavior understandably relevant to what the other can come to perceive is going on. Whatever else, our activity must be addressed to the other's mind, that is, to the other's capacity to read our words and actions for evidence of our feelings, thoughts, and intent (Erving Goffman, 1983, p. 51).

When we are alone and imagine what others not in our presence might think of what we are doing, this becomes social action without symbolic communication.

Social Interaction Is Ongoing Social Action Among Actors

When others are around us, we normally are social actors and we intentionally communicate something. When they see us and act back as social actors *social interaction* is created. Social interaction means that *actors take one another into account, symbolically communicate to one another, and interpret one another's actions*.

> What are some examples of social interaction? A conversation, a knife fight, a chess game, love-making. None of these things can be done by one. It takes two to tango, just as it takes two bodies to produce gravitational attraction or two electrons to produce electro-static repulsion. None of these things can be viewed simply as a result of two independent units simultaneously unwinding their self-determined lines of action. The action of one unit is dependent upon the action of the other, and *vice versa*. ...There must be mutual influence. (McCall and Simmons, 1966, pp. 48–49)

Games are interaction in slow motion. When I move a chess piece, I may have a plan. However, after I act, you make a decision and you act (on the basis of your definition of my act). Now that you have moved, I must move again—this time on the basis of my original plan *and* of my interpretation of your move. So it is in real life: what we each do depends in part on what others in the situation do. If I begin a conversation with you, the things you say in relation to me become important to me as I form what I want to say as we go along. If I want to sell something to you, what I say and do will depend on your actions; I must adjust to you, and you must adjust to me. We can say the same for two world leaders in a meeting, a public debate, two people on a date, a discussion group, a committee, a gang making plans, or musicians trying to play together for the first time.

Such interaction becomes the basis for what human beings decide to do in situations. What we do unfolds over time as we act back and forth, altering our plans and actions on the basis of what others do—or more exactly, on our definition of what others do. Goals change or are reaffirmed, directions change or are reaffirmed, perspectives and definitions change or are reaffirmed. Almost always when we enter a situation it is not simply what we bring to the situation, but it is tempered, altered, or ignored by the actors in the situation, defining and redefining one another's actions. "This process of interaction," Blumer (1969) writes, "consists of making indications to others of what to do and in interpreting the indications as made by others" (p. 20). Other animals gesture back and forth but the "conversation of gestures" has no symbolic meaning, and thus they become a "conversation" that is characteristically stimulus–response arising from instinct or conditioned learning.

It is fairly easy to understand social interaction among people who are engaged in face-to-face actions. However, we need to broaden what interaction is. An instructor may lecture and students take notes. This is social action but not interaction—until students somehow act back and communicate to the instructor. We might say that in some classes there is a lot of interaction; in others, very little. In some neighborhoods there is a lot of social interaction; in others, people interact with outsiders a great deal. Is Minneapolis and St. Paul one community or two? It depends on the social interaction within and between people in these communities. Integration involves social interaction; segregation divides social interaction. People who travel all over the world and interact with others in many societies will undoubtedly be different from those who stay home and never leave their neighborhood. World leaders interact, and musicians around the world interact, and scientists do. Social interaction as we are examining here is applicable to all of these situations and to many others we cannot possibly begin to list here.

It should be obvious that social action and social interaction always involves taking the role of the other. Communicating, interpreting, and adjusting what we do involves understanding the actions from the perspective of the other. We develop expectations, and sometimes we are accurate, sometimes off the mark, sometimes simply wrong. However, if we are going to continue social interaction, accurate role taking and interpretation are necessary (Joas, 1985, pp. 115–16).

THE GENERAL IMPORTANCE OF SOCIAL INTERACTION

It is impossible to exaggerate the role of social interaction in all that we do, think, and are. Everything described in this book is related to it. The title of this perspective and book is "symbolic interactionism," the study of human social and symbolic interaction. Therefore, it is imperative that we consider at this time the different ways social interaction enters into human life. It is probably best to break this analysis down into four general categories:

1. Social interaction creates our qualities as human beings.
2. Social interaction is an important cause of what the individual does in situations.
3. Social interaction forms our identities.
4. Social interaction creates society.

1. SOCIAL INTERACTION FORMS OUR BASIC HUMAN QUALITIES

What are we? What does it mean to be human? What is our nature? What are we as a species in nature? These are profound questions. They are questions that have a lot to do with hot issues in our society. To the symbolic interactionist the most important qualities that humans possess are not something we are born with, but are all dependent on social interaction: social objects, symbols, perspectives, self, mind, taking the role of the other, and being able to make decisions are all socially created. None of these would exist if it were not for social interaction. Human nature, writes Charles Cooley (1909, p. 30), is not what we are born with; it arises as other people begin to communicate symbolically to the developing child and the child learning to intentionally act back. To be human is to possess qualities that arise only from social interaction.

Social objects are objects we come to understand through social interaction. We learn about what exists, we give objects names, and by using objects, we become active in relation to our environment. Instead of response there is definition and manipulation of our environment. Blumer (1969) writes that objects for humans arise socially, that they are "creations that are formed in and through the defining activities of people as they interact" (p. 5). Social objects include *symbols* and *perspectives*. Thus, these too are created in social interaction. Our symbolic acts of communication toward others and ourselves would not be possible without social interaction. Perspectives too arise from interaction. Without interaction perspectives would not be possible, and without perspectives we would not be able to define or understand our world.

Self and *mind* are central to what we are and they too arise in social interaction. As a social object, the self is socially developed and the actor is able to perceive, assess, judge, communicate to self, and establish identity. Mind—the ability to think, to carry on conversation toward ourselves—is something unique not because we are born with brains, but because it is an ability formed through social interaction. *Role taking* too develops out of our interaction, and it becomes more and more a part of us through our interaction.

Our very humanity arises out of our social interaction. Of course, many people would argue that our essence is that we have a God-given soul, or that God makes us free or that disobeying God makes us evil. Our essence arising from such supernatural qualities cannot be easily refuted or proved, but that does not necessarily make them unimportant to our philosophies of life. It is also important, however, to assess the importance of all the qualities developed out of social interaction and discussed thus far if we are to understand the nature of what human beings are.

2. SOCIAL INTERACTION IS AN IMPORTANCE CAUSE OF HUMAN ACTION

Social interaction is a cause in its own right. It is not simply other people that matter; it is *interaction* with those people that matters. Others do not simply cause our action: instead, others act; we interpret their acts; we adjust our acts to theirs; and they act again (after interpreting and adjusting their acts to ours). No one knows where we all will end up. It depends on the continuous alignment of acts in relation to one another. Parents do not simply socialize their children; children interpret what is going on and in turn actually socialize their parents. Instructors teach classes, but if there is interaction, students alter the instructors' directions too.

> Put simply, human beings in interacting with one another have to take account of what each…is doing or is about to do; they are forced to direct their own conduct or handle their situations in terms of what they take into account. Thus, the activities of others enter as positive factors in the formation of their own conduct; in the face of the actions of others one may abandon an intention on purpose, revise it, check or suspend it, intensify it, or replace it….One has to *fit* one's own line of activity in some manner to the actions of others. The actions of others have to be taken into account and cannot be regarded as merely an arena for the expression of what one is disposed to do or sets out to do. (Blumer, 1969, p. 8)

I act….You act….I act….You act. I act with you in mind….You act with me in mind. We each interpret the acts of the other and form our action accordingly. Wherever we each begin in our social interaction does not determine where we end up. Our actions depend on one another. Two children try to persuade each other to let "me" have the piece of cake with the most frosting. Back and forth they go, until they get into a shouting match, then into a fistfight. One hurts the other, and both are punished for something that started out so innocently. Who knew that things would end this way? When I first asked Susan for a date, who knew then that interaction over time would lead both of us to alter our streams of action so that we would end up married, interacting for thirty-five years or more? World War I was clearly caused by the interaction of world leaders, each symbolically communicating, interpreting, and adjusting actions to one another until all of Europe found itself in war. I interact with my son, and through that interaction we are both influenced; yet, what he ends up doing in real situations depends also on the interaction that takes place with friends and even strangers as he acts along his stream of action. As a parent, I do not simply *form* him; instead, his action changes in social interaction with a lot of people besides just me, and what he ends up doing depends on much more than how I have "shaped him."

Our streams of action have long histories, and at almost every point there is social interaction, which results in decision making and the altering of our action. It is not that I commit murder because something happened to me fifteen years ago, or that I got a college degree because I became interested in school at the age of six, or that I have a job teaching school because that is what my father did. Each decision along the stream of action is influenced by a long history of decision making, and each decision in that history must be understood as influenced by the ongoing give-and-take of social interaction. It is important to step outside of the traditional perspectives most of us use in order to see action as being caused by more than a single predispositional factor within the individual and by more than what other people do to us in a particular situation.

> The central point [is] that human interaction is a positive shaping process in its own right. The participants in it have to build up their respective lines of conduct by constant interpretation of each other's ongoing lines of action. (Blumer, 1966, p. 538)

The dynamic nature of interaction and definition is lost on the printed page. We can capture only the very basics. Definitions and interpretations of the acts of other people are rapidly developed in interaction with self. Where there is time for deliberation, such as in games or in dealing with serious problems, all of the steps are evident. However, in most situations the process is very rapid and accompanies overt action.

An exciting, classic, and clear illustration of the centrality of interaction to decision making and action is this description by a college student in a sociology text that I read as a college freshman (from *The Gang* by Frederic M. Thrasher, 1936). It is fascinating as well as illustrative, and it will probably have more than a passing significance for understanding events in your own life:

> We three college students—Mac, Art, and Tom—were rooming together while attending V_____ University, one of the oldest colleges in the South. On the day of our crime all three of us spent over three hours in the library—really working. That was on Sunday and our crime was committed at 1:30 that night (or rather Monday morning).
>
> The conversation began with a remark about the numerous recent bank failures in the state, probably stimulated by one of us glancing at a map of the state. It then shifted to discussion of a local bank that had closed its doors the

day before. Tom, who worked at the post-office occasionally as special mail clerk, happened to mention that a sack containing a large amount of money had been received at the post-office that afternoon, consigned to a local bank that feared a run.

The conversation then turned to the careless way in which the money was handled at the office—a plain canvas sack thrown into an open safe. We discussed the ease with which a thief could get into the building and steal the money. Tom drew a plan showing the desk at which the only clerk worked and the location of the only gun in the office. At first the conversation was entirely confined to how easily criminals might manage to steal the money. Somehow it shifted to a personal basis: as to how easily we might get the money. This shift came so naturally that even the next morning we were unable to decide when and by whom the first remark had been made.

A possible plan was discussed as to how we might steal the package. Tom could go to the office and gain admittance on the pretense of looking for an important letter. Then Art and I, masked and armed, could rush in, tie Tom and the clerk, and make off with the package. We had lost sight of the fact that the package contained money. We were simply discussing the possibility of playing an exciting prank with no thought of actually committing it. We had played many harmless pranks and had discussed them in much the same way before; but the knowledge that there was danger in the prank made it a subject to linger over.

After about an hour and a half of talk, I started to take off my shoes. As I unlaced them, I thought of how it looked as if I were the one to kill our interesting project. I foolishly said something to the effect that if Tom was going down town, I thought I would write a letter that was already overdue. Tom was anxiously awaiting a letter that should be in that night. He suggested that I go down also as it was a very decent night. I consented and Art decided to join us. I sat down and wrote the letter—meanwhile we continued our talk about the money package. My letter finished, something seemed to change. We found further inaction impossible: we had either to rob the post-office or go to bed. Tom brought out his two guns; I hunted up a couple of regular plain handkerchiefs, and Art added some rope to the assortment. At the time we were still individually and collectively playing a game with ourselves. Each of us expected one of the other two to give the thing the horse laugh and suggest going to bed and letting the letters wait till morning. But it seemed that we forgot everything—our position in school, our families and friends, the danger to us and to our folks. We all made our preparations more or less mechanically. Our minds were in a daze.

Putting on our regular overcoats and caps, we left the rooms quietly. On the way down town we passed the night patrolman without any really serious qualms. Tom entered the post-office as was his usual custom, being a subclerk, and Art and I crept up to the rear door. Tom appeared at a window with his hat, a signal that there were no reasons why our plan would not be effective. At the door, in full illumination of light, we arranged our handkerchiefs over our faces and took our guns out of our pockets. We were ready.

"Have you enough guts to go through with this thing?" I asked, turning to Art, who was behind me.

"If you have," he answered.

Frankly I felt that I had gone far enough, but for some unknown reason I did not throw out a remark that would have ended it all then and there. And Art didn't. He later said that he was just too scared to suggest anything. We were both, it seems, in a sort of daze.

Tom opened the door and we followed our plan out to the end. There was no active resistance by the regular night man.

Then after we left the office with thousands of dollars in our hands we did not realize all that it meant. Our first words were not about getting the money. They were about the fact that our prank (and it was still that to us) had been successful. When we reached our rooms, having hidden the money in an abandoned dresser, the seriousness of the thing began to penetrate our minds. For an hour or so we lay quietly and finally settled on a plan that seemed safe in returning the money without making our identity known. Then I went to sleep (pp. 300–03).*

Definition by the narrator, action, definition by the others, action, definition and action by the narrator again—here is action building up among people, each of their streams of action being influenced by the ongoing interaction. The example is perhaps dramatic, but it illustrates what we all do in almost every situation. We end up acting in ways that were unintended at first, in ways that others might assume were intended right from the start. However, the act of robbing the post office must be understood in terms of the history of decisions made by the actors as they took each other into account. Why did you do that? Are you immoral? Are you stupid? Are you evil? Are you a criminal at heart? Did your poverty or your riches lead to that? We constantly ask such questions about ourselves and others. We look for easy answers—that was his choice, the environment caused it, his personality is that way—but we must look to the interaction with self and others for the reasons we act the way we do. "The direction taken by a person's conduct is seen as something that is constructed in the reciprocal give and take of interdependent men and women who are adjusting to one another" (Shibutani, 1961, p. 23).

3. SOCIAL INTERACTION SHAPES IDENTITIES

One of the most important qualities that we all develop over time is some idea of who in the world we are—our identity. Identity is really a process; who we are is an ongoing development. Indeed, we actually have many identities, some important one day, others important the next. Recall that identities are the names we call ourselves, and identities are important because they guide our actions. We present who we are to others, and others, in turn, are able to guide their actions according to what they believe our identities are. Social interaction is the context within which identities are created, recognized, negotiated, and lost. Everyone in an instance of interaction presents his or her own identities, defines what others are presenting, and forms his or her actions accordingly.

On the one hand, in social interaction *we attempt to label others*, recognizing their identity through out actions and words. We tell them *who we think they are*. And they, in turn, attempt *to tell us who they think we are*. The acts of students, faculty, and administration toward instructors creates the instructor, the acts of doctors and nurses toward patients create the patient. The acts of

---

*Reprinted from *The Gang* by Frederic M. Thrasher by permission of the University of Chicago Press and William E. Girton. Copyright © 1927 by the University of Chicago. All rights reserved.

prison guards toward prisoners create the prisoner. It is, however, also true that the instructor, in turn, tells students, other faculty, and administrators who they are, patients help create the identities of nurses and doctors, and prisoners help create the identities of the guards. Each action and word are statements that represent each actor's view of the identities of all the others. It becomes difficult for one who is being the object of others to completely put aside the identities created by others in their actions. One often becomes what others are creating; sometimes one quietly rejects the labels; and sometimes one even aggressively rejects the labels. In some situations others in social interaction attack the identity that one presents, and this can become an important source of anger and destructive conflict. We normally value who we are, and if we do not, we do not enjoy others attacking and reminding us who we are.

On the other hand, in social interaction *we also attempt to present ourselves to others.* We try to communicate to others, for example, that we are a lover of animals, a senior in college, a knowledgeable rock star, an African American, a married woman, a heterosexual, a cool guy. As we act back and forth we try to establish out identity so others know who we think we are, and are able to act toward us appropriately. Of course, since the process is negotiation, others may ignore, belittle, or reject the identity we present, or may become suspicious of it, or confused, or simply be reassured, happy, and even become excited.

"This is who I am!" "No; this is who you are."; "Wrong; This is who I am; can't you see?" "No way! I really don't believe you are who you think you are. To me you are a liberal...or con man...or a nut...or a genius ... or a great leader...or an atheist...or a wonderful choreographer...or a phoney." These are not usually the exact words through which we negotiate identities in social interaction (although on occasion they are); instead, it is in our acts toward one another that we constantly create one another. As I interacted with my children, wife, parents, friends, and school teachers, my identity as a father became increasingly important to what I thought I was and this influenced my actions. When some high school students addressed me as Mr. Charon for the first time I began to realize that I was becoming a teacher. As others recognized me as an author, I gradually saw that I indeed had become an author. And as I took on these identities, I continuously presented which identities were important to me, and what kind of actions would be appropriate by them toward me. I once directly told friends they should not call me "Joey" anymore, because I wanted to become "Joel." Once I directly told students to call me Mr. Charon rather than Charon or Joel. Once I directly told friends to stop making fun of my attempt to be a nonracist, and several times I have directly told others that being a teacher was a noble pursuit.

Our identities are not always easily understood by others. It is relatively easy to recognize and label ourselves and others where situations are standardized and communicated clearly. We can easily distinguish men from women, whites from nonwhites, quarterbacks from cheerleaders, and so on. Even then we can be fooled, so we still must evaluate how important these identities are to the other, and we need to show respect, indifference, or disgust for these identities. Most identities given off by others are even more ambiguous to us and thus there needs to be a lot more interpretation.

In conversation it is common to ask others who they are. We might ask where they grew up or where they live now, we might ask them what work they do, where they went to college, or if are they religious, or what they believe about the President, the stock market, the Yankees, or the state of the world. In part, we are fishing for a better handle on "who they are": what identities are important to them. Often we jump to conclusions before we know very much about them, or we overestimate the importance of the various identities that are obvious.

Many of our identities become important to us, emotionally attached, precious, and when others put them down one way or another we become defensive and even angry. Political, professional, gender, and ethnic identities are obvious examples. It surprises me how some people in interaction give out negative opinions about certain identities without knowing this may upset someone who values that identity. Much of our anger toward others is because others say or do something that intentionally or unintentionally attacks identities we hold dear. "You are going to go to hell because of your religious choice!" "Are you a bleeding-heart liberal?" "Dancing is for girls" "Chicago is the pits!" "I can't understand how anyone can become a teacher!" "Islam creates terrorism!" Even if actors might say to someone without malice; even if they truly believe it, where these these identities are sacred to the receiver, anger will usually result. Identities are important to all of us. It is who we think we are.

Robert Merton (1957, p. 421) describes the situation where we end up wrongly labeling others, and through this we actually influence their action, and they eventually become and act according to the label which then reaffirms our original label. "You are a dumb student"; you begin to act like a dumb student; eventually you come to think of yourself and act as a dumb student. And then we, in turn, are able to proudly declare that we knew who you were a long time ago. Merton calls this "the self-fulfilling prophecy." Labeling someone an "idiot," labeling a man as "sexist," labeling students as "cheaters" will often simply influence students to believe and act accordingly. "Yes, I guess this is who I am." Identity is a powerful aspect of everyone's definition of the situation "Who we are" and "who they are" guide almost everyone in social interaction one way or another.

Harold Garfinkel (1956) describes how one can be effective in degrading someone in public. To denounce someone the denouncer must somehow convince people that the victim has not simply done something that is wrong, but it is important to show that it is the person—who they are, their identity—that is the problem. To be successful, the denouncer must show others that the person possesses qualities that make him or her outrageously different from all others, who acts outside the community standards, who is strange or deviant. It is the essence of his or her identity not simply the act itself. The denouncer convinces the people in the community—"good upstanding people"—that they need to be aware that they are in danger because of the person who is denounced.

These are the conditions that must be fulfilled for a successful denunciation. If they are absent, the denunciation will fail. Regardless of the situation when the denouncer enters, if he [or she] is to succeed in degrading the other [actor], it is necessary to introduce these features (Garfinkel, 1956, p. 422–23).

Garfinkel describes degradation as a situation where "the public identity of an actor is transformed into something looked on as lower in the local scheme of social types" (p. 402). Criminal, liar, abuser, traitor, terrorist, and whore are examples of attempts at degradation. The "degradation ceremony" is often played out in the courtroom, in the office, in the newspaper, in the business, in the classroom, in the family, in some religious community, or in the military. It can actually exist in any interaction situation where someone decides to degrade someone else. The identities that each of us hold dear to us are not always certain and unshakable. Some are even so shaky they can be easily undermined by someone who is knowledgeable as to how to denounce us.

Successful attempts to denounce others by attributing negative identities in public for the purpose of degradation are often found in the political world. Gary Hart, who was a presidential candidate in 1988 had to eventually remove himself from the race because of a successful denunciation based on what he called an innocent encounter with a woman. When he tried to reenter the race, no matter how hard he tried, the successful denunciation of him could not be shaken. President Nixon was denounced as "a crook," and eventually he could not convince people the identity that his enemies attributed to him should be ignored. Much of Clinton's presidency was characterized by denunciation by those who opposed him, followed by denials by him and his supporters. It even resulted in his impeachment on television for all Americans to see. Although he was not convicted and was able to continue in office, the successful denunciation seriously affected his presidency, his public image, and his life. Imagine his embarrassment at the successful attacks on his identities as husband, as president, as a caring person, as a leader of the Western world. It seems remarkable how well he was able to get up each morning, do his work as well as he did, and appear in public as though none of this bothered him. He probably will "never live it down"; it will remain with him and probably taint his presidency over many years. Historically, the political arena has almost always been full of the denunciation of others who may be guilty, who sometimes may commit an act over the line, or sometimes are quite innocent.

Erving Goffman reminds us that we are not helpless. Actors are often able to be in charge; actors are often able to effectively present themselves to others. They announce their identity in obvious or subtle ways. They may dress to kill, put on a smile, decorate their office or house the "in" colors, or present toughness or honesty. Usually these are honest attempts to present identity; sometimes they are trying to fool us. Gregory Stone (1962, p. 100) describes dress as important for telling others who we are, announcing our identities. He points out that our appearance is a substitute for our past and present action, and it tells others what to expect from us. Clothing tells others our proposals in the situation Alison Lurie (1981) makes this same point in *The Language of Clothes:*

> More generally, the idea that even when we say nothing our clothes are talking noisily to everyone who sees us, telling them who we are, where we come from, what we like to do in bed and a dozen other intimate things, may be unsettling. To wear what "everyone else" is wearing is no solution to the problem, any more than it would be to say what everyone else is saying. We all know people who try to do this; but even if their imitation of "everyone" is successful, their clothes do not shut up; rather they broadcast without stopping the information that this is a timid and conventional man or woman, and possibly an untrustworthy one. We can lie in the language of dress, or try to tell the truth; but unless we are naked and bald it is impossible to be silent. (p. 261)

One of the very best descriptions of how we each try to influence others' views of us is Goffman's (1959b) description at the beginning of *The Presentation of Self in Everyday Life*. Goffman's analysis begins with a simple idea: when we interact, we know that what we say and do makes a difference to others, that others do indeed figure us out and act toward us accordingly; therefore, we make efforts to give off acts that influence others to think of us in the way that we want; in a real sense interaction is a stage where we all act out parts that we choose to present to others. In other words, we take an active role in telling others who we are, and we control our actions in order to give off the image that we want. It is in our own interests "to control the conduct of the other" in interaction, especially in how they act toward us. "This control is achieved largely by influencing the definition of the situation which the others come to formulate." There is always some reason to "mobilize" and control our own action, therefore, "so that it will convey an impression to others" that we wish to convey (p. 4).

The presentation of self in situations reminds us once again that human beings are symbol users. We try to communicate messages to others. In the case of identity, we control our actions so that what we do represents our identity to others. In fact, it even goes further than our actions: our friends, cars, religious objects, neighbors, clothes, and hair tell others what we want them to know about us, the identity we wish them to see. T-shirts and hats make a statement as to who we think we are, the opinions we express, the people a rock star surrounds himself or herself with, every single choice we make that others see us do can become important clues as to who others think we are. Even our spouses matter in our presentation of our self to others:

> As performers giving off impressions of public morality and fitness for office, public figures try to maintain the idea that they are indeed fulfilling the standards of civic conventionality, by which they are to be judged. At the same time, the activity of "engineering" convincing impressions of those standards makes them "merchants of morality." ... The public wife appears on that stage ... to nurture impressions of that "steady moral light." (Gillespie, 1980, pp. 119, 123)

The work of Goffman reminds us that creating identity is an active negotiation process between who others tell us we are and our continuous attempts to present who we think we are to others.

Social interaction, then, takes on further importance now. It is not only the basis of our human nature qualities; it is not only an important cause of how we act in situations; but it is also the negotiation process through which we create one another's identity. Through social interaction we become who in the world we are.

4. SOCIAL INTERACTION CREATES SOCIETY

Interaction is also responsible for society. It is through it that society is formed, reaffirmed, and altered. It is through the absence of continuous interaction that society ceases to exist. Society depends on individuals' continuously interacting with one another and with themselves. It is to this important topic of *society* that we now turn in Chapter 11.

Summary

It should be obvious by now how central social interaction is to the human being. This whole symbolic interactionist perspective comes together with the introduction of this concept. Let us briefly put together the central ideas concerning social interaction—its meaning and its importance:

1. Human beings are social symbolic actors. We take others into account as we act; we symbolically communicate in our actions; we interpret one another's actions.
2. Social interaction is simply mutual social action that involves symbolic communication and interpretation of one another's acts. Social interaction also involves role taking and organizing our acts as we take one another into account.
3. Social interaction creates our qualities as human beings, social objects, symbols, self, mind, and our ability to take the role of the other.
4. Social interaction is a cause of action in its own right. What we do in a situation depends on our interpretation of other people's actions; their action depends on their interpretation of ours. Action unfolds over time.
5. Social interaction shapes our identities. It is not others who create who we are, and it is not simply who we "really are" inside. Instead, identity results from a negotiation process that arises in social interaction. We label others in interaction; we present our identities to others in interaction; we tell others who we think they are in interaction. Through it all we come think of our self as something; an identity is formed, and our action is now influenced by who in the world we think we are.
6. Finally, social interaction creates society.

CHAPTER ELEVEN

Society

My friend Leonard moved to Portland many years ago. Leonard, a very bright and sensitive guy, knows a lot about mathematics and computers. He also has a great curiosity about subjects he has not formally studied. He is truly a person who listens to others, and seeks to learn from them.

A year or two after he moved he called me. "Joel," he said, "I've got a problem. How can I start a poker club in Portland like the one we had in Minnesota? I have tried and it just isn't the same. Do you have any suggestions?"

Our poker club lasted for more than twenty five years in Minnesota. Indeed, as people moved away we invited others to join us, and for some miraculous reason, it worked very well. Members learned what we did, put our games on their calendar, and started to feel part of the group.

Leonard's question to me got me thinking. Why were we able to succeed? Why was he having difficulties? Indeed, why do larger groups—even large societies—work, and why do some fall apart?

The answer I gave to Leonard was that groups do not usually just magically work out, but people have to work to keep them together. There have to be ways to encourage—even entice—people to choose to be active. There needs to be commitment, a feeling of camaraderie, a way that people are not simply coming to play a game, but realize that to enjoy themselves they should look forward to ongoing social interaction. Ultimately, they need to believe that their place in the group is necessary for the group's continuation.

So it is for every organized stable continuous social interaction we might call "society." They do not simply accidentally continue. There are reasons why they succeed. My advisor at the University of Minnesota, David Cooperman, on many occasions reminded me that the real goal of the sociologist must be to examine the reason why a bunch of individuals pursuing their own interests could ever agree to come together, sacrifice some of that individuality, and work together in organization. He was really telling me that society should not be taken for granted. Families dissolve; poker groups dissolve; whole communities dissolve; empires dissolve. Why some continue and some break up is a puzzle to be examined and understood. The answer would be a lot easier if we could isolate one quality: instinct, for example. For many animals who live in society, biology directs them, or it is kinship that matters, or sometimes it is imitation or simple conditioning.

However, human society—all human organization—is much more. It always starts with social interaction, and out of social interaction a unique society emerges. Society depends on cooperation and interdependence fostered by social interaction. Society continues because a culture is developed that becomes important to the individuals who make up society. Take away social interaction, or take away the desire to cooperate, or take away the belief in the society's culture, and we end up with a bunch of individuals seeking their own personal goals, individuals who come to follow others only by fear, and/or a society that dissolves because it cannot meet the needs of the individuals who make it up. Ultimately, Leonard's first try to create a poker group could not nurture social interaction, was not able to convince the actors to work together to have fun, and thus could never build a culture that people were willing to accept.

To the symbolic interactionist, society has three important qualities that make it viable: ongoing social symbolic interaction, cooperation or interdependence, and culture. Any instance of these qualities constitute a society, and to the extent these qualities continue to exist and become more established, society will be stable. In a nutshell, this is the approach the symbolic interactionist takes understanding society.

TWO VIEWS OF SOCIETY

Sociology was defined as the "science of society" by the French philosopher Auguste Comte in the early nineteenth century. Although sociologists may differ on what exactly should be the emphasis in what they study, all seem to agree that society must enter into the analysis somewhere, that one goal must be to understand the nature of society as well as the interrelationship between the individual and society. Therefore, it is imperative for a social psychology that has relevance to sociology to consider society.

Comte divided the study of society into statics (structure) and dynamics (change). Throughout the history of sociology, thinkers have clustered around two poles, some emphasizing structure, others dynamics; some describing the permanence of society's controls, some emphasizing the ever-changing nature of society and even shying away from terms such as *structure* and *society*.

Those who have emphasized structure have tended to examine the historical reality of society: society is a set of forces developed over time that exert themselves on the individual. Society is a set of institutions, stratification systems, and cultural patterns into which individuals are born and socialized, playing roles according to scripts laid down by others, living and dead. Society has a permanence that shapes each individual. Society socializes the individual; the individual internalizes society. The major criticism of this view is that it is a highly deterministic perspective that leaves little room to conceptualize the active person who defines and changes society. It shows how we all are shaped by society, but it does not show how the individual is able to shape society; it does not see how society is always being formed and shaped through interaction.

The second view of society is one that emphasizes a dynamic, changing nature and deemphasizes structure and the historical development of institutions, stratification systems, and cultural patterns. It focuses instead on change, on individuals interacting—influenced by the past, but also defining that past—developing new definitions of the present, and shaping society. Society is described as a process; society is individuals who interact. The criticism of this view is that it tends to overlook the power of society, the deterministic nature of institutions, of structure, and of cultural patterns. And a second important criticism is that it focuses too much on interacting individuals' constantly redefining society, changing society: it becomes a wonder that society is able to exist at all and maintain its structure with the constant self-direction that takes place.

Both perspectives of society are useful, and, although some theorists attempt to integrate them, it is difficult to do, and most end up emphasizing one or the other view. Most sociologists fall on the side of society as structure, society as historical, society as permanent, society as determining, although they will often attempt to look casually at the dynamics of human interaction and change. *The symbolic interactionists, probably more than any other school in sociology, conceptualize society in the dynamic sense: as individuals in interaction with one another, defining and altering the direction of one another's acts.* Certain qualities are necessarily emphasized, whereas others are ignored. "Human society might best be regarded as an on-going process, a *becoming* rather than a *being*. Society might be viewed most fruitfully as a succession of events, a flow of gestural interchanges among people" (Shibutani, 1961, p. 174). Symbolic interactionists recognize that society has a history and exists as a somewhat stable entity, but they are not able to give this side its due, simply because the focus is on interaction and change.

GROUPS, ORGANIZATIONS, SOCIAL WORLDS, AND SOCIETIES

There is, in symbolic interactionism, no reason for a distinction between types of organization. Each dyad, each group, each organization, each interaction situation, each social world, even the most temporary, is a society, or at least a society in an early stage of development. Even the crowd, where interaction might be considered "primitive," is the beginning of society. Through studying the crowd we come to understand the nature of society, for many of the same dynamics that characterize the crowd characterize all organizations.

Crowds, groups, organizations, communities, and societies all are made up of individuals who interact. Society—all group life—is defined here as *individuals in interaction*, doing the kinds of things discussed in earlier chapters: role taking, communicating, interpreting one another, adjusting their acts to one another, directing and controlling self, sharing perspectives. The terms *group, society, organization,* and *social world* will be used inter-changeably; we will regard all groups as societies. In other contexts, it may be useful to distinguish them, but for purposes of understanding the nature of organization from a symbolic interactionist perspective, distinguishing them is not necessary.

1. SOCIETY IS SYMBOLIC INTERACTION

In Chapter 3, the ideas of Tamotsu Shibutani were introduced, and his article "Reference Groups As Perspectives" was analyzed extensively. Shibutani emphasizes that "social worlds" are made up of individuals who communicate with symbols, who come to share a perspective in interaction. He describes these social worlds as lacking geographic unity, held together primarily by this communication, and shared reality (p. 185). Fine followed up with studies of the workers in restaurant kitchens (1996), the culture of mushroom collectors (1998), and the world of high-school debaters (2001). In each attempt, he isolated the dynamics of communication, expectations, action, and definition in various social worlds.

The fact that a social world needs no geographic unity but instead is tied by symbolic interaction is significant here. In a basic sense, a society and a social world are the same. The essence of any society is not geographic unity as much as it is the interaction of people and the ongoing communication by means of symbols. Society arises in social interaction; it continues through social interaction; it ends without social interaction.

Social interaction means, first of all, that *actors take one another's acts into account, and they decide on action dependent on that fact.* A group is made up of individuals whose acts matter to one another. They consider one another: their acts "are intertwined," "joint," "fitted together," "interdependent." This does not mean that they imitate one another, or that they necessarily do the same things, but at least each individual's acts matter to the others (Blumer, 1969, p. 109). A group or society, then, is made up of social actors who act back and forth and form their acts in relation to one another. Herbert Blumer (1966) refers to this process as "joint action" and points out that it ranges "from a simple collaboration of two individuals to a complex alignment of the acts of huge organizations or institutions" (p. 540). An employer and an employee each may have his or her own reasons for taking the other into account, each has something different at stake, but they are involved in joint action—ongoing coordinated interaction. Participants "fit their acts to one another"; they change their actions "on the basis of compromise, out of duress, because they may use one another in achieving their respective ends, because it is the sensible thing to do, or out of sheer necessity" (p. 544).

A family unit, the First Baptist Church, the crowd at a football game, two people who meet at Sam's bar—to the extent that each one of these examples of social interaction is characterized by individuals who act with one another in mind, by individuals who take account of one another as they act—to that extent we call it a society. Sometimes a society has only a short existence, but more often it has a much longer life. The United States is a society to the extent that we can identify interaction among those who live within its borders. To the extent that such interaction is segregated, then, to that extent, we might identify many separate societies instead of one larger one.

Society, however, is more than just interaction; society is *symbolic* interaction. It involves communication and interpretation by the actors. Blumer (1969) emphasizes that societies consist of people who are able to work together because they construct their actions together, and they are able to do this through communicating to one another and understanding one another's communication. Cooperative action is possible as long as we know what one another is doing and we are able to communicate what we are doing and interpret what others are doing (p. 16).

It is through *understanding* the act from the other person's perspective that society is made possible. It is through *communicating* to others what one is doing, what one believes, and what one is about to do that society is able to exist. It is through *socializing others* through symbolic acts that interaction continues over time. *Cooperation* depends on symbols, actors communicating and interpreting one another's acts as they go along:

> Communication involves a totally new phenomenon, that of a *collective* meaning. Although this collective meaning exists in the separate minds of the individual actors its content is defined by their communication and by the implicit and explicit agreements that this is the meaning that things shall have for them *in their interaction* (Warriner, 1970, p. 133).

The worldwide revolution in continuous and immediate social interaction through cell phones, easy travel, outsourcing, fiber optic cables, multinational corporations, and internet is increasingly making the world one society as never before. Interaction is the point; it allows people to communicate, cooperate, and create a common culture, and another level of society is being created. A worldwide society may have many roots, but during the past 25 years it has accelerated immensely. This does not eliminate other societies—Cuba, United States, New York, Harvard University—but all will now be influenced more easily by what the world society will become, and as people interact more easily with people in other societies, each society we identify now will be changed at an accelerating rate.

Society, then, is individuals interacting over time: acting with one another in mind, adjusting their acts to one another as they go along, symbolically communicating and interpreting one another's acts.

2. SOCIETY IS SYMBOLIC INTERACTION THAT IS CHARACTERIZED BY COOPERATIVE ACTION

Society involves individuals engaging in cooperative action. Almost all cases of interaction involve cooperative problem solving, but some do not. Enemies who are eternally hostile to one another may take one another into account and may communicate; they may even understand one another very clearly and may even act alike, but they will not constitute a society because their action is not characterized by a cooperative effort to deal with a situation. Society is coordination of action, joint action, action in which actors work together despite their individual goals or interests.

When two enemies are threatened, they may join forces, and they begin to become a society. The United States is a society to the extent that people cooperate in dealing with situations. Cooperation may involve having common goals, but not necessarily. Cooperation depends on interaction which allows actors to achieve their separate goals through contributing to one another's resources. Society exists as long as people work together despite their personal differences. Society is a matter of interdependence in social interaction where people pursue goals that are compatible, complimentary, sometimes the same. A student may want to graduate, a teacher may want to teach something vial, a janitor may desire to keep the school clean and safe, and a counselor may desire to help students handle difficult problems, but they are together in a society called a university or college, cooperating even though they each may have different goals.

Individuals interact. *When they interact cooperatively, a society is formed.* Individuals who act without taking others into account, without communicating or interpreting one another's actions, or who fail to work together, do not constitute a society.

The meaning of cooperative social interaction was investigated at the University of Iowa under the direction of Carl Couch. Although this research has focused on interaction between two actors, it has attempted to understand the nature of all cooperation, or more exactly, how actors in social situations work together to complete a task.*

Typically, a problem situation is set up in a laboratory, and people must decide to ignore that situation or to join forces and deal with it. Their actions are videotaped and analyzed. The critical question is: "What exactly takes place between people for them to participate in a cooperative act?" The research looks at cooperation that lasts for a few moments; society, of course, is ongoing interaction, but the process involved is basically the same. There

---

*The remainder of this section was written cooperatively with Professor Joel Powell, a graduate of the University of Iowa. It also relies heavily on Dan E. Miller, Robert A. Hintz Jr., and Carl J. Couch, in "The Elements and Structure of Openings," *Constructing Social Life*, pp. 1–24. Champaign, Ill., Stipes, 1975.

are five processes that must occur, and these are identical to what is meant here by cooperation:

1. *Ongoing communication.* For cooperation to take place, actors must be "co-present." That is, actors must be together in a situation where there is opportunity to communicate, where each is available for the other as both a subject and an object of communication. Cooperation depends on the ability of the actors to exchange ideas, requests, and orders about how each is to deal with the situation at hand. Communication may be vocal, but it also can be writing, eye movements, or gestures. From interaction between two people to interaction in large societies, cooperation depends on people's communicating as they go along.

2. *Mutual role taking.* Actors must be "mutually responsive." That is, actors must be in the position for taking each other into account over time. We must be in the position of observing the acts of the other and making a good guess concerning the future acts of the other in order to know what we should do. Those who do not note what others are doing cannot cooperate. In fact, it is also important for each actor to recognize that the other is also taking him or her into account.

3. *Defining the others as social objects.* Actors must develop "congruent functional identities." That is, they must recognize who the other is in the situation—a learner, a fullback, a single woman interested in going on a date—and these identities must be important to the goals of the actor in that situation. In turn, the actor's identity must be seen to be useful for the others too. Cooperation involves each actor recognizing that the other actor has an identity that is useful for completing the task that they are both facing.

4. *Defining social objects together.* Actors must develop a "shared focus of attention." That is, in interaction, an object in the situation must become important to each actor. An object is shared; it is around this shared object—a scream from another room, hostages, a topic of conversation, the opportunity to make money, a piece of music to perform—that people organize their actions.

5. *Developing goals in interaction.* Actors must develop goals that are either the same or complementary. A shared goal or cluster of goals emerges: to win a game, to help someone in need, to negotiate a contract, to study for an exam, to plan a business.

Cooperation means then, that people communicate (are copresent) and take one another's roles on an ongoing basis (are mutually responsive); they regard one another as important in their actions (regard one another as having congruent functional identities); they generally agree on what is important in their environment (have a shared focus of attention); and they develop common or complementary goals. Without any one of these, the interaction becomes something other than cooperation and society is no more. If they are no longer copresent and cannot communicate or role take, then they cannot know what to do in relation to one another. If they do not see one another as necessary partners in order to achieve their goals, then they do not find it important to act in accordance with one another. If they do not come to share a definition of objects in their environment, they cannot coordinate their actions in relation to those objects, and if they develop goals that are in conflict with the goals of the others then it is not until such goals can be made the same or complementary that cooperation exists.

Let us suppose, for example, that some people decide to have a party. For them to cooperate effectively, they must somehow perform all of these five processes. That is, they must decide when to get together in order to organize the party: either now, on the telephone next week, or at lunch on Monday (they must decide when they are going to communicate; when they plan to be copresent). Even if they decide to delegate the planning to one person, they must be copresent to make this decision. They must communicate to and understand one another in terms of what each wants at the party (menu, guests, time, place, and so on). They must also take the role of the others, becoming sensitive to and taking into account each individual's desire (in effect, they must become mutually responsive). As they interact they must recognize that at this point each is a participant in planning and that each will be expected to participate in carrying out assigned tasks. Each becomes a partner in the future: "It is *our* party" (each is an important social object; each takes on a congruent functional identity). In social interaction the actors might discuss bad parties, cool people, good music, but the discussion continues to focus on the plan (a common focus of attention; a shared social object). Of course, a shared goal continues to be reaffirmed (having a good party). All go away, continue to work, communicate as to how things are going, continue to take one another's work into account, alter their plan as they go along, and even redefine the goal.

So it is in every instance of cooperative social interaction: negotiation over hostages, planning a wedding, starting a business, playing checkers, conserving energy, teaching and learning sociology in the classroom, studying together for an exam, dancing, giving emergency care in a hospital, and fighting a war. There is communication, taking others into account, recognizing one another as useful in dealing with situations, defining objects in the situation in a similar way, and developing similar or complementary goals. All are examples of societies being formed; all are examples of cooperative symbolic interaction.

Interaction that does not involve cooperation is not society. In fact, actors can be copresent and mutually responsive but still lack either congruent functional identities, a shared focus, or complementary goals. For example, violent conflict is interaction that stands in marked contrast to what society is. Violent interaction normally disrupts society rather than maintains it. Some of us love, marry, and form a family group that ends up riddled with violent conflict. Over time such violence may become the primary way that actors relate to one another in a family:

> If not checked, it [violence] turns back on itself and destroys its participants and their relationships with one another.... The family becomes a network of violent,

interacting individuals. No one trusts anyone else. They have collectively passed through that thin wall that divides a "normal" family from a "deviant," "different," violent family. They become outsiders to one another. An emotional climate of violence attaches itself to the family. They are participants in a progressively differentiated system of negative symbolic interaction. The actions and utterances of each member call forth violent and violence-repressed reactions on the part of every other member. The potentiality for violence becomes the veil through which all thought and action in the family is first screened (Denzin, 1984b, p. 490).

This is applicable to more than a family; it characterizes some small towns, big cities, nations, and the world order on occasion. Here there is social interaction; here actors communicate symbolically and align their acts; but here also there are negative emotions, an inability to cooperate, a lack of trust, and alienation that undermine a societal order. "The course of daily interaction between the family members becomes problematic and unpredictable.... Situations get out of control, and the actions each member takes become consequential for all future dealings they have with each other" (p. 494). This stands in marked contrast to the cooperation necessary for society. There is no question that constructive social conflict contributes to society and is necessary for cooperative problem solving, but when it fractures the society, when violence prevails over peaceful disagreement, when destruction of others becomes a primary goal, society is likely to collapse or evolve to a very different cooperative order.

Two qualities are therefore central to society: symbolic interaction and cooperation. There is one more: *culture.*

3. SOCIETY IS SOCIAL INTERACTION THAT IS SYMBOLIC, THAT IS CHARACTERIZED BY COOPERATION, AND THAT DEVELOPS CULTURE

Culture Is a Shared Perspective

Over time, cooperative symbolic interaction creates culture. Every society has a culture; culture helps create continuity over time and is taken on by the actors as guides to action. Individuals enter situations with all kinds of tools to guide them as they interact with others, but the longer they interact with those others, the more likely something new will enter into their guides for action—the emerging culture of the group:

> In the course of their collective discussion, the members of the group arrive at a definition of the situation, its problems and possibilities, and develop a consensus as to the most appropriate and efficient ways of behaving. This consensus thenceforth constrains the activities of individual members of the group, who will probably act on it, given the opportunity (Becker, 1982, p. 520).

Culture means the "consensus" of the group, the agreements, goals, knowledge, understandings, shared language and values that emerge together.

Culture becomes a constraint on each individual; individuals who become part of the group agree to some extent to control their own actions through applying the consensus that has arisen.

Culture is really a shared perspective, a viewpoint from which people in a society see reality. Shibutani (1955) called it a frame of reference, a group, an anchor through which they think and act. Individuals become to some extent actors who see and control themselves in relation to the whole. Individuals are able to see their own action "from the generalized standpoint, anticipate the reactions of others, inhibit undesirable impulses, and thus guide [their] conduct." We use the culture to set standards for ourselves and we use them to judge others. Through this process social control becomes self-control (p. 564).

Culture Is a Generalized Other

Culture should not only be considered a way of defining reality—a perspective—but it also should be extended to include a body of rules, a *generalized other*. Mead's idea of generalized other is the socially created conscience, the guides to correct behavior in the group. A generalized other contains the law that is supposed to be obeyed; it is the system, it is the customs, informal and formal rules, procedures, taboos, traditions, morals. It is a guide to right behavior in the group that each individual takes on that allows actors to interact, communicate, and work together in a society. It is a guide for how people should control themselves when interacting with others in the group. It is a recognition that the rules we follow must not simply be our own but the rules of a "whole" we are calling society.

Lonnie Athens (1986, pp. 376–79) applies the concept of "generalized other" to an understanding of violent offenders. He describes four types of people: the pacifist, the marginally violent person, the violent person, and the ultraviolent person. These types are different from one another in the generalized other they assume in situations within which they act. The pacifist, for example, has an antiviolent generalized other—one that "provides him or her with pronounced and categorical support for never acting violently toward other persons." In contrast is the ultraviolent person: one who has a generalized other that "provides him or her with pronounced and categorical support for acting violently toward other persons even when it is not required to defend him or herself or an intimate or to deal with extreme provocation." The other two types are, of course, in between these two extremes. The point, however, is that our generalized others are guides to how we deal with situations—they set our limits, they inform us as to how best to deal with problems—and they arise from our society. Generalized others support or discourage violence by the individual.

The generalized other is the moral system that the individual takes on as his or her own. Continuous interaction depends on individuals who share a generalized other, who share a set of rules to some minimal extent.

Society—cooperative symbolic interaction—works because people agree to use a body of rules to direct their own action.

Culture then should be understood as (1) a shared perspective through which individuals in interaction define reality, and (2) a generalized other through which individuals in interaction take on rules that control their own acts. Culture arises in symbolic interaction; it is a central quality of any society; it becomes an important social object to individuals who continue to cooperate in that society; it guides their thinking and their self-control.

Culture Maintains Society

The product of symbolic interaction—culture—becomes important for the continuation of society. It is because people come to share and use a perspective and a generalized other that a continuing society is possible.

A *shared perspective* is necessary for understanding one another in order to accomplish difficult tasks. Charles Warriner (1970) writes that people are able to act with others because they "come to share notions as to what they will do. And they can come to share such notions (expectations) only through the communications involved in interaction" (p. 98). A shared perspective is necessary (at least to some extent) in order to perceive one's own place in the interaction. A shared perspective is important for ongoing communication, which in turn, is central to cooperation. A *shared perspective* is "agreement" on very basic matters, "shared meanings," "a common terminology" that people together use to understand "further shared experience" (Strauss, 1959, pp. 148–49).

A *generalized other* is necessary for self-control and self-direction, which make action consistent with what others are doing, allowing the action to go in an agreed-upon direction established in interaction rather than according to the whims of each individual. We can afford to act alone without a generalized other when our actions do not need to be coordinated with anyone else's; however, once others are needed for cooperation a generalized other needs to enter into what we do.

Society continues, therefore, at least in part because individuals share a culture from which they define reality and control their actions. "Human society rests upon a basis of *consensus*, i.e., the sharing of meanings in the form of common understandings and expectations" (Meltzer, 1972, pp. 13–14).

A study by Linda Smircich (1983) of the executive staff in an insurance company illustrates the central place of cultural consensus in maintaining organization. Her article is entitled "Organizations As Shared Meanings," and her conclusion is that an organization gets things done on a day-to-day basis through "the development of shared meanings for events, objects, words and people" and through the development of "a sense of commonality of experience that facilitates their coordinated action" (p. 55). In this particular organization, the dominant cultural belief was that differences, problems, and conflict were not to be brought out in the open. People knew that the way to maintain the smooth operation of the organization was to maintain a surface conformity. The executive staff also shared a belief as to why this had to be the case: the president wants things that way. This emerging culture gave the executive staff "a sense of commonality and unity to their experience. These beliefs contributed to coordinated, albeit restrained, interaction and an aura of passivity among the staff members" (pp. 57–58). The Monday morning staff meeting, important to the president, was ritual to the executive staff, who saw it as an "empty formality," where nothing of substance was ever done. The emerging perspective was used by members to control their own acts and to cooperate to achieve goals in the organization.

Sometimes a consensus does not emerge in interaction, and society is impossible. In *The Derelicts of Company K*, Shibutani (1978) specifically examines the problem of demoralization in groups—how groups fall apart and individuals are not able to cooperatively problem solve. His focus was on the morale of Company K, a unit stationed in Minneapolis at the end of World War II. Here is a description of individuals without commitment to a generalized other, a refusal to internalize rules, individuals without self-control in line with cooperative problem solving:

> Company K had all the symptoms of a demoralized group. The most common form of resistance was evasion of duties, but opposition often went well beyond mere recalcitrance. Shouting obscenities and insults from ranks was commonplace. Violence erupted, and a brief reign of terror developed. Local officials, though held personally accountable for the accomplishment of military objectives, found it impossible to maintain order; at times the men became so unruly that the officers simply left them to their own resources (p. 8).

Shibutani described more examples of demoralization and lack of unity: going AWOL, walking off work details, fighting with and embarrassing supervisors, and refusing to salute. One officer who was particularly disliked ended his lecture with: "You must obey orders regardless of how stupid or absurd they may seem." The entire company burst out in laughter (p.123). This is the nightmare of an organization that fails to work because there is no commitment to a shared culture either as a generalized other or as a perspective that individuals are willing to use as guides to action.

Culture acts to make society possible because it minimizes obedience and conformity by force. The culture, itself, may often support force onto individuals who are labeled "criminals," "deviants," "scapegoats," "terrorists," "enemies," but when a society relies on force to assure conformity by its actors, it is usually disintegrating as a society or has become an oppressive system of powerful individuals.

Culture Is Ever-changing

There is a paradox, writes Howard Becker (1982): "On the one hand, culture persists and antedates the participation of particular people in it: indeed, culture can be said to shape the outlooks of people who participate in it." On the other hand, however, everything is always changing: cultural understandings "have to be reviewed and remade continually, and in the remaking they change." This is not a true paradox, Becker continues, as "the understandings last *because* they change to deal with new situations" (pp. 522–23). Societies deal with an ever-changing environment. Culture is communicated, tried out, applied, and altered by cooperative individuals in real situations. Like anything else, if it works there is reason to continuously use it; if it does not work exactly right, then it is altered. Culture represents the stability of the group, yet stability cannot be complete, because situations always involve some adjustment on the part of the cooperative group. Society is a complex interplay of consensus and change, carried on through ongoing interaction or communication. It is never complete; it changes in symbolic interaction; and each actor in his or her actions reaffirm, add to, or challenge that consensus. Interaction validates past culture, and it revises what is known. It involves conflict and negotiation where actors compete; interaction is "almost like a battle over whose and which definitions prevail as the basis for future interaction" (Stryker, 1980, p. 57).

Culture is negotiated. It arises as actors "do battle." What is negotiation? Negotiation means that an idea or rule among actors emerges out of the acts of all to one another. Each does not get his or her own way exactly, but instead the input by each affects the net result to some extent. Ideas, rules, direction of the group, direction of the individuals—all are negotiated in interaction.

In one simple example, Fine (1987) reports an episode in a Little League baseball game. Of course, there is one rule book that all are supposed to follow. The book tells all that one needs to know. Yet, in specific games, rules must be interpreted to fit the situation, and that interpretation is a result, in part, of negotiation. In one instance, a pitch was thrown that was the most important pitch of the whole game. The batter moved in order to avoid getting hit. However, he actually moved his head into the strike zone and was hit. Should he take his base or was he out? One coach came running out of the dugout. The umpire declared: "I don't know what it is. I've never had a kid get hit in the head like that before." The umpire decided to go over to the other coach for advice and then declared that the batter should continue batting. The first coach then ran out, the fans began screaming foul play, and then the umpire declared the boy out: "He intentionally put his head in the strike zone." Actually, there were several rules that touched upon this situation, but none of them dealt with it exactly. "Even a finely attuned set of rules requires interpretation, and this process of interpretation allows negotiation by the coaches" (p. 23).

A role is also a set of rules, and it, too, is governed by negotiation. Traditionally, roles have been treated as an objective reality confronting the individual entering into organization. Role is normally defined as a set of expectations—or a script—that tells the individual what to do. The symbolic interactionist sees this view as overly structured: the fact is that roles are fluid, vague, contradictory. They should be seen as a general outline. Actors shape their own roles to an extent, to meet their own goals. Roles are thus social objects that we learn in interaction and alter according to our definition of the situation. We announce to others what it is we are doing—playing a certain role—but this is an active human being doing that, and we do it until it is not useful to us anymore. We change how we play it when we see that what we are doing does not work or when others tell us through their actions that it is unsatisfactory. How we make our roles, in the end, is through a continuous negotiation process, rather than passively entering into a role and doing what others tell us. Roles are loosely defined guidelines, and individuals make ongoing decisions concerning those guidelines as they act and other individuals act back. So, for example, Peter Manning (1977) identified a negotiation process in two police departments he studied: although formal rules describe what each individual should do, actual action is determined by individuals' using and applying and altering those rules as they make ongoing decisions in their actual actions.

All aspects of culture are negotiated. What sociologists sometimes call social structure—class, power, roles, and authority, for example—like all other rules that are part of culture, may exist and exert themselves on the individual, yet they are also defined, altered, legitimated, used, and shaped by each individual.

Both the external existence of rules and the definitions matter. All organized life is ordered—guided by rules—yet that order is renewed, altered, acted out time and time again as people in real-life situations interact. It is an exaggeration to say that each rule that is part of culture is negotiated all of the time, yet it is equally an exaggeration to say that rules are fixed for people to follow and obey. All orders are negotiated; acts of people in interaction determine the patterns that prevail (Fine, 1984, pp. 240–43).

Society—social interaction, symbolic communication, and cooperation—creates culture. Culture becomes important for ongoing social interaction. Culture is used by the actors to guide their own action. Culture is ever changing and negotiated.

THE MEANING OF SOCIETY: A SUMMARY

Society then can be defined as *any instance of ongoing social interaction that is characterized by cooperation among actors and that creates a shared culture.* The culture is something that becomes an important social object for the individual's view of reality and for the rules he or she uses to control self. In turn, this agreement to use the culture becomes an important reason people can continue to cooperate. Without social interaction society ceases to exist. Where cooperation is replaced by social conflict there is no society. And without a culture used by the participants in social interaction, society becomes an aggregation of individuals who are thinking and acting without

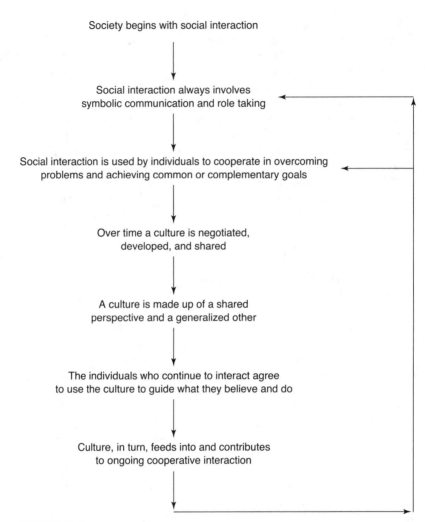

Society begins with social interaction

Social interaction always involves
symbolic communication and role taking

Social interaction is used by individuals to cooperate in overcoming
problems and achieving common or complementary goals

Over time a culture is negotiated,
developed, and shared

A culture is made up of a shared
perspective and a generalized other

The individuals who continue to interact agree
to use the culture to guide what they believe and do

Culture, in turn, feeds into and contributes
to ongoing cooperative interaction

FIGURE 11–1

concern for the whole, and ongoing cooperative interaction cannot continue. We might try to conceptualize society as shown in Figure 11–1.

Sociologists continuously debate the relative importance of a society such as the United States and a society such as a Little League baseball team or an individual family group. It is, first of all, important to regard all societies—from the very largest to the very smallest—as sharing certain qualities, and this point has been emphasized throughout this discussion. All organized life is characterized by ongoing symbolic interaction, cooperative problem solving, and shared culture. I can be a consultant invited to evaluate a business organization or a university, or I can be a social worker who must try to help a community organize itself, or I can be a family counselor whose job it is to help people lead a more cooperative family life. In each case we are examining a society, and in each case it is social interaction, symbolic communication, role taking, cooperative problem solving, and culture that must be evaluated and improved for the society to work. If I am asked about what types of problems are created by having a segregated United States I can point to problems of unity that break down where ongoing social interaction, symbolic communication, role taking, cooperative problem solving, and shared culture are no longer in evidence. We can examine why the Soviet Union collapsed, why Lebanon dissolved, or the nation of Yugoslavia eventually broke up into many distinct societies. The success or failure of South Africa, Iraq, Israel, China, NATO, the European Union, the United Nations can all be analyzed using these same qualities.

THE INDIVIDUAL EXISTS WITHIN MANY SOCIETIES

It is when we look at all of these various societies that we can come to appreciate how many societies we enter throughout our lives. We are all part of many societies, very diverse, each with its own social interaction, cooperation, and culture. The society that matters to me the most on a day-to-day basis may be my family. Here is the society where I try to achieve my goals cooperatively, through ongoing social interaction with those who share with me a common culture. However, I also live within the United States, and that, too, is a society with people interacting, communicating, cooperating, and using a common culture. When these qualities are not evident, the United States becomes much less of a society, perhaps ready for dramatic change. We all exist in other societies too: Minneapolis, Augsburg College, the art department, and a bunch of friends who hang out together at Bud's Coffee Shop. My societies changed as I left my university in Minnesota to a community in Nevada. One of my sons lives in New York City as an active member of the society of modern dance, and the dance company he performs with is itself a society for him. My other son who lives in Minneapolis is a photographer, artist, and computer expert, independent in his work, yet part of a working community where interaction, cooperation, and a common culture still exists and is important to him.

Some of our societies are very small and some are very large and spread out. Each of the smaller ones exists within larger ones. The larger ones may have an impact on the smaller ones in many possible ways (for example, it may be important to the larger cultures that smaller societies develop). Norman Denzin (1978) investigated the U.S. liquor industry. It is made up of tiers of organization: distilling, producing, rectifying, wholesaling, retailing, and drinking. He found that the larger culture of the industry affected all the interaction within the various tiers and between those tiers. The larger culture was characterized by informal wheeling and dealing, often illegal, and this affected interaction throughout the industry:

> This industry engages in corrupt, semi-legal and illegal behaviors [and] these behaviors have roots that predate prohibition and the Eighteenth Amendment. We have identified—on the part of all or some of the participants in the liquor world—misrepresentations of financial statements, manipulations of stock holdings, commercial and personal bribery of public officials, misrepresentation of funds and products, and at times clear-cut instances of conflict of interest. The liquor industry, as Al Capone suggested, is a "legitimate racket" (p. 110).

Harvey Farberman (1975) found that this same pattern existed in the automobile industry. The rules at the top affected the interaction throughout the industry. He found that the price policies of top managers affected the way everyone—wholesalers, retailers, and customers—interacted with one another. That interaction was "criminogenic," involving illegal aspects consistent with the larger culture.

Smaller societies may also have an impact on the larger society. If they work effectively, they can alter the rules or influence the larger society to include their goals and interests. They can disrupt the cooperative problem solving in society, and they can influence the larger society to change how people act and think there. They can separate themselves from the larger society, or they can be seen as too different or threatening to be allowed to interact in the larger society. Their differences can bring diversity to the larger society and new creative ways to achieve goals and solve problems.

Often, the larger encourages and even forms the smaller (a business may encourage an office to develop its own society, or a university may encourage a department to), and often the smaller works to reinforce cooperation in the larger (learning rules in school may ultimately be very important for encouraging the individual to follow the rules of the larger society). Societies can become highly integrated with other societies, or they can be increasingly separated or forcefully segregated. However, if you link everything back to social interaction, you will understand the essence of ongoing society: Where cooperative interaction is made easy, society will continue to exist, where it is lost somehow, so will society be lost.

Society, as any sociologist would argue, is therefore highly complex. We live in many. Our interaction links us to some and simultaneously separates us from others. Sometimes one society matters to us; at other times a very different society matters. Larger societies affect the smaller, and sometimes smaller societies have an impact on the larger. Sometimes societies exist for a long time, and sometimes they exist as momentary instances of social interaction. Each society, because of social interaction, will be unique and separated from others, yet where there is interaction among people from different societies, a larger society can be established. Every society begins wherever people interact; every society can be understood by examining that interaction (including symbolic communication and role taking), the way people cooperate in that interaction, and the elements of and importance of the culture that arises.

THE ACTIVE HUMAN BEING IN SOCIETY

We are born into societies that have been around for a long time. We enter into interaction that has gone on between other individuals for a long time. America was here before we were born and will probably be here after we are dead. We interact with other Americans, with our family, with the Joneses, and with the workers at General Motors. It is correct to see each of these as instances of social interaction: each is a society where people cooperate, solve problems together, communicate, and share rules and perspectives. It is also important, however, to recognize that each has a history, a stream of action in which people have interacted and worked together over time. Each situation people face together is not a brand-new society but is influenced by interaction that has gone on before. People have interacted in America for a long time, and through that interaction, a generalized other and perspective have developed among them, ever changing, but also to some extent retaining some consistency over generations. The culture, continuously shared and continuously being redefined, leads those who interact to define one another, self, and the world outside in somewhat the same way as those who interacted earlier.

But that which has the longest history is actively defined by real live thinking actors. Lest we forget: every human society is made up of actors with selves, minds, and the ability to take one another's roles. This means that society cannot simply stamp out its members, but that people are active in society: they shape it. They *use* the culture to deal with their own problems and to reach their personal goals. It becomes a social object to them rather than simply a force causing behavior. And new situations arise that demand new definitions, new kinds of problem solving, and the culture is transformed by the acts of people back and forth in social interaction. Society may exist over time, but at all times what has developed is evaluated, negotiated, and changed.

You will not find the essence of human society in the study of ants or bees or even other primates. That is because the societies that we form are formed with actors who possess selves and engage in ongoing mind action. That makes human society problem solving just like the actors who make it up. It is not by instinct or simple imitation that society continues but by symbolic interaction by beings with self and mind.

Blumer makes this point over and over: *Human society is made up of actors with selves.* Social interaction is not something out there that stamps itself on the individual, nor is culture. Instead, "human association is a moving process in which the participants note and gauge each other's actions," where they organize their action in relation to one another, and where they inhibit themselves, encourage themselves, and guide themselves as action unfolds over time (Blumer, 1953, p. 197). Self-control is not passive control; it is individuals considering others and actively directing themselves in relation to those others.

Cooperation is accomplished through controlling self in line with others for the purpose of achieving a goal. Each works with the others; all coordinate their activities, dealing with the environment together. Human society is not humans who blindly imitate one another, but instead it is humans who actively direct themselves to cooperate. Coordination of action comes from self-control; voluntary cooperation assumes a self we direct; to see ourselves in relation to a society involves an ability to actually see our selves in the situation within which we act (Shibutani, 1961, pp. 92–93).

And Mead also reminds us that human society is unique: *It is made up of actors who engage in mind action.* Society means cooperative problem solving. As they act, humans must think about that which they do. They consider their own acts in relation to others, and they role take the other's acts. Mind enables the actor to figure out situations, to evaluate the acts of others, to determine ways to deal with the problems at hand, to turn on society "and thus in a degree, to reconstruct and modify in terms of [his or her] self the general pattern of social or group behavior in terms of which [his or her] self was originally constituted" (Mead, 1934, p. 263). Rules do not exist "out there" determining what we all do. Interpretation of society's reality—as does interpretation of all reality—occurs in interaction with self and others. Rules are social objects *used* by actors in situations to control their action.

So it is that symbolic interactionism departs from the general view of society that is so often a part of the discipline of sociology. Society does shape us: it gives us our selves, symbols, mind, our ability to role take, our social objects, our culture. *Yet human beings—possessing self and mind—act back on society and shape it, putting forth ideas, actions, directions that arise from within and that influence the direction of others in the ongoing cooperative order.*

Yes, we are socialized to accept the culture. But in our acts we turn on our socializers and we act in directions we choose. People are not robots, Shibutani (1978) reminds us in *The Derelicts of Company K.* The soldiers' refusal to obey was a reaction to an authority perceived to be unjust. It was not in their interests to obey, and they caused problems for the army (p. 436).

Whereas most theories of society almost dare us to show how it is possible for freedom and creativity to exist, the symbolic interactionist shows that freedom and creativity arise *from* society, not despite it. In truth, society does make us as we interact with others. But with what society provides—symbols, self, mind, role-taking ability—we turn around and make society.

Summary

To the symbolic interactionist, society is always developing as people interact. Society is said to have the following qualities:

1. It is characterized by social symbolic interaction. Actors take one another into account as they act; they intentionally communicate; and they interpret one another's acts.

2. It is characterized by a certain type of interaction: cooperation. Society is cooperative problem solving.
3. It possesses culture, a shared perspective (a general view of reality), and a shared generalized other (a general body of rules), all of which facilitate social interaction and cooperation.

Every instance of social symbolic interaction that is cooperative and develops culture is a society, from very small groups to very large entities. Each individual is a member of many societies, each playing a role in his or her definition of reality and self-control.

Like everything else in the symbolic interactionist perspective, human society is thought to be something created, defined, altered, and used by actors who are active beings, who possess selves, and who engage in mind action.

CHAPTER TWELVE

Erving Goffman

Written by Spencer Cahill, University of South Florida*

GOFFMAN AND SYMBOLIC INTERACTIONISM

No introduction to symbolic interactionism would be complete without some discussion of Erving Goffman's contributions to the perspective. Both before and since his unexpected death in 1982, Goffman's many books and essays have influenced not only symbolic interactionists but also sociologists more generally and, perhaps less extensively but still notably, cultural anthropologists and psychologists. The tradition of thought now known as symbolic interactionism also undoubtedly influenced Goffman but probably not as much as he has influenced it.

When Goffman came to the University of Chicago as a graduate student in the late 1940s, the legacy of George Herbert Mead, Charles Horton Cooley, and other forerunners of symbolic interactionism still loomed large. Professors there at the time, such as Herbert Blumer and Everett Hughes, as well as many of Goffman's fellow graduate students, later became known as important figures in the history of symbolic interactionism. Goffman, too, is often called a symbolic interactionist, but he strongly objected to that label (Goffman, 1988). Although Goffman did address many of the same topics as symbolic interactionists, he drew at least as much inspiration and guidance from the ideas of the early French sociologist Emile Durkheim and the British anthropologist A. R. Radcliffe-Brown as from those of Mead or Cooley.

Goffman's abiding concern was with what he came to call "the interaction order" (Goffman, 1983)—the structure, process, and products of social interaction. Goffman's approach to the study of social interaction is often called *dramaturgical*, meaning that he viewed social life as something like a staged drama. Although that is an important aspect of Goffman's general perspective, there is an equally if not more important component. Goffman also

---

*Revised by Joel Charon for purposes of style.

viewed interaction as something like a religious ceremony *filled with ritual observances.* For Goffman, these two characteristics of social interaction—drama and ritual—are complementary, and both are implicated in the *collaborative manufacture of selves.*

As do most symbolic interactionists, Goffman gives "self" a prominent place in his writings. His focus is not the self-concept carried by an actor from situation to situation but the socially situated self developed in and governing specific interactions. According to Goffman (1959b, p. 253), the self is "something of collaborative manufacture" that must be produced anew on each and every occasion of social interaction. It is both the product of the drama of interaction and the object of the interpersonal rituals that Goffman analyzes.

These three themes—drama, self, and ritual—form the core of Goffman's perspective, and these will be briefly introduced in the description that follows. It should be noted that all three are central to the morality that is the foundation for all society, and each, in turn, exists in and is influenced by a larger social context, which Goffman calls the "social environment."

DRAMA IN INTERACTION

Impressions and Performance

Goffman's (1959) analysis of the dramatic processes of social interaction begins with a rather simple observation:

> When an individual enters the presence of others they commonly seek to acquire information about him or to bring into play information about him already possessed. They will be interested in his general socio-economic status, his conception of self, his trustworthiness, etc. Although some of this information seems to be sought as an end in itself, there are usually quite practical reasons for acquiring it. Information about the individual helps to define the situation, enabling others to know in advance what he will expect of them and what they may expect of him (p. 1).

Even with those we know well, when they act in a situation we must determine their current mood, their view of us, and which of their many social identities they consider relevant at the moment. We need to acquire even more information about those with whom we are not acquainted in order to know how to treat and what to expect from them. Yet we rarely ask one another to supply such information; instead, we depend on an individual's "front" or appearance, manner, and the setting where we meet to define the situation (pp. 22–30).

Although we are forming impressions of others on the basis of such readily apparent expressions of self, we are aware that they are doing the same with us, and we act accordingly. The way we act and dress for a job interview is different from the way we and dress for a party. Through our appearance and manner, or "personal front" (Goffman, 1959b, p. 24), we manage others' impressions of us, influence their definitions of situations, and affect their conduct. Goffman (p. 24) aptly describes the activity that serves to influence others in these ways as a "performance." Some of our performances may be thoroughly calculated to evoke a particular response; others may be less calculated and much easier to do because they seem more natural to us or more "authentic." In either case, we must dramatically convince others that we are who and what we want them to consider us to be:

> Whether an honest performer wishes to convey the truth or whether a dishonest performer wishes to convey a falsehood, both must take care to enliven their performance with appropriate expressions, exclude from their performances expressions that might discredit the impression fostered and take care lest the audience impute unintended meanings (p. 66).

Whenever we interact with others, we are not only performers but an audience for their performances as well. Each participant in social interaction expresses a self and forms an impression of each of the other participants on the basis of their appearance and manner and the setting of the interaction. In most cases, they quickly arrive at what Goffman (1959b, p. 10) describes as a "working consensus" about definitions of one another and the situation that then guides their interaction. Like stage actors, social actors enact roles, assume characters, and play through scenes when engaged in interaction with one another. Although Goffman (pp. 254–55) acknowledges that these dramas of everyday social life are somewhat more fateful than theatrical productions for those who enact and witness them, he points out that both kinds of drama involve use of the same techniques. Social actors, like theatrical actors, rely on costume, makeup, body carriage, dialect, props, and other dramatic devices to produce a shared experience and sense of reality.

Goffman points to the way we commonly divide social settings as evidence of the staged character of everyday social life. In his words, most social settings consist of a front region—or frontstage—where a performance is given and a back region—or backstage—"where the impression fostered by the performance is knowingly contradicted" (p. 112). To protect the vital secrets of shows visible there, we generally separate the backstage from the frontstage by barriers to perception and restrict the audience's access to that region. Thus, in the backstage kitchen of most restaurants food is placed back on plates after falling on the floor and staff ridicule customers. It is well out of sight and hearing from the frontstage dining area, where the impression of careful food preparation and polite service is dramatically fostered.

Of course, audiences are aware that performers are likely to present themselves and the social entities they represent in a favorable light. Thus, they often look for evidence of deception. They may try to overhear or catch a glimpse of what is happening backstage. More often, they check aspects of performances that are easily controlled by actors against supposedly less controllable and controlled aspects such as the tightness of a smile. This is a common method of evaluating the honesty of performances perfected by parents who always know when their children are lying.

On the other hand, performers may exploit the dramatic effect of seemingly automatic expressions for their own purposes. That is, they may actually control expressions that appear spontaneous and uncontrolled. The verbal discharges of internal states that Goffman (1981a) calls "response cries" provide examples. The "strain grunts" we sometimes emit when exerting ourselves may be purposefully enacted to dramatize for the benefit of some audience the effort we are expending (p. 104). Similarly, revulsion sounds, such as "Eeuw," which dramatically demonstrate the limits of our tolerance, may sometimes be premeditated to foster the impression that we are the kind of person who is disgusted by certain sights and smells.

Goffman (1961b, p. 107) recognized that individuals do not always or even usually expressively "embrace" their formal roles in a situation. He describes numerous instances of individuals' expressing "distance" from social roles and the images of self they imply. For example, a teacher may mention a popular song or recount a personally embarrassing incident indicating that she is not as different from the students in the class as her official role in the classroom implies. And students may listen to her lecture with a bored look or disdainful smirk, dramatizing their lack of enthusiasm for their current role.

However, Goffman (1961b, p. 139) argues that individuals thereby free themselves from social roles and projected definitions of self, not to be free, but because other social roles and identities have a hold on them. Goffman empirically illustrates this argument with the example of physicians who distance themselves from the role of surgeon while performing operations. They sometimes announce their identity as fishermen by telling of a recent fishing trip, proudly claim the identity of family man by recounting some story of domestic life, and demonstrate their identity as a sexually vital male by flirting with nurses. Goffman (1961b, p. 144) argued that such expressive "dances of social identification" or constant changes of dramatic "footing" (Goffman, 1981a) are evidence of individuals' multiple social identifications and how they manage those competing commitments. We may take an individual's graceful gliding in and out of social roles and identities as indicating his or her "real" or "true" self, but that is as much a dramatic effect as any of his or her specific role identities.

Performance Teams

In addition to dramatically enacting roles and characters, social actors attempt to manage others' impressions of the groups, establishments, and organizations that they represent. The members and personnel of such social units often constitute what Goffman (1959b, p. 79) calls "performance teams" that cooperate in "staging a single routine." For example, family members often cooperate in staging shows of domestic bliss and respectability. Similarly, pilots and flight attendants sometimes cooperate in staging shows of calm confidence and competence under life-threatening circumstances. Staging such routines takes teamwork. The team members often rehearse their lines in audiences' absence, provide one another stage directions through such subtle cues as a raised eyebrow or a kick under the table, and otherwise support one another's individual performances.

Goffman emphasizes that the routine staged by a performance team is precariously dependent on the loyalty of each of its members. The show of domestic bliss and hospitality being carefully staged by a husband and wife can be quickly spoiled by their child, unschooled in the arts of impression management, who tells the houseguests how mad Mommy was with Daddy for inviting them. Like this child, every member of a performance team usually possesses some information that can give away the team's show because maintaining a fostered impression almost always involves concealing or playing down certain facts. As Goffman (1959b) notes, "since we are all participants on teams we must carry within ourselves the sweet guilt of conspirators" (p. 105). To have a job, to be a member of a family or virtually any other social entity is to be part of a dramatic conspiracy to control the information that is available to others and their definitions of situations.

To Goffman, therefore, human beings act on a stage; they perform for others; they impress and they are impressed. They are both actors and audiences. And they often form a cooperative performance team that works to present a united front to others. We know we do this; others know we do this; we know that others know we do this. Life is drama, and to understand interaction, self, or society we must consider this fact.

Reaction to Goffman's Dramaturgical View

Although Goffman's ideas are not embraced by all symbolic interactionists, his dramaturgical view does represent a view of the human being that is attractive to many. The attractiveness is in the fact that he makes the human actor into an active being who has some control over what takes place in interaction. To perform is to control how others define and treat you. It is not simply to respond to what others do. Although we are performing actors, we use our performances to our advantage in real situations; and, as the play begins to change because of the performances of others, we change. Together we dramatically construct one another's self and the social situations in which we act.

Goffman's dramaturgical analysis of social life has been emulated by other sociologists (e.g., Brisset and Edgley, 1990), but it has also provoked considerable criticism. Critics of Goffman's dramaturgical view argue that his analysis of social life verges on a kind of perverse cynicism. They contend that human beings are not mere performers. This is too much of an exaggeration that reduces individuals to little more than superficial hypocrites. In the words of one reviewer:

> You come away ... seeing artifice and histrionics everywhere. But Mr. Goffman's
> moral is very sad, because his skepticism is ... unrelieved ... he seems to say we
> can't assemble authentic characters out of the bits of business that actors show
> (Numberg, 1981, p. 11).

Along similar lines, other critics accuse Goffman of reading "a Machiavellian kind of manipulation into human interaction" (Karp and Yoels, 1986, p. 80) and of depicting social life as little more than a continuous con game (Cuzzort, 1969, pp. 173–92).

Although Goffman did focus attention on the trickery and pretense of everyday social life, he did not see contrivance and chicanery everywhere, as many of his critics suggest. Instead, Goffman (1959b, p. 66) wrote that we are both honest and dishonest social performers: we sometimes express who we truly believe we are, and sometimes we try to present an image of self that benefits us but is false. However, what is important is that honest and dishonest performances are still performances and have the same general characteristics. Goffman therefore reasoned that we could "profitably study performances that are quite false to learn about ones that are quite honest" (p. 66). By concentrating on how easily dramaturgical techniques could be exploited for self-serving and unsavory purposes, Goffman shows not how often but how seldom individuals take unfair advantage of the dramatic character of social interaction and reality.

Rather than reading a kind of Machiavellian manipulation into human interaction, Goffman emphasizes its intrinsically cooperative and moral character. That is, he shows us that mutual performance creates the mutually acceptable rules that form the basis of orderly social interaction. I perform for you and present myself in a way I choose. You perform for me and present yourself in a way you choose. Some of this performance is honest, some dishonest. Yet, if there is no clear evidence of deception, we agree to respect each other's performance and treat each other accordingly. Out of this agreement arises the morality that guides our acts and allows for the continuation of our interaction. Goffman leaves little doubt that the drama of interaction is a deeply moral matter.

THE SELF OF SOCIAL INTERACTION

Goffman's View of Self

As do many symbolic interactionists today, Goffman viewed the self as something cooperatively built up on each and every occasion of social interaction. In this respect, he took Mead's (1934, p. 140) characterization of the self as essentially *social* more seriously than did Mead himself. According to Goffman (1967) "the Meadian notion that the individual takes toward himself [or herself], the attitude that others take toward him [or her] seems very much an oversimplification" (pp. 84–85). Rather, the individual "must rely on others to complete the picture" of self that his or her performance merely outlines. Others fill in and sometimes reshape that outline of self through their actions toward the individual. For Goffman, then, a self is not something an individual owns but something others temporarily lend him or her.

Social Control and Self

Goffman (1967) once observed that "societies everywhere, if they are to be societies, must mobilize their members as self-regulating participants in social encounters" (p. 44). The key word here is *self*. Through the respect and regard or lack thereof others show us, they instruct us in what we must and must not do to gain their cooperation in constructing a socially acceptable self. The parent who sharply rebukes a child for creating a public scene and the peers who ridicule him or her for crying when excluded from their play teach the child how to act to present a viable self—a self others will accord him or her. These are the kind of lessons that encourage *self*-regulated participation in social interaction.

Over time, we learn to have feelings attached to the selves that we present to others. We come to care how others see us and to care about the positive social value we effectively claim through our performances, or what Goffman (1967 pp. 5–45) called "face." We become attached to the image of hard-working student that earns us the respect of our teachers and family and to the image of class clown that earns us the respect of our peers. Our emotions are thereby mobilized in support of the interaction order that sustains those selves and claims. We are always prepared with informed answers to our teachers' questions and are always ready with the humorous quip. And, when we fail to fulfill social expectations, we are embarrassed, turning red-faced and flustered over the projected self we have shattered and the face we have lost (pp. 97–112). The answer that the teacher corrects or the joke that brings frowns rather than laughter results in the burning sensation of shame creeping up the back of our necks.

Goffman (1967, p. 8) suggests that *this emotional attachment to projected selves and face is the most fundamental mechanism of social control leading us to regulate our own conduct*. It deters us from misrepresenting ourselves to others because of the danger of being discovered "in the wrong face" and exposed as a dishonest performer. Similarly, our emotional attachment to face leads us to avoid situations in which we would be "out of face" and in which others would refuse to recognize and respect the self we present. The straight-A student may avoid a notoriously demanding and difficult teacher. An individual who has not learned which fork goes with which course may decline an invitation to an elegant dinner party. And individuals who possess what Goffman (1963b) terms a social "stigma," such as a visible disability, will often prefer the company of those who share that stigma to strained and uncomfortable interaction with "normals." Like the socially "stigmatized," most of us learn from others' hints and glances and tactful cues what our places are, and we generally keep them:

> Social life is an uncluttered, orderly thing because the person voluntarily stays away from the places and topics and times where he is not wanted and where he might be disparaged for going. He cooperates to save his face, finding that there is much to be gained from venturing nothing (Goffman, 1967, p. 43).

Then again, our emotional attachment to face is also why there is not more deception and chicanery in social interaction.

When individuals reach a working consensus regarding the definition of the situation that will guide their interaction and treatment of one another, they form a moral pact to support one another's fostered impressions of self (Goffman, 1959b, p. 13). They not only "defend" their own projected self and face but also protect one another's by employing practices such as "tactful blindness," politely ignoring one another's slips of the tongue, memory, clothing, and body if at all possible (Goffman, 1967, p. 18). And they have good reasons for doing so. When events or information hopelessly contradicts the impression of self fostered by one of the participants, the definition of the situation that was governing the interaction is shattered. In Goffman's (1967) words, "the minute social system that is brought into being with each encounter" is disorganized, and the participants feel "unruled, unreal and anomic" (p. 135). Lodged in assumptions that no longer hold, all of the participants' projected selves and faces are threatened.

Goffman (1971) movingly illustrates what can happen when the collaborative manufacture of selves goes awry with the example of a manic family member. According to Goffman (p. 356), what are considered the mental symptoms of the manic individual in effect involve enactment of a self that other members of his or her family can neither accept nor allow. The life of the entire family is consequently disorganized:

> The individual's failure to encode through deeds and expressive cues a *workable* definition of himself, one which closely enmeshed others can accord him through the regard they show his person, is to block and trip up and threaten them in almost every movement that they make. The selves that had been the reciprocals of his are undermined.... In ceasing to know the sick person, they cease to be sure of themselves. In ceasing to be sure of him and themselves, they can even cease to be sure of their way of knowing...for there is no place in possible realities for what is occurring (p. 390).

The havoc that a manic member brings to a family is only an extreme and extended instance of the trouble any individual who fails to sustain the self that others have accorded him or her can cause. In Goffman's words, the manic "reminds us of what everything is, and that this everything is not very much" (p. 390). That everything is the selves and realities that we collaboratively manufacture and maintain through interaction with others.

We sometimes do gamble with that everything, however. We may challenge our skills as a performer by seeking what Goffman (1967) calls "action," or situations, such as games of skill and daring, in which a projected self can easily collapse. We may also test our poise by engaging in what Goffman (pp. 239–58) terms "character contests," such as playful or more serious exchanges of insults. Although often harmless, these attempts to gain face at the expense of someone else's face are always risky because we evaluate one another in terms of not only how we handle ourselves but also how we handle one another. Instigators of a character contest can suddenly find that they have gone too far, destroying their own face in the eyes of those whom they had hoped to impress. One strategy for minimizing this risk is to choose a victim for whom the audience will have little sympathy. That is why a man among male companions may verbally harass passing women and an individual among those of similar ethnicity may hurl humiliating insults at someone of another ethnicity. Whatever such an individual may gain through this "aggressive face-work" (pp. 24–25), something of our everything is lost. The mutual protection of projected selves and face that shelters us all is cracked.

As we shall see, Goffman also maintains that an individual's socially situated self and face depend in part on the larger context or environment of interaction. In his words, "an environment...is a place where it is easy or difficult to play the ritual game of having a self" (Goffman, 1967, p. 91). For example, some social environments, such as the back wards of mental hospitals, make it nearly impossible for a resident to present a self that others will accept and respect. Other social environments erode what Goffman considered the intrinsic morality of the interaction order by promoting dishonest performances. Although some social environments, such as a small-town neighborhood, may encourage sincere presentations of self, others, such as secretive governmental bureaucracies and more than a few business organizations, encourage individuals to engage in conspiracies of dramaturgical deception.

To Goffman, therefore, self is intimately linked to interaction and society. Selves are cooperatively constructed in interaction, and interaction is influenced by the larger social environment. On the other hand, the dramatic realization of selves in interaction has a distinctive moral character that links individuals to one another and holds society together.

RITUALS OF INTERACTION

The Meaning of Ritual

The brilliance of Goffman's work is that he focused attention on commonplace elements of social interaction that most of us seldom notice. The following is his description of the common pattern of eye contact between strangers who meet on a city sidewalk or in some other public place:

> What seems to be involved is that one gives to another enough visual notice to demonstrate that one appreciates that the other is present (and that one admits openly to having seen him), while at the next moment withdrawing one's attention from him so as to express that he does not constitute a target of special curiosity or design (Goffman, 1963a, p. 84).

This fleeting and virtually automatic pattern of social behavior may seem trivial, but Goffman's description suggests that it is not. By quickly glancing at one another and then looking away, strangers, mutually establish that they can be trusted to let one another alone. Exceptions prove the rule. When a stranger does stare at us, we usually feel uncomfortable and anxious, if not frightened. Life among strangers in our modern, urbanized society would be one of constant terror without some standard method of establishing mutual trust, such as the pattern of eye contact Goffman called "civil inattention." In Goffman's (1967) words, "the gestures we sometimes call empty are perhaps the fullest things of all" (p. 91).

For Goffman, apparently empty gestures, such as quickly glancing away from those we do not know, are interpersonal rituals but not simply because they are conventional and performed almost automatically. He also maintains that such conventional and perfunctory acts are expressions of respect and regard for what we value most highly—each individual's "sacred" self (Goffman, 1971, pp. 62–63). By avoiding prolonged eye contact with or talking or sitting next to strangers, we express our respect if not reverence for what Goffman (pp. 28–41) calls one another's "self territories" and, thereby, for one another. On the other hand, when we unthinkingly blurt out "How ya doin'" as we pass an acquaintance even if we are not interested in his or her health, we are showing regard for our relationship to that individual and, thereby, for him or her. These interpersonal rituals attest to our own goodwill and to how highly we value one another. As Goffman (1967) once observed:

> ... this secular world is not so irreligious as we might think. Many gods have been done away with, but the individual himself stubbornly remains a deity of considerable importance. He walks with some dignity and is the recipient of many little offerings (p. 95).

Borrowing a distinction from Durkheim, Goffman (1971, pp. 62–65) classifies interpersonal rituals as either positive or negative. Negative interpersonal rituals are those acts through which we avoid intruding upon one another's many self territories. We usually refrain from looking at, talking to, and touching strangers and often treat their possessions similarly. As Goffman (pp. 41–44) notes, we usually treat "markers" of an individual, such as a jacket draped over the back of a chair or an open notebook on a library table, as extensions of their owner, showing those objects the same respect and regard as we would show that individual. If, for example, there are other options, we are as unlikely to sit at a table where there is an open notebook as we are to sit at a table that is occupied by an individual. However, our ritual treatment of those we do know is almost opposite. Rather than briefly glancing at and then looking away from a friend we meet on a city sidewalk, we widen our eyes and raise our eyebrows in a sign of recognition, verbally greet, and sometimes hug or otherwise touch him or her. This is an example of the kind of positive interpersonal rituals that we employ to affirm and signal initiations or extensions of relationships (p. 58). Whereas negative interpersonal rituals express a kind of reverence for the individual's self through the regard shown its inviolable boundaries, positive interpersonal rituals do so by celebrating past, present, or anticipated contact with such a revered object.

The Importance of Ritual

As Goffman (1963a, 1967, 1971) repeatedly argues, our routine observance of such interpersonal rituals or common courtesies demonstrates our commitment to a vast array of shared rules of interpersonal conduct. In an important respect, what we commonly call etiquette is a complex code of ceremonial or ritual prescriptions and proscriptions governing our interactions with one another. That does not mean that we always observe these rules. Rather, they are "enabling conventions" (Goffman, 1983, p. 5) that provide a background of common expectations against which almost anything someone does or does not do is seen by others as meaningful. Because strangers are expected to look away from one another, they can show that they are curious about or interested in further interaction with one another by not doing so. That is why flirtatious or menacing glances are flirtatious or menacing. Because acquaintances are expected to greet one another, friends can express disappointment or anger with one another at the moment through an obvious snub. Because touching is expected between intimates, a lover who recoils from another's touch and angrily snaps "Don't touch me" conveys that all is not right with their relationship. These are all examples of what Goffman (1971, p. 61, fn 54) terms "meaningful nonadherences," and their meaningfulness results from mutually understood but usually unnoticed rules of ritual conduct.

Then there are the many times we violate our shared code of ritual conduct either inadvertently or for good practical reasons. We sometimes accidentally bump into strangers or stop to ask them for directions or the time. We sometimes pass by friends while lost in thought. However, when we commit such ritual offenses and realize that we have done so, we almost always engage in what Goffman (1971, p. 108) calls "remedial work of various kinds." Most often we offer potentially offended parties an apology such as "Excuse me" or "I'm sorry." Sometimes we also offer an explanation or account: "Excuse me, but I'm lost" or "Sorry, I was daydreaming." Other times we request the approval of those who might be offended by an act before committing it. For example, before sitting in one of the few empty seats in a crowded theater, we usually ask the stranger sitting in the adjoining seat if he or she minds if we sit there.

Perhaps the best evidence of our commitment to a shared code of ritual conduct is the number of times a day we employ remedial expression such as apologies, accounts, and requests. Even when we address someone like a sales-clerk, who is paid to assist us, we often preface inquiries—for example, whether a particular item in a certain size is in stock—with an apologetic

"Excuse me." This virtually automatic and tired expression is an abridged form of an elaborate plea for mercy:

> I know that I have violated a ritual expectation, do not take that violation lightly, and beg you to judge me not on the basis of this violation but in terms of the knowledge of and regard for ritual expectations that I am now showing (Goffman, 1971, p. 108).

In most cases, others graciously grant this implicit request, relieving us of responsibility for our violations of ritual expectations.

According to Goffman (1971, pp. 95–187), what usually ensues when ritual expectations are not fulfilled is itself an interpersonal ritual. These remedial interchanges have a standard form projecting an expected sequence of "moves." For example, when an apology is not accepted, we often repeat it in more and more elaborate forms until the potentially offended party accepts it and completes the sequence. When an expected apology is not forthcoming, the offended party may sarcastically say something like "Hey, no problem," emphasizing the offender's failure to offer an expected apology. Of course, the absence of an apology may be a meaningful nonadherence expressing how little respect and regard the offender has for the offended.

We clearly do not consider everyone equally deserving of ritual expressions of respect and regard. We feel little ritual obligation toward those who do not fulfill their own toward us. We also feel similarly about those whose unkempt appearance or strange manner suggests that they have little self-respect, pride, or concern for our opinion of them. When we come upon such persons on city sidewalks, we may stare disapprovingly, make disparaging remarks loud enough for them to hear, or treat them as "nonpersons" not worthy of a glance (Goffman, 1963a, p. 83). In Goffman's (1967, p. 83) words, individuals must show proper "demeanor" to "warrant deferential treatment" or ritual offerings of respect and regard. The demeanor we show through our "deportment, dress, and bearing" conveys to others that we are persons of certain desirable or undesirable qualities and largely determines how much deference they will give us. In simpler terms, how we present ourselves to others influences how they treat us. That dramatic process largely determines the ritual structure of our interactions with others.

Through this analysis, Goffman leads us in yet another direction. He is showing us that ritual acts are an essential part of all of our interaction and are necessary for the continuation of that interaction. Interpersonal rituals are the source of mutual trust, social relationships, and the moral order of society.

THE ENVIRONMENTS OF SOCIAL INTERACTION

Goffman never sees interaction as existing in a vacuum. Our performances take place in social environments that influence them. Critics of Goffman often miss this important point. The "false" performances that Goffman studies in order to learn about ones that are quite "honest" occur in social establishments where a great deal of importance is placed on the control of audiences' definitions of the situation. They occur in restaurants, where waiters and waitresses try to foster an impression of personal concern for each and every customer to maximize tips (Goffman, 1959b, p. 122), in hospitals where doctors and nurses present a front of professional competence in order to gain patients' cooperation (Goffman, 1961a, pp. 340–50), and in funeral homes where the illusion that the deceased is in a deep and tranquil sleep would be shattered if the bereaved witnessed the preparation of the body (Goffman, 1959b, p. 44).

The seemingly Machiavellian individuals whom Goffman describes engage in deceptive performances because they act within social establishments that encourage control of others' definition of the situation and conduct. The control of the bereaveds' impression of the deceased in funeral homes and of patients' conduct in hospitals may seem harmless and even desirable, but not all organizationally encouraged subterfuge is intended to be harmless, as Goffman (1974) makes clear in his description of undercover police work:

> . . . it transforms self-interest into selflessness and insulates a misrepresenter from the immorality of misrepresentation. Insulates as might a game. But here the game engulfs the world and is played against persons who may fail to recognize that they have become players (p. 175).

Although Goffman argues that social life is built on dramatic artifice, he also clearly points out that dramaturgical deception can have negative consequences. The organization of social establishments and of society more generally may encourage social actors to break others' implicit trust that individuals are what they claim to be, undermining the intrinsic morality of the interaction order and the foundation of society. It may also deprive some individuals of any reason to observe that morality.

In a very influential book called *Asylums,* Goffman (1961a) illustrates how social arrangements can pervert the morality of the interaction order with the example of social life in a mental hospital. In his words, the mental patient "starts out with at least a portion of the rights, liberties and satisfactions of the civilian and ends up on a psychiatric ward stripped of almost everything" (p. 148). Cut off from contact with the outside world, patients are subject to the diffuse authority of a small supervisory staff who manage virtually every aspect of their lives. Defined by their very presence in the hospital as very sick, inmates do not get support from the staff nor from one another in their attempts to project a more viable self. Some inmates, with the help of sympathetic members of the staff, do find cracks in the social arrangements of the hospital where they can intermittently have a more viable self (pp. 173–320). Yet such minor victories are small consolation for patients' many defeats. Their only hope of regaining some of the rights, liberties, and satisfactions that they have lost is to accept the hospital's conception of them as ill. They are made to purchase those privileges at the expense of face.

Goffman's (1961a, p. 158) primary point is that "an all embracing conception of the member" is built right into the social arrangements of "total institutions" such as prisons, nursing homes, and mental hospitals. For inmates of mental hospitals at least, that conception provides them no defensible line for projecting a viable self and effectively claiming positive social value. Goffman notes that the fate of mental patients has unique interest for exactly this reason:

> ...it can illustrate the possibility that in casting off the raiments of the old self—or in having this cover torn away—the person need not seek a new robe and a new audience before which to cower. Instead he can learn the amoral arts of shamelessness (p. 169).

Thus, the very social arrangements that are designed to encourage self-regulation and morally responsible conduct may have the opposite effect. Mental patients, prisoners, and inmates of many other total institutions pay in advance for whatever sins they may commit against the intrinsic morality of the interaction order and have never had better reasons for doing so. Shamelessly amoral acts are their only means of expressing outrage over what is being done to them.

Throughout his writings, Goffman shows us how fragile society, interaction, and self are. All three depend on our willing observance of the intrinsic morality of the interaction order. Social arrangements that encourage dramaturgical deception, restrict individuals' control over their presentations of self, and deprive them of social respect and regard undermine that morality, threatening our everything. Everything from society to interaction to self ultimately depends on authentic performances, mutual trust, and support of one another's presented self and face.

Summary

Goffman focuses attention on "the interaction order." All is tied to interaction: definitions of reality, self, moral order, and the surrounding social environment. Using his own concepts and emphases, Goffman analyzes what happens as people act in relation to one another. He shows how the actor forms his or her own acts, how individuals cooperatively construct selves, and how, through ritual, social control becomes the kind of self-control necessary for the continuation of society. His work enriches the perspective of symbolic interactionism and simultaneously shows its links to sociology.

As did both Durkheim and Mead, Goffman (1974) held "society to be first in everyway" (p. 13). All agreed that society is central to forming what the human being is. However, more than either Durkheim or Mead, Goffman spelled out how the intrinsic morality of the interaction order provides the bindings of society. In Goffman's view, the real cornerstones of society include (1) presentation of selves that are consistent with the facts of individuals' social lives, (2) support of one another's projected selves, (3) protection of one another's face, and (4) ritual expressions of respect and regard for one another. Social arrangements that diminish individuals' commitment to these basic moral principles erode the very foundation of society itself.

Regardless of whether one fully accepts Goffman's views, it is virtually impossible to look at the world or oneself the same after reading his insightful analyses of social life. Goffman (1981b) once suggested that the purpose of studying social life is to "cause others to see what they hadn't seen or connect what they hadn't put together" (p. 4). That was Goffman's goal, a goal that his own studies of social life continue to accomplish.

CHAPTER THIRTEEN

Symbolic Interactionism:
A Final Assessment

Take any situation: a dinner party, an athletic event, a club meeting, a meeting of the United Nations, a battle, a family feud, a revolution, a conflict between ethnic groups—look at any of these in depth and one has to be amazed at the complexity of human social life. Every one of these—in fact, all situations—can be approached and analyzed from a number of perspectives, each telling us something more, each unlocking new and enlightening aspects of human beings. The lesson has to be humility: no perspective, no matter how useful, can tell us all there is about any situation. A Marxist perspective sensitizes us to inequality, conflict, power, and economics. A sociological perspective will point us to social structure, roles, social stratification, and institutions. A psychoanalyst reveals to us the subconscious at work in situations, drives, defense mechanisms, personality. Psychological social psychologists tell us how individuals are influenced by others in situations and how attitudes are formed and changed in situations. It is easy to criticize each of these perspectives. We can say that each one is *incomplete,* each ignores some important aspects of the situation, and each undoubtedly overemphasizes certain things.

This criticism is true, of course, of the symbolic interactionist perspective. When the focus is on interaction, both personality predispositions and social structure fail to be examined in great depth. Unconscious reactions are deemphasized. The symbolic interactionist emphasizes that humans are dynamic, that they are rational problem solvers, and that society is a process of individuals in interaction—cooperating, role taking, aligning acts, and communicating. The human engages in overt and covert action in the *present*—recalling past, planning for future—and the action that takes place between individuals is an important influence on the direction of individuals and societies. The choice of concentrating on interaction is a bias in the same way that perspectives must concentrate on some things at the expense of others—but this concentration is central to the understanding of what humans do. The symbolic interactionist focuses on concepts few scientists have seriously considered, and thus the perspective has always been a criticism of mainstream social science. Expecting symbolic interactionism to explain everything is erroneous, but, in my opinion, it is correct to say that symbolic interactionism is an exciting and useful perspective for understanding human social life. It has made important contributions to social science, sociology, social psychology, to those who "work with people," and to students interested in understanding themselves and society.

SYMBOLIC INTERACTIONISM AND HUMAN FREEDOM: A REVIEW

Tamotsu Shibutani (1978) finishes his book *The Derelicts of Company K* with this final appraisal of an army unit that simply did not work:

> Human beings think for themselves. Although some may be prevented from speaking for a time, no one can be forced to believe something that is not plausible to [him or her]. Furthermore, it is doubtful that conversations among intimate friends can be controlled. This suggests that high morale ... can only be offered by those who make the contribution. High morale, like affection and respect, is something that has to be earned (p. 436).

Here Shibutani is telling us that freedom enters into refusing or giving allegiance, obeying or disobeying, conforming or refusing to conform, accepting the generalized other or directing yourself away from it. Organized life as well as our own individual streams of action depend on decisions, which are to some extent freely made by actors.

Symbolic interactionism is an attempt to break away from traditional social science and to view the human as maker, doer, actor, and as self-directing. It is an attempt to locate what Kant and other philosophers were looking for: a free spirit, a "soul," individual freedom in humans. It is an attempt to locate the freedom that many say scientific sociologists cannot really find. It is, of course, naive to believe that humans are completely free, but this perspective of symbolic interactionism does focus on human qualities—socially created qualities—that break us out of the determining prison of traditional social science. For a moment, perhaps, it might be beneficial to summarize how symbolic interactionism conceptualizes the "free" person:

1. Freedom has something to do with making choices in what we do, deciding for ourselves what our thoughts and action shall be. It means control over oneself. It means thinking, evaluating, planning, holding back action, determining what we do next, applying past knowledge and events to the present, considering consequences. It is not impulse, environment, or biology that creates what we do. Thus, it seems that freedom always means definition, ongoing covert action toward ourselves.

2. Freedom assumes that the actor has a self, a socialized self, that allows the actor to perceive and act back on himself or herself, and through this take control over other forces around him or her. Self-awareness, self-judgment,

self-communication, self-concept, and identity are all actions that allows the actor to make choices and act them out in situations.

3. Freedom means that the actor does not simply respond to the environment, but instead, is able to stand back from the environment, appraise it, define it, understand it, label it, categorize it, and act on it in creative ways. Such acts assume the actor has tools necessary for such a relationship toward the environment. These tools are abstract, socially understood, and intentionally used internally in order to manipulate whatever exists. These tools are symbols.

4. Freedom means that the actor is constantly defining and redefining self, others, and environment. It assumes that the actor has many perspectives, much knowledge, identities, societies, and choices that are able to be applied in situations. The actor must understand the environment he or she encounters, so that he or she can use it rather than simply be used by the environment.

Freedom, of course, is limited. We act freely, but only within a situation that has parameters. Some of us are very free; some not very free. Some acts are very free; some are not. Some societies will encourage freedom to some extent; others will try to control. Some limits, from the symbolic interactionist perspective, are the following:

1. *The situation will provide some important constraints on what we can do.* We are confronted by situations that we must define, but these situations have an existence in themselves. They have a history independent of us: a war is a reality; others may reject us or love us; a class structure in society may place us within its limits; poverty may limit much of our action and concerns; and others may have more resources and, therefore, more power advantage over us— they may at times coerce us, manipulate us, or persuade us. Central here is the fact that actors constantly define situations for others, and people can be and are manipulated by the definitions of others. It is difficult to ignore the situation that confronts us; it is an important parameter.

2. *Action is not always directed by symbolic interaction with the self.* Alternatives include nonconscious action, habit, and impulse. These alternatives are responses to stimuli without thinking, without problem solving, without considering past and future, without role taking. There are elements of nonconscious action, habit, and impulse in much of what we do, and to the extent that we rely on only these in our action, we are not "free" in the sense that freedom is described above. These alternatives tend to make us unable to deal appropriately with new situations or toward new variables in situations, unable to interact effectively with others, unable to role take, unable to cooperate, and unable to communicate effectively. Actively making a choice is made difficult or impossible. Freedom is limited.

3. *Lack of knowledge, understanding, inability to think clearly, few perspectives, and limiting perspectives will discourage freedom.* Thus our interaction and what we come to believe in social interaction will encourage or discourage what we

learn, understand, and apply what we learn. Definition of situation and choices become highly limited, and one is influenced to go in the direction of the socializers. By creating a situation where individuals are highly controlled in their social interaction, they will not have access to the tools necessary for self-direction and making choices from alternatives. They will also lack much ability to evaluate what they and others are doing. Think of symbols and how they are able to be used, and we can recognize that our ability to be free depends on our ability to think, control our self, and make choices in situations along our stream of action.

These limits, or parameters, should not cause us to lose sight of the freedom that is human. Perhaps it is better to call it "our active nature": Humans do not respond to situations but are actively involved in both definition and self-direction in these situations.

SYMBOLIC INTERACTIONISM AND SCIENCE

George Herbert Mead argued forcefully for the understanding of human beings through the study of what they *do*, through their action. Action, according to Mead and to the symbolic interactionist perspective, is always overt *and* covert action, what we do in relation to the other and in relation to ourselves. The subtle combination of overt and covert action may be difficult to study scientifically, because self-action is difficult to measure and difficult to predict. This perspective also seems to go against most of our notions of science because it suggests that there is an important element of human freedom in what we do.

There has always been disagreement over the meaning and purpose of science. All seem to agree that science is a method of discovery that relies on empirically gathered evidence and emphasizes a systematic and objective approach to the accumulation and analysis of evidence. Most social scientists have regarded science as a means of testing hypotheses related to causes of human behavior. This inquiry has usually involved defining two or more variables and testing a causal relationship between them. Social scientists, in their attempt to be scientific, have adopted from some natural scientists a certain model of science for studying human behavior. As a result, the symbolic nature of the human being has been neglected; covert-minded activity has been considered "outside of science"; action in the present has been overlooked as a cause; and, in the end, "the definition of the situation" by the actor has not been considered an important element in the situation.

Symbolic interactionists take a different approach to science than most social scientists. Instead of using physics as a model, they are much closer to cultural anthropology, which investigates people through observing them talking and acting in their everyday lives. Symbolic interactionists are closer to those biologists who go off and observe nature in the field rather than in the laboratory, animals in nature rather than in captivity. As a result, there are certain principles of investigation that symbolic interactionists follow that we should briefly describe here.

The central principle of symbolic interactionism is that we can understand what is going on only if we understand what the actors themselves believe about their world. The actor lives and knows his or her world. It is imperative to understand what the actors know, see what they see, and understand what they understand. We must understand their vocabulary, their ways of looking, and their sense of what is important. What the researcher must do is interact with the actors, observe and partake in their activities, conduct formal interviews, and try to reconstruct their reality. Always, it is imperative to understand from their particular point of view what it was that influenced them to act as they did (Schwartz and Jacobs, 1979, p. 179). Herbert Blumer (1969) clearly makes this point:

> The contention that people act on the basis of the meaning of their objects has profound methodological implications. It signifies immediately that if the scholar wishes to understand the action of people, it is necessary to see their objects as they see them. Failure to see their objects as they see them, or a substitution of his [or her] meaning of the objects for their meanings, is the gravest kind of error that the social scientist can commit. Simply put, people act toward things on the basis of the meaning that these things have for them, not on the basis of the meaning that these things have for the outside scholar (pp. 50–51).

To understand how others define reality is to interpret their acts not from our own perspective but from theirs; not according to our scholarly interpretation but from their own socially based interpretation. It is imperative to understand the definitions actors give to their actions, even if doing so means simply asking them for "retrospective accounts of past actions" (Denzin, 1971, pp. 166–67).

Symbolic interactionists believe that it is important to gather data through observing people in real situations. Typical social science research is done in laboratories or through questionnaires. Research on people, however, should describe people in real settings—how they work out real situations. This research should not be impressionistic and journalistic, but as careful, critical, systematic, and objective as possible. Experiments and videotapes of more controlled situations may be used to supplement what is learned in the real world, but always the real world must be the central laboratory for understanding human action.

Symbolic interactionists do more than go out and watch people in real-life situations; however, these other techniques often indirectly examine real-life situations. Howard Schwartz and Jerry Jacobs (1979, 179) describe *participant observation* and *interviewing actors* as two techniques used to understand the perspectives of groups of actors. *Personal accounts* and *life histories* are two attempts to capture the perspectives of individual actors. *Nonreactive techniques*—such as analyzing nonverbal communication, content in written materials, and audiovisual tapes—aim at understanding perspectives and action without direct involvement with the actors themselves.

Symbolic interactionists are critical of traditional social science, its use of scientific methodology for the study of human beings, and its definition of "important causal variables." The way we study humans, as anything else in nature—for instance, bugs, stars, rocks, or rats—must be determined first and foremost *by the nature of the empirical world under study.* We must develop empirical techniques that take into account the central qualities of *human* behavior. Science must understand how humans *define situations,* how they *act in the present* by applying past experiences and future plans, how they *solve problems* confronting them. This means that scientists must recognize that past events alone do not *cause* present action without an active person's defining the situation and directing the self in the present. The purpose of symbolic interactionism as a scientific perspective must be to understand the cause of human action. But "cause" is transformed to mean human definition, self-direction, and choice in situations. We must better understand how humans think, solve problems, role take, apply their past, and look to the future in situations. Science for understanding human action must recognize that part of human action is choice, is creative, and is free, and thus, paradoxically, the role of science becomes one of understanding how, and to what extent, freedom plays a role in what we do.

The symbolic interactionist regards a careful description of human interaction to be a central goal of social science. Careful observation of action, description of the important elements involved, and a careful description and redefinition of these elements should be achieved. That does not necessarily mean understanding which variable causes which variable, although the important elements at work in social situations may someday be causally linked. In a sense, a "formal sociology" is one of the goals of the symbolic interactionist, the purpose of which is to isolate and carefully describe such central concepts as conflict, role taking, cooperation, negotiation, problem solving, rehearsal of action and situations, definition of the situation, identity, self-direction, symbol, social objects, embarrassment, appearance, poise, and the like. It is important to see such concepts at work in a number of situations, comparing and contrasting instances of them, clarifying them, describing their role and, where appropriate, their absence. I might observe human action and recognize some important process taking place. Then I describe it: "This is what *negotiation* is; this is what happens when people *negotiate;* this is what people think, what they do; this is what happens to the ongoing interaction and the emerging culture." Then I describe a number of situations in which *negotiation* exists and also analyze where it is absent. There are many models for this type of analysis: Anselm Strauss's work on negotiation, Edward Gross and Gregory P. Stone's on embarrassment, and many recent studies cited throughout this text, such as works on emotions, identity, demoralization, vocabulary of motives, violence, rules, disclaimers, and so on.

Blumer described two modes of inquiry that should be used to describe the real world: exploration and inspection. *Exploration* is using any ethical procedure that aids in understanding "what's going on around here." Ideas, concepts, leads, and so on are altered as the observer goes along. Preconceptions are always open to change. One attempts to describe in detail what is happening in a social situation. The purpose is to become acquainted with an area of social life and to develop some focus of interest. *Inspection* is the second step. It involves isolating important elements within the situation and describing the situation in relation to those elements (e.g., conflict, alienation, domination, and cooperation). Inspection also involves forming descriptive statements about that element in a situation, then applying that to other interaction situations. The procedure of inspection must be "flexible, imaginative, creative, unroutinized" (summary borrowed from Stryker, 1981, p. 10).

The symbolic interactionist in studying the human being believes it is very important to move from mechanical models of causation (characteristic of natural science) to processual models. Mechanical models emphasize single variables as inevitably leading to certain outcomes. The job of the traditional social scientist has been "to identify the specific antecedent factors which under certain specified conditions produce specific kinds of observable outcomes" (Athens, 1984, p. 241). Processual models emphasize processes—a string of developing factors—"whose initial stages do not automatically determine their later ones," and therefore "the job of the scientist is to discover the stages which are necessary for a given phenomenon to come into existence and once in existence to sustain itself" (p. 249). For example, becoming deviant is a process, never inevitable because of certain isolated factors, but highly probable when a string of factors come together. Cause is complex, multifaceted, developed over time rather than simple, singular, and isolated.

Symbolic interactionism stands as an important criticism of using traditional scientific methods in social science. It is to always understand action from the perspective of those who act. It is to observe people in real situations. It is to broaden our understanding of cause to include definition of the situation in the present. It is to describe the elements of human interaction as well as to understand cause. It is to emphasize cause as highly complex and including a string of factors rather than as simple and single-faceted. The study of attitudes, values, animals in laboratories, and people in experimental situations gives some insight into human behavior, but it is not enough. The symbolic interactionist calls for a different direction, as summarized by Blumer (1969):

> It [symbolic interactionism] believes that this determination of problems, concepts, research techniques, and theoretical schemes should be done by the *direct* examination of the actual empirical social world rather than by working with a simulation of that world, or with a preset model of that world, or with a picture of that world derived from a few scattered observations of it, or with a picture of that world fashioned in advance to meet the dictates of some imported theoretical scheme or of some scheme of "scientific" procedure, or with a picture of the world built up from partial and untested accounts of that world. For symbolic interactionism the nature of the empirical social world is to be discovered, to be dug out by a direct, careful, and probing examination of that world (p. 48).

SYMBOLIC INTERACTIONISM: SOME REPRESENTATIVE STUDIES

The studies that have been inspired by this approach are too numerous to include here in any systematic way. However, six interesting examples might help give some idea of what can be done.

A Study of Pregnant Drug Users

In the summer of 1993, I heard an excellent paper presented at the American Sociological Association meetings. It was written by three researchers who applied the ideas and methods of symbolic interactionism to studying pregnant drug users. Margaret H. Kearney, Sheigla Murphy, and Marsha Rosenbaum (1993) reminded me that it is easier to condemn others than to understand them. It is hard for outsiders to understand how someone who is shortly going to give birth continues to use illegal drugs. It is easy to:

> judge them as less than human, as violating our deeply-held expectations for mothers: to protect their unborn at the expense of their own pleasure. We assume that because they don't comply with expected maternal behavior, they must not feel maternal feelings (p. 2).

Do they understand what they do? Do they care for their unborn child? Do they feel guilty in any way? How are we to answer those questions without investigating definitions of the situation by those caught up in it? Kearney, Murphy, and Rosenbaum investigated these women's definitions by interviewing 120 pregnant and postpartum women who had used illegal drugs at least once a week during pregnancy.

Of all the emotions labeled and described by these women, *guilt* was the most common. The women described guilt as having arisen from a realization that they were harming another human being whom they were supposed to protect. To these women "guilt was remorse at failing to keep the promises of a relationship" with an unborn child (p. 2). Their actions were not something they made light of. They bothered them, and the women defined themselves as failures as mothers or potential mothers. They knew they were pregnant; they knew that taking drugs was harmful; and they believed that they could have refrained from drug use if they had really wanted to. When all three ideas were believed, the result was acute guilt.

Guilt was the central emotion. How was it dealt with? Kearney, Murphy, and Rosenbaum identify five strategies: *using more drugs* so they did not have to think about what they were doing, *using fewer drugs* in order to convince themselves they were trying to deal with the problem, *putting off acknowledging pregnancy* as long as possible, and *seeking reassurance* from others that their baby was okay. A fifth strategy was to try to *change beliefs that fed their guilt.*

The women tried very hard to reject to themselves the idea that drug use was their own fault, rather than something that arose from poverty or other social conditions. It was very difficult for them. They continuously blamed themselves for the drug use, "for not being in better circumstances at the time of pregnancy, for not having made better choices in life and for not having the self-control and resolve to leave drugs alone" (p. 10), Some tried to rid themselves of blame by blaming some outside force, but their efforts were doomed to failure. And, instead of leading to the women's seeking help, self-blame for their situation only increased their guilt and their drug use.

There is more to the study than what has been described here. However, the points made are tragic, fascinating, and important. The researchers found out how people felt by asking them, not by interpreting their actions as outsiders. They pulled out from the interviews how these women defined their babies, their own behavior, and their situations. They informed me, the reader, that it is too easy to pass judgment through jumping to conclusions without trying to understand how others actually feel. The authors conclude:

> Guilt was a constant companion for these women when they weren't high on drugs. It arose from reflexivity and was a physical and emotional pain. Guilt was remorse for a loss of self-control that had risked harm to a loved one.... Strategies to relieve the pain were directed at reducing reflexivity—by numbing awareness or seeking alternatives to the rhetoric that fueled the guilt (p. 13).

A Study of Sam's Definition of Pain and Injury

In contrast to Kearney, Murphy, and Rosenbaum, who interviewed 120 women in order to understand how they acted in a particular life situation, Timothy Jon Curry (1993) interviewed a single person by the name of Sam in order to understand how he took on a certain identity over time: the identity of an amateur wrestler. Curry was interested in how Sam's definition of pain and injury changed over his wrestling career.

Curry found that (1) Sam's definition of pain and injury, as well as his identity as a wrestler, arose through social interaction and interaction with self and that (2) in the early stages of his wrestling career, pain and injury were defined as unimportant and something a *man* must endure, but eventually they became something to be avoided and what *good wrestlers* must endure.

To understand someone's career, one must ask the actor to reconstruct moments in a stream of action that seem to matter in influencing why he or she took on a certain identity rather than another. Sam reported that his parents always assumed that he would be an athlete, and throughout his precollege years they encouraged his participation in sports and attended all of his events. Whereas his mother would react to injury in a very serious and negative manner, his father reacted as if injuries were normal and part of being an athlete. Sam remembers having to make a choice: "being treated like a baby" or being "rough and tough" (p. 278). Early in his career he defined pain and injury as unimportant, normal, and masculine. This was a way to separate himself from femininity, and it also brought him closer to his father. Injury and pain were defined by Sam as things to be endured; serious injury was defined as a threat to both his wrestling career and his relationship with his father.

Sam recalled going to a summer camp where he learned to be "super-motivated." He learned to associate pain with physical growth and athleticism. To practice hard and train until he hurt was defined as good for the soul. He learned that "what is disdained is not injury or pain themselves, but allowing pain or injury to stand in the way of accomplishing a goal" (p. 279).

In his senior year of high school, Sam had a serious knee injury, over-came the pain with a shot of cortisone, and was able to win a tournament. Here he demonstrated to himself that he had truly arrived as a wrestler. Sam used this injury as an important step; he came to believe that in order to succeed he had to protect himself more carefully. Pain and injury took on yet another meaning: for him to become an elite wrestler, he had to endure pain, yet keep from seriously injuring himself.

In college the presence of trainers at all times and easy access to a sports physician highlighted the constant threat of serious injury. The coach made sure that no one was excused from practice because of injury. If nothing else, injured wrestlers were expected to exercise while others wrestled. Pain and injury were defined as something to be faced directly and overcome, never as something to get in the way of performance. Sam and others, if they were going to become "real" wrestlers, needed to assume this definition of pain and injury.

Through his wrestling life, Sam's definition of pain shifted from a symbol of masculinity to something that must be endured and overcome in order to succeed as a wrestler. To grin and bear it is simply part of what a good wrestler must do, knowing that a serious injury can end a career (p. 286).

Definition of our world, in this case the pain one feels, is central to the whole perspective of symbolic interactionism. Understanding such a defini-tion is best accomplished by asking the one who is actually doing the defining. Understanding the history of our stream of action as well as our changing view of self is to look back and isolate different acts or moments.

A Study of Identity Formation in a Maximum-Security Prison

Identity was also the subject of a study by Thomas J. Schmid and Richard S. Jones (1991). Here the focus was on identity transformation in a maximum-security prison. How does one see self in such a situation, and what happens to identities that are formed on the outside that one brings to the situation? This study was the result of one researcher's actual experience at a maximum-security prison for men over a one-year period as well as field observation by the second researcher and interviews with twenty first-time inmates.

The research shows that, before their arrival at prison, first-time inmates do not yet possess criminal identities. They see other prison inmates as violent "with whom they have nothing in common" (p. 417). They arrive afraid, and they arrive convinced that they do not want to change who they are while they are at prison. Part of their strategy is to protect themselves from hostilities, other inmates, and guards, to "resolve not to change, or to be changed, in prison." The researchers describe this process as self-dialogue, probably "the most extensive self-assessment he has ever conducted" (p. 418).

Once in prison, each inmate is faced with how others in the prison have come to see themselves. Insulation becomes impossible because he cannot avoid social interaction. As he comes to understand the prison world through social interaction, both his behavior and his identity are influenced. There is an ambivalence: a desire to hold on to the identity brought to the prison and a desire to interact and to know what to do in the new situation. He draws a sharp line between the identity he brings, which he calls his true identity, and the one he develops in the prison world. In a sense he is forced to put aside the identity he brought with him in order to survive. The prison identity is "a false identity created for survival in an artificial world" (p. 421). At first the inmate must control how he presents himself to others, simultaneously hiding what he considers his true identity and acting on the basis of an identity he does not really want to accept. Over time, he becomes used to presenting himself according to his temporary identity, and his actions become increasingly habitual. He slowly becomes an "insider."

As the inmate faces release, he must again shift to his old identity, taking on the outsider's view of the prison. He puts aside his prison identity, recalls again the outside world, and develops a plan to recapture his suspended identity. An interesting realization confronts him: he has changed in prison much more than he wanted to. He asks himself how permanent his changes are and how outsiders will perceive him when he leaves. He wonders if he can make it, and, above all, "he repeatedly confronts the question of who he is, and who he will be in the outside world" (p. 426). This is something that he must do within himself; some factors favor a shift, while others retard it. And, once he leaves, it is difficult to completely ignore the changes that have taken place as a result of his experiences:

> To the extent that these men draw upon their prison survival tactics to cope with the hardships of the outside world ... their prison identities will have become inseparable from their "true" identities (p. 428).

Here we have a study that tries to understand how people change identities in interaction with others and in interaction with self. It is not a radical or permanent shift, since there is a self-conscious attempt to make the prison identity temporary. The prison identity is important for survival while he is in prison, but never does he give up the identity he came with. There is the expectation that eventually he will go back into the world he was used to, and there is a recognition that his outside identity will once again become important. It is through interviews and field observation that the researcher comes close to capturing the actor's definition of the situation and view of self altered in interaction with others and with self.

A Study of First-time Tattooees

Identity is also important to Katherine Irwin (2001) who, because of her personal interest in the world of tattooing, observed that first time tattooees faced a conflict between what they wished to do and a middle-class society that disapproved. She wanted to understand their conflict and how they came to resolve it. In the process of her study, she came to understand that informal social interaction within the social world of tattooing was an important way that first-time tattooees changed their views and resolved their conflict. Through interaction, tattooees, socialized by friends and family to treat tattoos as outside middle-class norms, overcame their fear of societal reaction and found tattooing acceptable and even exciting. Irwin believes this is not simply important for the individual but for the views in the larger society: Legitimizing tattoos in the eyes of middle-class America was an example of real social change brought about not by media, educational, political institutions or widespread protest, nor by any other broad societal change, but instead by simple informal interaction among individuals who resolved a personal conflict through altering views that came to legitimate actions that they were taught to be reserved for people "not like themselves."

Irwin eventually focused her study on forty-three interviewees, some of whom had one or two tattoos, some who eventually decided not to be tattooed, some heavily tattooed, and some professional tattooists. She also interviewed ten parents of those tattooed.

Irwin wanted to understand both the conflict and its resolution by those who eventually were tattooed. It was clear that tattoos were symbols. To the young women it represented liberation, independence, and freedom. Many reported that it was a way to stay outside the dominant peer politics surrounding them. Others saw the tattoo as a passage from one life phase to another. Some believed it was a way to control their own bodies, to take their bodies away from men. Some also saw it as a way to gain entree into a fringe social world.

Yet tattoos symbolized something different to their parents and to people in middle-class society. Parents openly disapproved, defining tattoos as risky for their children's future, as an association with undesirables, and as a reflection on themselves as parents. The problem shared by those attracted to tattoos was how to reconcile their desires, yet not lose social status in the eyes of parents, friends, employers, and others who disapproved.

Irwin discovered four strategies used. (1) They exhibited "mainstream motivation": Tattooing was being done in order to commemorate a special time in their life, a rite of passage, an achievement in their lives, a personality trait they possessed, or a skill they were proud of. Thus they wrapped their tattoos within a conventional framework. (2) They attempted to continue acting conventionally, exhibiting the fact that they continued to remain who they were before they were tattooed, and showing that tattooing was "no big deal." (3) They defended their actions by condemning those who would condemn. (4) They treated their tattoos as pieces of art, and tattooists as artists.

Irwin's study is quite simple and informative. It helps us understand the meaning and importance of tattoos as symbols, the different ways people define the same activity, and how people resolve personal conflict and conflict with others. It is an attempt to understand how people think, how thinking influences action, how actions come to legitimate that which others normally think are not legitimate, and ultimately how ongoing interaction alters what the larger society eventually comes to accept.

Definition of the situation is a key to the whole symbolic interactionist perspective. Irwin shows the importance of definition for people's desire for a tattoo and their conflict with those who see it as outside middle-class norms. She underlines the strategies taken so that tattooing becomes acceptable and relationships with certain others are not undermined because of tattooing.

A Study of Compulsive Gamblers

Josh Rossol (2001) is also interested in the importance of how people define situations, but his focus is not on tattooing but on gambling, specifically how people come to define their own gambling as illness, as something they need to control or to stay away from. Of course, what is and is not "illness" is a matter of definition, and whether or not something that needs correction is actually an illness or a problem or a sin or a weakness is also a matter of definition. Like alcohol, problem gambling has come to be defined as an illness, an affliction, a disorder that must be controlled or cured.

Rossol studied a therapy group that was set up to help problem gamblers. He tried to analyze how the group defined gambling, problem gambling, and how to help others. He observed group discussions and interviewed problem gamblers who sought help in the group. In the interviews, he examined the reasons individuals decided to join the therapy group. The most important commonality was that they described a crisis in their lives—financial, family, employment, legal—a crisis they linked to their gambling. Either the crisis already occurred or it was about to occur.

Instead of focusing on the individual's reasons for gambling, the past was set aside and the present and future were emphasized by the group. What became important was the individual's choice to recover from an illness that he or she somehow developed. Although each individual may have a different reason for gambling, the group emphasized that everyone who sought help had the same illness, and the group aimed at making many individuals believe they were basically the same in this regard. People were taught that cure rather than cause was important to understand, that this illness would get worse over time if untreated, and that to overcome it one must go through twelve stages, with shortcuts out of the question. The individual's past was interpreted in relation to the gambling illness existing in the present. Through interaction the gambling status became one's central or master status, a status shared with everyone else in the group, and a status that was stigmatized and one that needed to be treated. A diversity of individuals came to share a definition of their problem through a medical vocabulary.

At meetings individuals spoke out about how their illness developed, describing gambling as an addiction, occasional blackouts while gambling, and withdrawal symptoms when they did not gamble. Whether or not the accounts were true was not assumed by Rossol. What was important was that this is what individuals reported, and through this, a culture emerged from the group that individuals came to accept. Each individual had a different story to tell, but the group influenced each individual to see his or her story within the perspective of the group, and tried always to focus on their actions since the last meeting rather than discussing what they thought and did before they joined the group. Did you gamble since the last meeting? How did you feel over the past week?

The culture was anchored in a book—called the yellow book—that individuals used to interpret their lives and their views of gambling. The purpose of the group was to show each person that the book was a good way of seeing their illness, and a good guide to treating their illness.

This study recalls the importance of the famous statement by William and Dorothy Thomas that underlines the importance of definition in human actions: "If you define a situation as real, it is real in its consequences" (1928, p. 572). This whole study is about definition: definition of problem gambling, illness, disease, deviance, crisis, and one's past. Each definition became a part of the group's culture, and each was used by the whole group and every individual in directing their actions away from a problem they came to recognize. There are certainly other ways of defining these terms, but for those who must face this problem these definitions and solutions work. Three principles arise out of these definitions: focus on your actions now instead of trying to figure out why you became a compulsive gambler, interpret your problem according to the culture of the group aided by a book describing what you must do, and recognize that your disorder is an illness that needs to be treated. Social interaction—cooperative problem solving—shared culture—directing self according to a perspective and body of rules that constitutes culture—all of this sounds like a society, and that is exactly what it is for these people.

A Study of Student Anxiety: Not Studying Hegel So Much as Doing Laundry

Most readers of this book have gone through what it means to be a student in a university, and can probably recall what it felt like being a high school senior wondering what university would be like. Lynda Holmstrom, David Karp, and Paul Gray (2002) examined upper-middle-class students who were about to enter a university away from home. After doing several pilot interviews with many high school students, thirty-one students were chosen to be part of a long-term study. These students, were interviewed in depth during the fall of their senior year in high school. Their parents were also interviewed. Later on in the year as students were admitted to universities twenty-three of the thirty-one were interviewed again, and their parents were interviewed in May.

Actually, the results of the study surprised me, but you probably knew them without reading the study. I remember my own experience: I worried whether or not I would make it, whether or not I could pass my classes, whether or not I was going to understand what was going on in class. And, of course, as an instructor for over twenty-five years I too readily assumed that incoming students were just like me. I was probably unique in 1957; and I was too involved in my job as instructor to really understand my students. The study did not find that students were anxious about classes, but they were much more concerned about the changes in their daily lives they were about to face. The students expressed a lot of uncertainty, fear, and anxiety, and although they recognized the greater academic challenges, they seemed to worry much more "about getting their laundry done, managing daily time, budgeting money, establishing friendships, and renegotiating family ties" (p. 438). The researchers entitled their article "Why Laundry, Not Hegel?" meaning that their sample seemed to be more worried about laundry than in understanding philosophy.

Three tensions were important to them: (1) maintaining the world they were familiar with and "venturing forth into unknown places," (2) being taken care of by others and living on their own, and (3) "gaining personal autonomy and simultaneously maintaining family attachments." The researchers see these tensions as part of a "status transition," a slow gradual steady transition from adolescence to adulthood, a four-year adjustment period where they were neither children nor yet adults.

The researchers were fully aware that their sample was upper-middle-class students who had decided to leave home and enter a four-year residential college. The students cared about academic success, but they worried about the issues related to everyday life. Overall, college was defined as a step toward adulthood, a halfway house between high school and the real world, being able to live on one's own, but not yet completely. Students clearly saw college as a gradual transition to adulthood, a phase that would help them in a personal and professional direction that would then lead them along an adulthood path after graduation. They wanted independence, but they also wanted to be helped out by their parents. If successful, at graduation they will be recognized as adults. The researchers conclude that a college education, therefore, simultaneously postpones adulthood and "maximizes the likelihood that middle- to upper-middle class youth will secure well paid employment, allowing them, at least to sustain their class position" (p. 456). Parents are able to steer their children into adulthood and middle-class life. In life directions, class matters:

> Upper-middle-class family life is centrally organized around the singular pursuit of children's education. Parents see it as their job to provide all the necessary infrastructural support to guarantee their offspring's educational sucess. Not

surprisingly, the high school seniors admitted scant knowledge of the logistics of everyday life. Ordinarily, parents simply do not expect them to manage finances, to cook, to clean, or to do their laundry completely on their own. Therefore, it follows that managing these everyday life tasks would be at the forefront of students' consciousness as they imagined being "on their own" for the first time (p. 456).

The researchers describe part of the process of retaining upper-middle-class status: those who adjust and succeed during these four years are treated to a pause in their journey. Their adult roles are deliberately delayed. The university experience allows them to postpone responsibilities related to marriage, parenthood, and fulltime work. This contrasts with those "disadvantaged and discouraged high school students" who do not see a university education in their future, and are relatively unsure what their future will be, "drifting into early parenthood and taking on one adult role while still unable to perform the economic provider role securely." The university is a "semi-independent environment" that:

> encourages increasing independence and deliberately delays aspects of adulthood in order to later maximize opportunities. Upper-middle-class parents are hoping to maximize the probability that their children will at least replicate their class position. They perceive correctly that college attendance creates a deliberate and gradual path to a particular type of adulthood, namely, to an upper-middle-class adulthood (pp. 457–58).

The researchers give us a clue to look at processes that perpetuate class position. Definition of the future college experience actually lay out routes that people follow. Through extensive interviewing, a view of how these high-school seniors define their upcoming university experience is uncovered, and those of us who are interested can better grasp what the authors argue are "long-term advantages associated with selective delays in the transition to adult status in late modern societies" (p. 458).

These empirical studies are good examples of research using the perspective of symbolic interactionism. All attempt to focus on interaction, definition, decision-making and the development of both societies and identities. All are examples of observation and/or interviewing, often asking people to tell their stories or show how their perspective is created, altered, or lost. All are interested in identity, on how people define themselves and others, and how people's identity influences how they act in situations. And all of them, through showing the importance of definition, examine the human being as actively forming his or her own life rather than simply being influenced by personality, past, attitudes, emotional response, habit, other people, or society. In the last study on college seniors, definition is heavily influenced by an upper-middle-class social world, thus emphasizing less active decision-making on the individual's part, and showing the importance of reference group. (Of course, the study does not tell us how definitions change in young people once in college, but that becomes an important and interesting subject for another symbolic interactionist study.) All these studies tell us that to understand the human being we must try to understand how humans think about situations; all tell us that taking the role of the person who is being researched is critical for researching human behavior.

SYMBOLIC INTERACTIONISM: SOME EXAMPLES OF APPLICATION

A student in my class on symbolic interactionism asked me: "This is all fine and dandy, but what in the world does this perspective have to do with anything? What is its relevance?" I could not believe that this perspective, so powerful for me, could not be applied by the student. "It's relevant to everything human," I began. "All situations can be described using this perspective—this classroom interaction, for example, race relations, war, a football game, a family, a party ...," and I went on and on, patting myself on the back as I proudly announced all the applications that occurred to me at the time. "But I'm going to work with delinquents," was the reply. "How can I use this to help them, to change them, to make them better?" Then I knew that relevance to this student meant changing people—how do we as teachers teach better, how can we alter behavior for the better, change attitudes, make a better world? For me, relevance has always meant just plain understanding—how well does Marx understand society, or Freud understand it, or Mead? In fact, the point of the symbolic interactionists seems to be that human beings are not easily manipulated, altered, or predictable. I realized that the perspective may aid *my understanding of human complexity* but not necessarily suggest how to successfully change or manipulate others.

Another student who was in business management told me: "The thing that symbolic interactionism taught me was that it is very difficult to manage people any way one chooses; people are active and thinking, and they determine their own directions in interaction with others and with themselves. This is important when I go out into the business world and deal with people." Symbolic interactionism may not yet be relevant to those who want to systematically alter people in a given direction, but it is a very relevant perspective for understanding human social situations. As it does this more and more accurately, prediction and the ability to change people may result (if that is what one chooses to do with knowledge).

The point of the business management student cannot be taken lightly: it is interaction that affects the direction of the individual, and the nature of interaction—overt and covert—is difficult for other people to control except in a small number of situations. We can teach our children our values, but these values will be effective in directing the child only if they influence the child's interaction or only if they continue to be important to new perspectives he or she may pick up. In most cases, it seems that the teacher or parent must be prepared to see these values transformed or put aside during the child's interaction with others who become the new significant others or reference groups. The convicted criminal can be put away in a prison community, can learn new values, can take on a different perspective, can have a different "personality," but when the prisoner is released these things will be effective only if *interaction* is influenced, and only if interaction does not lead the individual to define the world in the same way he or she defined it before imprisonment. To change the person is to change his or her interaction, social worlds, reference groups, and perspectives, and thus to alter the person's definition of self and situations. Given the nature of modern society this goal seems difficult for one person to set for another.

Symbolic interactionism is a perspective that can be applied to all social situations and can help illuminate them. This goes for two people on a date, for a college classroom, for any game, such as chess or football, for bringing up children, and for social problems such as crime and inequality. All of these involve interaction among individuals as well as interaction within each individual. And all of these individuals have a self and a mind, symbols, and perspectives; they analyze, problem solve, cooperate, share, communicate, and align acts. I have tried to apply this perspective to my world, and I find it full of insights. If it is going to be useful, one must take the concepts and use them to analyze situations. Here are some ways I have applied the perspective to some of the issues that are important to me. It is not the only perspective I use, but over time, symbolic interactionism has become a central identity and has encouraged me to thoughtfully understand many puzzles of human behavior.

An Understanding of Society

Society and morality are very appropriate and important subjects for the application of this perspective. Nothing human is as complex to understand as the nature of society, and nothing is as important to society as the relationship between morality and society. It is so easy in this modern age to worship the individual and to be attracted to a perspective (such as symbolic interactionism) that supports the fact that the human being is free to some extent and is the creator of society. Most of us want to believe this.

Yet Erving Goffman reminds us that society exists only through an agreement by people to cooperate, to respect one another, and to act according to a generalized body of rules. Only when we agree to support one another's face in interaction, to accept what one presents himself or herself to be, is society possible. In short, society rests on respect for one another, the acceptance of a shared body of rules, and the use of a common perspective that allows all to understand one another. Mead, too, returns again and again to the moral basis for society: society is possible only through the agreement by individuals to use the morals of society as a generalized other—as a guide—to control action in light of the needs of the whole.

Society seems very tenuous in the symbolic interactionist perspective, almost always on the verge of collapse, always negotiated, always changing, always new. This is not an inaccurate picture: society does not continue automatically; every group's existence today is not guaranteed tomorrow. The Soviet Union no longer exists. Interaction, cooperation, and culture once unified the Soviet Union. Different interaction, cooperation, and culture caused it to crumble. It has broken apart as separate societies have now become separate nations. My group of friends can be lost tomorrow—if we no longer interact, share a culture (including rules we agree to control ourselves by), cooperate (in discussion, playing poker together, going on fishing trips together every summer, investing in the stock market), talk out the problems that concern us and our families. The group will be no more when we do not respect one another's identities and when we are unwilling to adjust our own actions in relation to the other individuals and in relation to the whole.

Symbolic interactionism—a perspective so involved in trying to understand individuals and their ability to act freely in the world—makes an important contribution to sociology and to those who are interested in the human being as a social being because it tells us so much about the nature of *society*.

An Understanding of Racism in Society

Symbolic interactionism also can help us understand social problems in this society and in the world. This is no small matter. The student has a right to expect that perspectives within sociology should contribute to understanding the problems of inequality, poverty, racism, sexism, crime, meaningless work, alienation, violent conflict, mental illness, and other problems that caring people should be concerned with.

To many sociologists, the society of the United States is characterized by racial inequality, racial segregation, racial conflict, and racism. Symbolic interactionism offers a fresh approach to understanding this problem.

We begin with the nature of society. People who interact with one another form society. They take one another into account; they communicate, role take, and cooperate. They share an understanding of reality, and they develop a set of rules to live by. At the same time, the development of society through cooperative symbolic interaction will, by its very nature, cut off interaction with those outside that interaction. This is the basis for the racial problems in this society, and it is the basis for similar problems in all societies. The United States has developed a segregated society; thus, in a basic sense it is not one society, but several. The reasons for segregation are several, all embedded in our history: slavery, exploitation, racist institutions, *de jure* and *de facto* segregation. Today, despite efforts to eliminate unequal treatment based on race, we still face conflict arising from segregation, conflict that can threaten whatever other gains we might have made in our history. Let us briefly examine some of the effects of segregation in our society (or in any society).

1. Where interaction creates separate societies, each will develop its own culture, and individuals will be governed by different sets of rules and will

share different perspectives. Without continuous interaction between people in various societies, actors in each will fail to communicate with and understand the other, and role taking and cooperation between them will be minimized. *Human differences, exaggerated and perpetuated through segregated interaction, are what bring about the creation of two societies in one, two societies that continue to be at odds to the extent that opportunities for interaction and cooperation between them are not available.*

2. If one of these separate societies has more power in the political arena of the nation, its representatives will be in the position to stigmatize the other. That is, its leaders will be able to define the other as less worthy; it will be able to define the other society as having a culture that is unacceptable and even threatening to the dominant culture. *Racism is a philosophy expressed in the public arena that condemns as inferior those societies that are different, and racism is action that retains the inferior position and continued segregation of societies.*

3. People in the dominant society through interaction develop a perspective—one that is useful for their understanding of reality. Included are their definition of those in the other society and the reasons for their differences, as well as a justification for the inequality that exists between the other society and the dominant one. *It is through this definition of those who are different as heathens, infidels, savages, slaves, or enemies that one society develops a justification for taking land, enslaving, discriminating, or segregating, or simply refusing to work for equality.* The dominant culture might include such ideas as the others are biologically inferior, the others are not motivated (as we are), the others are threats to what we stand for, or if the others would only be like the rest of us they could be equal. Many ideas in the dominant society would not be blatantly racist, but the implications might be: "Ours is a society where anyone can be whatever he or she wants to be" (thus, the reason why some people— often minorities—are poor is that they do not work hard enough), or "Our educational system gives equal opportunity to all our citizens" (so those who do not make it do not take the opportunities offered to all).

4. Where interaction is segregated, and people are unable to develop a culture shared by all, the others will continue to be seen as different. No matter if real differences do in fact exist; where segregation exists differences will be perceived, exaggerated, not understood, and often condemned. It is almost too much to expect people who form their own culture to be able to see other cultures as equally good. *To the extent that people in the dominant society see their own culture as right and true, others who are different will be defined as threats. To members of the dominant society, this perception makes destructive actions against the others appear justifiable.*

5. Destructive action against others also seems justifiable if we can somehow make them into objects rather than people. It is easier for us to see those people similar to us as people; people who are different from us—who are part of societies separate from us—we do not understand and we cannot easily take their roles. *We do not regularly interact, communicate, and cooperate with them.*

How much easier it is to see them as objects who do not seem to have equally important problems, concerns, interests. Seeing them as objects not only encourages destructive actions, but it also works against efforts to aid the other.

6. *It is conflict rather than cooperation that characterizes segregated societies.* Without interaction, which includes communication, role taking, and recognizing the mutual identities of actors who are necessary for cooperative action, no shared culture is likely to develop, and the different definitions will continue.

It is difficult to illustrate here all the ways that the symbolic interactionist perspective can be usefully applied to this serious problem, but these six points should be a start. Remember: we can understand social problems such as racism and racial conflict through focusing on interaction, cooperation, communication, culture, and definition, and such an analysis can bring us very far. Symbolic interactionist ideas can be applied to understanding problems between all ethnic groups in society, between people of different classes, between labor and management, and between nations. When interaction is cut off between societies, a perspective cannot be easily shared; the acts of each cannot be understood by the other; problem solving becomes impossible; aligning acts no longer materialize, and emotional and habitual responses replace cooperative symbolic interaction among people.

An Understanding of Gender Differences

"Nearly all feminists agree that women have historically been denied the opportunity to construct their own separate identity, their own sense of selfhood and purpose apart from the definitions imposed on them by men" (Ferguson, 1980, pp. 128–29).

Who are we? What does it mean to be a woman—or a man? Symbolic interactionists see men and women as they see everything else in nature: these are classifications that we regard as useful—otherwise we would not see people this way. But why is it that distinction is useful? The answer is that we probably have so defined this classification minimally for purposes of having sex, having children, and socializing children. It has proved useful to us, and so we continue to make it.

In most societies this distinction is a primary one, and the biological distinction has grown to be enlarged to include many of our actions, from color of blankets to power relationships and opportunities in life. We might point out that such distinctions have been especially useful for men, who claim a privileged position in society. The definition of who women are in the world may have originally arisen among men (in interaction with one another), or even between men and women, but over time that definition has influenced the views that women have of themselves. My purpose in life—my reason to be—is an integral part of my definition of myself, and if I see myself as an object to be used by men, as an instrument of reproduction, as a servant to others, then this is how I will act and how I will present myself in my actions to others. Others will continue to see me this way, recognizing my identity, and generally approving it through their actions.

The symbolic interactionist tries to understand gender differences by investigating the questions of how the individual is socialized and how we come to take on our identities and define what we are supposed to do. Spencer Cahill (1986) observed children in a nursery specifically to understand the process of "gender identity acquisition": At first children act in ways that have little to do with how sex-appropriate those acts are. As adults begin to distinguish through language which of these acts are male and which are female, the children learn who they are and which types of behavior belong to their identities. Then, in play with one another, they increasingly try to take on appropriate actions that others have identified, and in interaction with one another they reaffirm those identities: "You be the mom!" "No, you should be the mom—you're the girl!"

> Through interactions such as these, children apparently learn that in order to gain recognition as full-fledged persons they must avoid appearing and behaving in ways that contradict, in the eyes of others, their socially bestowed sex identity. Because of children's desire to be recognized as such persons, most children become increasingly concerned with doing so (p. 300).

Who are these people we call women? Who am I, one who is a woman? This reality, like all else, is defined in interaction, and this, like all else, changes in interaction. What is happening today is that women are increasingly defining who they are in interaction with one another rather than primarily in interaction with men. Women in the United States are increasingly forming their own social worlds and are claiming that they are something other than what men have traditionally claimed they are. Women have organized in part to change the dominant definitions of men and women, and they have attempted to change how political leaders, media, schools, and families limit people through such definitions. More and more we are finding subtle and powerful ways people define gender, and as a society we are recognizing that men and women are far more socially defined categories than biologically created ones.

Always there is in symbolic interactionism the underlying idea that people are not stamped out by their environment or by their socializers, that regardless of how others define us, there is also the fact that individuals will interact with themselves, develop their own identities apart from others, overcoming in part the power of social interaction. Throughout history many women have been able to do this. Probably people have recognized from the beginning that "I do not necessarily have to be who I have learned from others I am." What has changed in our society is that many people are joining to say this, and the result is an emerging definition that includes real alternatives by which people can guide their lives and go in directions most in the past would not have chosen.

An Understanding of Childhood Socialization

Symbolic interactionism can be useful for almost every aspect of our lives. One of the problems many of us will face is parenthood. What does it mean to be a good parent?

Symbolic interactionists have a view that is different from many other perspectives of what is important in the socialization of children. Most other perspectives assume the stable view of the human being: We are personalities; we develop traits in childhood; and those traits will be carried by us into adulthood. The symbolic interactionist view looks at the human being as an ever-changing actor, communicating, role taking, cooperating, problem solving along a stream of action. We are all capable of going in many directions. What we value at one point will be different from what we value at another point. What we believe— about the world and about ourselves—will constantly change, as will our significant others and our reference groups. Does parenthood matter? If it does, how?

Parenthood does in fact matter. To begin with, all along we have emphasized that actors are influenced in the directions that they take along their stream of action by decisions they make due in part to interaction with others. *All the acts that we perform in relation to our children can have an influence on the directions they go in life.* What we do in our lives, they are able to observe; what we intentionally communicate to them, the words we use to describe them, the identities we give them—all have an effect. Continuous interaction has a good chance of influencing direction. Even though it is unlikely that ongoing interaction will continue to any great extent as they become adults, the directions they were influenced to take through interaction with us at an earlier point in their lives may always remain important.

In addition, if we remain significant others to our children, our perspectives will be used by them to define their world. Without continuous social interaction, it is probable that these perspectives will cease to be important or will become less important; as others replace us as significant others, our perspectives will probably become less useful to our children. However, if they continue to find our perspective useful even without our interaction with them, or if they continue to regard us as important others in their lives, then our perspectives will continue to be important to them.

Parenthood is far more complex than simple influence over directions or remaining significant others to our children. *If the human being is the kind of actor that the symbolic interactionist claims, then there are certain qualities that parents should encourage in their children,* including the following:

1. *The ability to problem solve.* Problem solving is not an inherent faculty; we don't know how to do it without someone's teaching us the skills necessary. Children should be encouraged to handle their own situations through a thoughtful approach to figuring out how to realistically handle situations as they occur. Problem solving is an ability to figure out for oneself how to study, how to find a job, how to perform well on a job, how to develop and maintain

friendships, how to counsel others who need our advice, and how to approach almost everything we can name. This ability to understand situations and to control them to achieve goals should be an important goal for parents to nurture. Instead of teaching a child how to act in specific situations, the parent must encourage the child to figure out situations in a thoughtful manner.

2. *The ability to communicate, understand others, and role take.* Many of the problems that we all have center on these abilities. Through constantly interacting with children, encouraging them to communicate, sensitizing them to understanding what others mean, we are teaching our children skills that will matter in situations they encounter.

3. *A moral sense.* It is very difficult to ensure that the morals we give our children will follow them through life. Whether they do depends on ongoing interaction to a great extent. If they continue to use us as their significant others, then our morals will certainly remain important; if they interact with others who reaffirm our morals, then our morals will also remain important. However, there is no guarantee that either will happen, and chances are that neither will happen in this society, which is so broken up into smaller societies, into many instances of interaction. Developing a moral sense is different from handing down a set of morals. A moral sense is a recognition that if one is going to live with other people then one should be willing to take on a shared morality, one should be willing to be governed by the rules of the society to some extent, rather than be governed simply by what one wants to accomplish at a particular moment. It means that one should constantly take the role of others and try to understand their needs as well as his or her own, and that, to remain together with them, one must respect their rights.

Finally, parenting matters for one more reason. The whole symbolic interactionist perspective is premised on the idea that ultimately human beings regularly define their situations and act according to those definitions. Because we live in human society and encounter many diverse situations and other human beings throughout our day, our successes depend in large part on our ability to think in the situations we act in. Causing children to respond emotionally to situations prevents thoughtful problem solving. The harmful effects of child abuse—physical, sexual, or emotional—eventually stand in the way of dealing with ongoing situations by causing an unconscious response rather than an attempt to usefully define the situation they are acting in. Situations will end up stimulating responses which are not actively adjusted by the actor who ends up acting without understanding consequences, the acts of others, or even his or her own acts. Action then becomes dysfunctional in relation to other people and in achieving personal goals.

All of these principles—and more—are inferred from the perspective of symbolic interactionism, and they are important guides for parents. Indeed, many of these principles are found in other perspectives too, and improving role taking, communication, and problem solving remain important goals in much of the therapy that psychologists and counselors emphasize today.

Symbolic Interactionism: A View of the College Experience

Symbolic interactionism, when applied to my own life as a teacher, is awfully humbling. I started my career hoping to influence students, to get them to look at the world sociologically, humanistically, or through the symbolic inter-actionist perspective. I hoped to teach something that would remain with students, to make a difference in some important way. I was a teacher, in part, to try to create a better world. I woke up one day when a student stated: "You know, this is all very interesting, this is even relevant to my life, but this class-room is the only place I ever discuss these things or hear anything about them. Outside this classroom there just is not any interest or knowledge about them. I won't remember any of this when the class is all over." I realized then why things are so easily forgotten after a final exam.

A perspective is remembered if it is applied and found to be useful in a number of situations. But this is unlikely to happen unless other people around us also use it regularly and share it in interaction. A perspective is remembered if one has a reference group that shares it, if it is associated with our significant others. The different perspectives gained in the classroom cannot be expected to be remembered and applied; they are forgotten unless they continue to be shared through interaction. College itself can be an important perspective that we remember—it can become a reference group providing a perspective for our present situation—but whatever was gained will be changed consider-ably as we interact *now* with new people.

Unhappily, for those of us who think we can actually teach something last-ing, what will probably happen to our students is this: they might learn an at-tractive perspective, barely remember it after the final exam, never take a class like it, and never have another opportunity to discuss it with others. They will leave college with a dim memory that will be transformed as they interact with others in the work world that seems to offer them a more attractive perspective.

Realistically, the classroom experience is part of a long stream of action for each person. A teacher may influence the direction that stream of action takes. He or she may influence the student's desire to interact with others who share an academic, sociological, psychological, or biological perspective or, at least, may influence the student's desire to continue to interact with those who are open to discussing these perspectives intelligently. But even if the teacher's perspective is forgotten or never used, there is one bright spot: The class has made the students aware, however briefly, of a new perspective, and the class-room interaction, if the symbolic interactionist perspective is correct, *has* changed them, one hopes in a way that will contribute to a better world.

Symbolic Interactionism: A Final Look at Application

It is impossible to show all the ways that this perspective can be applied because in fact it can be applied to any human experience. It is a refreshing view, for it explains human action in a way that most perspectives miss. The perspective describes everyday situations as well as complex social problems. The perspective is regularly applied in sociology to understanding social deviance in society. It has illuminated the problems of mental health, racism and racial conflict, and substance abuse. It has been applied to understanding society, education, and communication. It serves as an important guide to all of us seeking to understand ourselves and others, and it helps explain how freedom is possible and society necessary.

THE IMPORTANCE OF THE SYMBOLIC INTERACTIONIST PERSPECTIVE

The symbolic interactionist perspective is important for all *social science*. It is a criticism of social science, calling forth an alteration of direction and a set of new assumptions about human action. It is revolutionary. By emphasizing the active nature of humans, it questions the scientific potential for fully understanding and predicting human behavior. It asks that we focus on a definition of the situation, which is an active process, impossible to predict exactly, but to some extent understandable through careful and systematic investigation. It questions the attempts to understand human behavior by studying attitudes or values the human chooses on a questionnaire. It sees experiments done with nonsymbolizing animals as limited approaches to the understanding of the human being, and it questions the validity of applying certain accepted scientific methods uncritically to the understanding of human action. Symbolic interactionism sees the human as too complex an organism to be studied by such methods. Action is seen as caused not by something from a distant past but by symbolic interaction between and within individuals. It emphasizes that actions have a long, continues history, that the cause of any isolated act is not easily located, and that action shifts direction from time to time. In the end, symbolic interactionism calls for social science to see humans from a different perspective and to adjust its scientific focus and techniques accordingly.

Symbolic interactionism also has much to offer the *disciplines outside of social science,* such as the humanities, communications, and philosophy. The nature of reality, the meaning of the self, the emergence and importance of society, the nature of symbols, the importance of human communication, and the future of humanity are all topics that symbolic interactionists share with these other disciplines. Mead seems to relate increasingly to more and more people outside of sociology, and other symbolic interactionists recognize this development. Indeed, the Society for the Study of Symbolic Interaction, an active academic organization that meets and discusses research being done and issues of concern for symbolic interactionists, draws from people all over the world and appeals to many who are not sociologists. The increasing importance of "identity" in psychology, humanities, women's studies, and ethnic studies, either parallel and supplement the work of symbolic interactionists or have been influenced by symbolic interactionists who have seen identity to be a central concept for understanding human action. Ruth Wallace and Alison Wolf in 1986 wrote that symbolic interactionism "can be seen as an alternative perspective providing theoretical tools which are missing in other perspectives" (p. 231). They were right.

Symbolic interactionism has a number of important implications for *sociology* specifically. It is critical of traditional sociology in the same ways it is critical of all social science. But it is also extremely enriching and adds immeasurably to the important insights of this field. For example, it adds to our understanding of the sociology of knowledge; it describes the social nature of reality, how our group life or our society creates our definition of reality, internal or external. It tells us of the power available to those who control symbols, perspectives, and definitions. The perspective can be applied to understanding further the "collective consciousness" in Durkheim, the "class consciousness" and "false consciousness" in Marx, the religious perspectives in Weber, and the "forms of interaction" in Simmel, to name only the most obvious ties with sociological theory. Symbolic interactionism has been applied to the theoretical and empirical study of deviance, emphasizing the importance of identity as a sociological concept. Symbolic interactionism has been applied to socialization, collective behavior, and social problems, studying questions that others tend to ignore, such as the importance of lifelong socialization, collective behavior as social interaction, and how some issue in a society comes to be defined as a social problem. Its definition of society is useful because it emphasizes both society's dynamic nature and the kinds of action between individuals necessary for its continuation. It seems to me that symbolic interactionism, more than any other perspective in sociology, clearly describes the intricate interrelationships between the individual and society: Society makes the individual through creation of the self, mind, symbols, generalized other, perspectives, and symbolic role taking. Conversely, it is the human individual who makes human society through active interpretation, self-direction, role taking, aligning his or her own acts with others, and communicating. By regarding the human as so thoroughly social and symbolic, and by describing the complex ways this is so, symbolic interactionism makes a major contribution to the sociological perspective.

It is difficult to know the precise place that symbolic interactionism fills within the more general sociological perspective. On the one hand, it is part of sociology and one of the leading contemporary perspectives. Its insights are sociological; its practitioners are among the leading sociologists. On the other hand, it differs from the work of most sociologists, asking serious questions about many of the directions we have gone. Wallace and Wolf (1986) emphasize this complexity:

> A perspective that places a primary value on subjective meaning and on process as opposed to structure, combined with a methodology that takes great pains to capture the "world of the other" as seen by that other, asks important sociological questions that cannot be answered by mainstream sociology.... It therefore deserves recognition as an approach that makes important and distinctive contributions to sociology (p. 231).

Finally, we must remember that the symbolic interactionist perspective is important to those of us who are *students of human action*, interested in understanding the nature of human life, society, truth, and freedom. That is the appeal the perspective has had for me, and that has been the underlying theme of this book. This perspective contributes to a liberal arts education: It deals intelligently and systematically with some of the most important questions concerning human life.

Summary

Symbolic interactionism is a perspective. Like all other perspectives, it is limited because it must focus on some aspects of reality and ignore or deemphasize others. It is different from all other social scientific perspectives, and is, in part, a criticism of the directions taken by these other perspectives.

Symbolic interactionism questions the determinism that prevails in much of social science. It tries to show that the possibility of freedom exists only through the use of symbols, self, and mind. And instead of blindly asserting that human beings are in fact free, symbolic interactionism shows many of the limits of freedom. Freedom is a complex issue; to symbolic interactionists its existence is possible, but it is always limited.

Most symbolic interactionists consider themselves scientists. Both George Herbert Mead and Herbert Blumer were committed to systematic and objective observation, the accumulation of knowledge through open discussion and critical evaluation of whatever understandings and proofs are put forward, and the accumulation of careful generalizations concerning human behavior. As the studies summarized in this chapter tried to indicate, that science is based on a methodology that emphasizes interviewing, observing people acting in the real world, and focusing on how and why people define the situations they act in. All of the studies used in-depth interviews (pregnant drug users, prison inmates, a wrestler, tattoos, compulsive gamblers, and high-school seniors about to enter college). One was a study of a single individual (the wrestler study), and one combined careful observation with interviews (compulsive-gambler study). Always the focus was on how people defined the world they lived in and how that definition influenced their action. Also, in every case the people studied belonged to a social world that most people do not know firsthand; thus, each gives us a glimpse of another world, showing how people in that particular world define their reality. What a key this becomes to understanding human action! And, for many of us, these are worlds similar to what we might encounter, and in which we might be embedded—and here, too, these studies become significant, because they can help us to understand our own actions.

Throughout the book I have tried to show how symbolic interactionism is a useful way to understand the real world. It is not simply a perspective to memorize for an exam, but one that can be easily applied. In this final chapter, I was more direct in showing its applications: from understanding society racism, and gender inequality to understanding personal situations such as socializing children and college life.

Finally, it is important to realize that symbolic interactionism is an increasingly influential perspective today: in the academic community, in social science, and in sociology.

REFERENCES

Adler, Patricia and Peter
    1998   *Peer Power: Preadolescent Culture and Identity.* New Brunswick, NJ: Rutgers University Press.

Ames, Van Meter
    1973   "No Separate Self." In Walter Robert Corti, Ed., *The Philosophy of George Herbert Mead,* pp. 43–58. Winterthur, Switzerland: Amriswiler Bucherei.

Anderson, Leon, and David A. Snow
    2001   "Inequality and the Self: Exploring Connections from an Interactionist Perspective." *Symbolic Interaction,* 24:395–406.

Aronson, Elliot
    1992   *The Social Animal,* 6th ed. San Francisco: Freeman.

Athens, Lonnie
    1984   "Blumer's Method of Naturalistic Inquiry: A Critical Examination." *Studies in Symbolic Interaction* 5:241–57.
    1986   "Types of Violent Persons." *Studies in Symbolic Interaction* 7:367–89.

Atkinson, Paul A., and William Housle
    2003   *Interactionism.* London: Sage.

Ball, Donald
    1972   "The Definition of the Situation." *Journal for the Theory of Social Behavior* 2:24–36.

Becker, Ernest
    1962   *The Birth and Death of Meaning.* New York: Free Press.

Becker, Howard S.
    1953   "Becoming a Marihuana User." *American Journal of Sociology* 59:235–42.
    1963   *Outsiders.* New York: Free Press.
    1982   "Culture: A Sociological View." *Yale Review* 71:513–27.

Berger, Peter L.
    1963   *Invitation to Sociology.* Garden City, NY: Doubleday.

Berger, Peter L., and Thomas Luckmann
    1966   *The Social Construction of Reality.* New York: Doubleday.

Best, Joel
    1997   "Victimization and the Victim Industry." *Society* 34:9–17.
    1999   *Random Voilence: How We Talk about New Crimes and New Victims.* Berkely: University of California Press.

Bjorklund, Diane
    1998   *Interpreting the Self: Two Hundred Years of American Autobiography.* Chicago: University of Chicago Press.

Blumer, Herbert
    1953   "Psychological Import of the Human Group." In Muzafer Sherif and M.O. Wilson, Eds., *Group Relations at the Crossroads,* pp. 185–202. New York: Harper & Row.
    1955   "Race Prejudice as a Sense of Group Position." *Pacific Sociological Review* 1:37.
    1962   "Society as Symbolic Interaction." In Arnold Rose, Ed., *Human Behavior and Social Processes,* pp. 179–92. Boston: Houghton Mifflin Co.

1966   "Sociological Implications of the Thought of George Herbert Mead." *American Journal of Sociology* 71:535–44.
1969   *Symbolic Interactionism: Perspective and Method.* Englewood Cliffs, NJ: Prentice Hall.
1981   "Conversation with Thomas J. Morrioni and Harvey A. Farberman." *Symbolic Interaction* 4:9–22.

Brissett, Dennis, and Charles Edgley, Eds.
1975   *Life As Theater.* Chicago: Aldine.
1990   *Life As Theater,* 2nd ed. New York: Aldine de Gruyter.

Brooks, Richard
1969   "The Self and Political Role: A Symbolic Interactionist Approach to Political Ideology." *Sociological Quarterly* 10:22–31.

Brown, Roger
1965   *Social Psychology.* New York: Free Press.

Burke, Kenneth
1966   *Language As Symbolic Action.* Berkeley: University of California Press.

Burke, Paul J.
1980   "The Self: Measurement Requirements from an Interactionist Perspective," *Sociological Quarterly* 10:22–31.

Buttny, Richard
1993   *Social Accountability in Communication.* Newbury Park, CA: Sage.

Cahill, Spencer E.
1980   "Directions for an Interactionist Study of Gender Development." *Symbolic Interaction* 3:123–88.
1986   "Socialization, Language, and Gender Identity Acquisition." *Sociological Quarterly* 27:295–311.

Cassirer, Ernst
1944   *An Essay on Man.* New Haven, CT: Yale University Press.

Charmaz, Kathy
1999   "Stories of Suffering: Subjective Tales and Research Narratives." *Qualitative Health Research* 9:362–82.

Chodorow, Nancy
1999   *The Power of Feelings.* New Haven: Yale University Press.

Clark, Candace
1997   *Misery and Company: Sympathy in Everyday Life.* Chicago: University of Chicago Press.

Clarke, Adele E.
1991   "Social Worlds Theory as Organization Theory," pp. 119–58 in *Social Organization and Social Process: Essays in Honor of Anselm Strauss,* by D. Maines, Ed. Hawthorne, NY: Aldine de Gruyter.

Cooley, Charles Horton
1909   *Social Organization,* 1962 ed. New York: Schocken Books.
1970   *Human Nature and the Social Order.* New York: Schocken Books.

Coombs, Robert, and Pauline S. Powers
1975   "Socialization for Death: The Physician's Role." *Urban Life* 5:250–71.

Crittenden, Kathleen S.
1983   "Sociological Aspects of Attribution." *Annual Review of Sociology* 9:425–46.

Curry, Timothy Jon
1993   "A Little Pain Never Hurt Anyone: Athletic Career Socialization and the Normalization of Sports Injury." *Symbolic Interaction* 16:273–90.

Cuzzort, R. P.
  1969   *Humanity and Modern Sociological Thought.* New York: Holt, Rinehart & Winston.
Darling, Jon
  1977   "Bachelorhood and Late Marriage: An Interactionist Interpretation." *Symbolic Interaction* 1:44–55.
Davis, Fred
  1984   "Decade Labeling: The Play of Collective Memory and Narrative Plot." *Symbolic Interaction* 7:15–24.
Denzin, Norman K.
  1971   "The Logic of Naturalistic Inquiry." *Social Forces* 50:166–82.
  1972   "The Genesis of Self in Early Childhood." *Sociological Quarterly* 13:291–314.
  1978   "Crime and the American Liquor Industry." *Studies in Symbolic Interaction* 1:87–118.
  1984a   *On Understanding Emotion.* San Francisco: Jossey-Bass.
  1984b   "Toward a Phenomenology of Domestic, Family Violence." *American Journal of Sociology* 90:483–513.
  1987   *The Alcoholic Self.* Beverly Hills, CA: Sage.
  1989   *Interpretive Interactionism.* Newbury Park, CA: Sage.
  1992   *Symbolic Interactionism and Cultural Studies: The Politics of Interpretation.* Oxford: Blackwell.
  2001   "Symbolic Interactionism, Poststructuralism, and the Racial Subject." *Symbolic Interaction* 24:243–49.
Denzin, Norman, and Yvonna Lincoln, Eds.
  1994   *Handbook of Qualitative Research.* Thousand Oaks, CA: Sage.
Desmonde, William H.
  1957   "George Herbert Mead and Freud: American Society Psychology and Psychoanalysis." In Benjamin Nelson, Ed., *Psychoanalysis and the Future,* pp. 31–50. New York: Psychological Association for Psychoanalysis.
Deutscher, Irwin
  2002   *Accomodating Diversity: National Politics that Prevent Ethnic Conflict.* Lanham, MD: Lexington Books.
  2004   "Little Theories and Big Problems: Chicago Sociology and Ethnic Conflicts." *Symbolic Interaction* 27:441–59.
Dewey, John
  1922   *Human Nature and Conduct.* New York: Modern Library.
Duncan, Hugh Dalziel
  1968   *Symbols in Society.* New York: Oxford University Press.
Duneier, Mitchell
  1999   *Sidewalk.* New York: Farrar, Straus and Giroux.
Duneier, Mitchell, and Harvey Molotch
  1999   "Talking City Trouble: Interactional Vandalism, Social Inequality, and the 'Urban Interaction Problem.'" *American Journal of Sociology* 104:1263–95.
Dunn, Jennifer L.
  2001   "Innocence Lost: Accomplishing Victimization in Intimate Stalking Cases." *Symbolic Interaction* 24:285–313.
Eames, S. Morris
  1977   *Pragmatic Naturalism.* Carbondale, IL: Southern Illlinois University Press.
Elkin, Frederick, and Gerald Handel
  1972   *The Child and Society.* New York: Random House.

Elliot, Anthony
    2001   *Concepts of the Self.* Cambridge: Polity Press.

Erickson, Karla
    2004   "To Invest or Detach? Coping Strategies and Workplace Culture in Service Work." *Symbolic Interaction* 27: 549–72.

Farberman, Harvey
    1975   "A Criminogenic Market Structure: The Automobile Industry." *The Sociological Quarterly* 16:438–57.

Felson, Richard B.
    1978   "Aggression As Impression Management." *Social Psychology* 41:205–213.

Ferguson, Kathy E.
    1980   *Self, Society, and Womankind.* Westport, CT: Greenwood Press.

Fine, Gray Alan
    1981   "Friends, Impression Management, and Preadolescent Behavior." In Gregory Stone and Harvey Farberman, Eds., *Social Psychology through Symbolic Interaction* 2nd ed., pp. 257–72. Lexington, MA: Ginn.
    1984   "Negotiated Orders and Organizational Cultures." *Annual Review of Sociology* 10:239–62.
    1987   *With the Boys: Little League Baseball and Preadolescent Culture.* Chicago: University of Chicago Press.
    1992   "Agency, Structure, and Comparative Contexts: Toward a Synthetic Interactionism." *Symbolic Interaction* 15:87–107.
    1993   "The Sad Demise, Mysterious Disappearance, and Glorious Triumph of Symbolic Interactionism." *Annual Review of Sociology* 19:61–87.
    1996   *Kitchens: The Culture of Restaurent Work.* Berkeley: University of California Press.
    1998   *Moral Tales: The Culture of Mushrooming.* Cambridge, MA: Harvard University Press.
    2001   *Gifted Tongues: High School Debate and Adolescent Culture.* Princeton University Press.

Fine, Gary, and G. W. Smith (eds.)
    2001   *Erving Goffman.* Newbury Park, CA: Sage.

Flaherty, Michael G., and Gary Alan Fine
    2001   "Present, Past, and Future: Conjugating George Herbert Mead's Perspective on Time." *Time and Society* 10:147–61.

Francis, Linda E.
    1997   "Ideology and Interpersonal Emotion Management Redefining Identity in Two Support Groups." *Social Psychology Quarterly* 60:153–71.

Fromm, Erich
    1973   *The Anatomy of Human Destructiveness.* New York: Holt, Rinehart & Winston.

Fujimoto, Naomi
    2001   "What Was that Secret? Framing Forced Disclosures from Teen Mothers." *Symbolic Interaction* 24:1–24.

Gardner, Robert
    2004   "The Portable Community: Modernization and Mobility in Bluegrass Festival Life." *Symbolic Interaction* 27:155–78.

Garfinkel, Harold
    1956   "Conditions of Successful Degradation Ceremonies." *American Journal of Sociology* 61:420–24.
    1967   *Studies in Ethnomethodology.* Englewood Ciffs, NJ: Prentice Hall.

Gecas, Viktor
  1982 "The Self Concept." *Annual Review of Sociology* 8:1–33.
  1995 "Symbolic Interactionism." *Encyclopaedia of Marriage and the Family*, vol. 2. New York: Simon Schuster/Macmillan.

Gecas, Viktor, and Peter J. Burke
  1995 "Self and Identity." In *Sociological Perspectives on Social Psychology*, edited by K.S. Cook, G.A. Fine, and J. House. Boston: Allyn & Bacon.

Giddens, Anthony
  1991 *Modernity and Self-Identity: Self and Society in the Late Modern Age*. Stanford: Stanford University Press.

Gillespie, Joanna
  1980 "The Phenomenon of the Public Wife: An Exercise in Goffman's Impression Management." *Symbolic Interaction* 3:109–26.

Glaser, Barney, and Anselm Strauss
  1964 "Awareness Contexts and Social Interaction" *American Sociological Review* 29:669–79.

Goff, Tom W.
  1980 *Marx and Mead*. London: Routledge & Kegan Paul.

Goffman, Erving
  1959a *Asylums*. Chicago: Aldine.
  1959b *The Presentation of Self in Everyday Life*. Garden City, NY: Doubleday.
  1961a *Asylums*. Garden City, NY: Doubleday.
  1961b *Encounters*. New York: Bobbs-Merrill.
  1963a *Behavior in Public Places*. New York: Free Press.
  1963b *Stigma*. Englewood Cliffs, NJ: Prentice Hall.
  1967 *Interaction Ritual*. New York: Random House.
  1971 *Relations in Public*. New York: Basic Books.
  1974 *Frame Analysis*. New York: Harper & Row.
  1981a *Forms of Talk*. Philadelphia: University of Pennsylvania Press.
  1981b "Program Committee Encourages Papers on a Range of Methodologies." *Footnotes* (9 August): 4.
  1983 "The Interaction Order." *American Sociological Review* 48:1–17.
  1988 "*Entretien avec Erving Goffman*." In Yves Winkin, Ed. and trans., *Les Moments et Leurs Hommes*, pp. 231–38. Paris: Seuil/Minuit.

Gross, Edward, and Gregory P. Stone
  1964 "Embarrassment and the Role Requirements." *American Journal of Sociology* 70:1–15.

Gubrium, Jaber F., and James A. Holstein
  1997 *The New Language of Qualitative Method*. New York: Oxford University Press.

Hall, Peter M.
  1981 "Structuring Symbolic Interaction: Communication and Power." *Communication Yearbook* 4:49–60.

Halliday, M. A. K.
  1978 *Language As Social Semiotic*. Baltimore, MD: University Park Press.

Hampden-Turner, Charles
  1970 *Radical Man*. Cambridge, MA: Schenkman.

Hardesty, Monica J.
  1987 "The Social Control of Emotions in the Development of Therapy Relations." *Sociological Quarterly* 28:247–64.

Harris, Scott R.
  2001   "What Can Interactionism Contribute to the Study of Inequality? The Case of Marriage and Beyond." *Symbolic Interaction* 24:455–80.

Hayes, Terrell A.
  2000   "Stimatizing Indebtedness: Implications for Labeling Theory." *Symbolic Interaction* 23:29–46.

Heilman, Samuel C.
  1976   *Synagogue Life: a Study in Symbolic Interaction.* Chicago: University of Chicago Press.

Hewitt, John P.
  1984   *Self and Society,* 3d ed. Boston: Allyn & Bacon.

Hewitt, John P., and Randall Stokes
  1975   "Disclaimers." *American Sociological Review* 40:1–11.

Hertzler, Joyce O.
  1965   *A Sociology of Language.* New York: McGraw-Hill.

Hickman, C. Addison, and Manford H. Kuhn
  1956   *Individuals, Groups, and Economic Behavior.* New York: Dryden Press.

Hindmarsh, Jon, and Christian Heath
  2000   "Sharing the Tools of the Trade: The Interactional Constitution of Workplace Objects." *Journal of Contemporary Ethnography* 29:523–62.

Hochschild, Arlie Russell
  1983   *The Managed Heart.* Berkeley: University of California Press.
  2003   *The Commercialization of Intimate Life: Notes from Home and Work.* Berkeley: University of California Press.

Hogg, Michael A., and Cecilia Ridgeway
  2003   "Social Identity: Sociological and Social Psychological Perspectives." *Social Psychology Quarterly* 66:97–100.

Horowitz, Ruth
  1995   *Teen Mothers: Citizens or Dependents?* Chicago: University of Chicago Press.

Holmstrom, Lynda Lytle, David A. Karp, and Paul S. Gray
  2002   "Why Laundry, Not Hegel? Social Class, Transition to College, and Pathways to Adulthood," *Symbolic Interaction* 25:437–462.

Holstein, James A., and Gale Miller
  1997   "Rethinking Victimization: An Interactional Approach to Victimology," pp. 25–47 in *Social Problems in Everyday Life,* G. Miller and J. A. Holstein, Eds. Greenwich, CT: JAI Press.

Holstein, James, and Jaber Gubrium
  2000   *The Self We Live By: Narrative Identity in a Postmodern World.* New York: Oxford University Press.

Irwin, Katherine
  2001   "Legitimating the First Tattoo: Moral Passage through Informal Interaction." *Symbolic Interaction* 24:49–73.

James, William
  1915   *Psychology.* New York: Holt, Rinehart & Winston.

Jarvinen, Margaretha
  2001   "Accounting for Trouble: Identity Negotiations in Qualitiative Interviews with Alcoholics." *Symbolic Interaction* 24:263–84.

Jenkins, Richard
  1996   *Social Identity.* London: Routledge.

Joas, Hans
     1985   *G. H. Mead.* Trans. Raymond Meyer. Cambridge, MA.: MIT Press.
Josselson, Rthellen and Amia Lieblich, Eds.
     1993   *The Narrative Study of Lives.* London: Sage.
Kant, Immanuel
     1952   *The Critique of Pure Reason.* (1781) Trans, J. M. D. Meiklejohn. *The Great Books of the Western World,* Ed. Robert Hutchins. Chicago: Encyclopedia Britannica.
Karp, David, Gregory Stone, and William Yoels
     1991   *Being Urban: A Sociology of City Life.* New York: Praeger.
Karp, David, and William Yoels
     1986   *Sociology and Everyday Life.* Itasca, IL: F.E. Peacock.
Kearney, Margaret H., Sheigla Murphy, and Marsha Rosenbaum
     1993   "At Least I Feel Guilty: Emotions and Reflexivity in Pregnant Drug Users' Accounts." Unpublished paper presented at the American Sociological Association 88th Annual Meeting.
Keller, Helen
     1954   *The Story of My Life.* Garden City, NY: Doubleday.
Kemper, Theodore D.
     1978   *A Social Interactional Theory of Emotions.* New York: Wiley.
Kendon, Adam
     1990   *Conducting Interaction: Patterns of Behaviour in Focused Encounters.* Cambridge: Cambridge University Press.
Kennedy, Leslie W., and Vicent F. Sacco
     1998   *Crime Victims in Context.* New York: Roxbury.
Kinch, John W.
     1963   "A Formalized Theory of the Self-Concept." *American Journal of Sociology* 68:481–86.
Kleinman, Sherryl
     1996   *Opposing Ambitions: Gender, Identity, and Inquality in an Alternative Organization.* Chicago: University of Chicago Press.
Kuhn, Manford H., and Thomas S. McPartland
     1954   "An Empirical Investigation of Self Attitudes." *American Sociological Review* 19:68–76.
Ladd-Taylor, Molly, and Lauri Umansky
     1998   *"Bad" Mothers: the Politics of Blame in Twentieth-Century America.* New York: New York University Press.
Lamb, Sharon
     1996   *The Trouble with Blame: Victims, Perpetrators, and Responsibility.* Cambridge, MA: Harvard University Press.
Lindesmith, Alfred R., Anselm Strauss, and Norman K. Denzin
     1988   *Social Psychology.* 6th ed. Englewood Cliffs, NJ: Prentice Hall.
Lofland, John, and Lyn H. Lofland
     1995   *Analyzing Social Settings: A Guide to Qualitative Observation and Analysis.* 3d ed. Belmont, CA: Wadsworth.
Lofland, Lyn H.
     1998   *The Public Realm: Exploring the City's Quintessential Social Territory.* New York: Aldine de Gruyter.
Loseke, Donileen R.
     1992   *The Battered Woman and Shelters.* Albany: SUNY Press.

Lurie, Alison
    1981   *The Language of Clothes*. New York: Random House.
Lyman, Stanford M., and Arthur Vidich
    1988   *Social Order and the Public Philosophy: An Analysis and Interpretation of the Work of Herbert Blumer*. Lafayette: University of Arkansas Press.
Maines, David R.
    2001   *The Faultline of Consciousness: A View of Interactionism in Sociology*. New York: Aldine de Gruyter.
    2003   "Iteractionism's Place." *Symbolic Interaction* 26:5–8.
Malcolm X and Alex Haley
    1965   *The Autobiography of Malcolm X*. New York: Grove Press.
Manning, Peter
    1977   *Police Work*. Cambridge, MA: MIT Press.
Mason-Schrock, Douglas
    1996   Transexuals' Narrative Construction of the "'True Self.'" *Social Psychology Quarterly* 59:172–92.
McCall, George J. and J. L. Simmons
    1966   *Identities and Interactions*. New York: Free Press.
Mead, George Herbert
    1925   "The Genesis of the Self and Social Control." *International Journal of Ethics* 35:251–77.
    1934   *Mind, Self and Society*. Chicago: University of Chicago Press.
    1936   *Movements of Thought in the 19th Century*. Merritt H. Moore, Ed. Chicago: University of Chicago Press.
    1938   *The Philosophy of the Act*. Merritt H. Moore, Ed. Chicago: University of Chicago Press.
    1982   "1914 Class Lectures in Social Psychology." In David L. Miller, Ed. *The Individual and the Social Self*, pp. 27–105. Chicago: University of Chicago Press.
Meltzer, Bernard N.
    1972   *The Social Psychology of George Herbert Mead*. Kalamazoo: Center for Sociological Research, Western Michigan University.
Merton, Robert K.
    1957   *Social Theory and Social Structure*. New York: Free Press.
Miller, David L.
    1973   *George Herbert Mead: Self, Language and the World*. Chicago: University of Chicago Press.
    1973   "Mead's Theory of Universals." In Walter Robert Corti, Ed., *The Philosophy of George Herbert Mead*, pp. 89–106. Winterthur, Switzerland: Amriswiler Bucherei.
Miller, William Ian
    1993   *Humiliation: And Other Essays on Honor, Social Discomfort, and Violence*. Ithaca: Cornell University Press.
Mills, C. Wright
    1940   "Situated Action and the Vocabulary of Motives." *American Sociological Review* 6:904–13.
Mischel, Walter, and Harriet N. Mischel
    1977   "Self-Control and the Self." In Theodore Mischel, Ed., *The Self*, pp. 31–64. Oxford: Basil Blackwell.
Natanson, Maurice
    1973   *Social Dynamics of George Herbert Mead*. The Hague: Martinus Nijoff.

Neuman, W. Lawrence
    2000   *Qualitative Evaluation and Research Methods.* Newbury Park, CA: Sage.

Newman, Katherine S.
    2000   *Rampage: The Social Roots of School Shootings.* New York: Basic Books.

Numberg, Geoffrey
    1981   "The Theatricality of Everyday Life." *New York Times Book Review* (May 10):11.

Power, Martha Bauman
    1985   "The Ritualization of Emotional Conduct in Early Childhood." *Symbolic Interaction* 6:213–27.

Perinbanayagam, R.S.
    2000   *The Presence of Self.* New York: Rowman and Littlefield.

Rapoport, Tamar, Edna Lomsky-Feder, and Angelika Heider
    2002   "Recollection and Relocation in Immigration: Russian-Jewish Immigrants 'Normalize' Their Anti-Semitic Experiences." *Symbolic Interaction,* 25:175–98.

Redfield, Robert
    1941   *The Folk Culture of Youcatan.* Chicago: University of Chicago Press.

Reynolds, Larry
    1993   *Interactionism: Exposition and Critique.* 3d ed. Dix Hills, NY: General Hall.

Rollins, Judith
    1985   *Between Women: Domestics and Their Employers.* Philadelphia: Temple University Press.

Rosenberg, Morris
    1979   *Conceiving the Self.* New York: Basic Books.
    1981   "The Self-Concept: Social Product and Social Force." In Morris Rosenberg and Ralph Turner, Eds., *Social Psychology,* pp. 593–624. New York: Basic Books.

Rosenberg, Morris, and Ralph Turner
    1981   *Social Psychology.* New York: Basic Books.

Ross, Ralph
    1962   *Symbols and Civilization.* San Diego, CA: Harcourt Brace Jovanovich.

Rossol, Josh
    2001   "The Medicalization of Deviance as an Interactive Achievement: the Construction of Compulsive Gambling." *Symbolic Interaction* 24:315–41.

Scheff, Thomas J.
    1999   *Being Mentally Ill: A Sociological Theory.* New York: Aldine de Gruyter.
    2000   "Shame and the Social Bond: A Sociological Theory." *Sociological Theory* 8:84–99.
    2003   "Shame in Self and Society." *Symbolic Interaction* 26:239–62.
    2005   "Looking-Glass Self: Goffman as Symbolic Interactionist." *Symbolic Interaction* 28:147–66.

Schmid, Thomas J., and Richard S. Jones
    1991   "Suspended Identity: Identity Transformation in a Maximum Security Prison." *Symbolic Interaction* 14:415–32.

Schwalbe, Michael, Sandara Godwin, Daphne Holden, Douglas Schrock, Shealy Thompson, and Michelle Wolkomir
    2000   "Generic Processes in the Reproduction of Inequality: An Interactionist Analysis." *Social Forces* 79:419–52.

Schwartz, Howard, and Jerry Jacobs
    1979   *Qualitative Sociology: A Method to the Madness.* New York: Free Press.

Scott, Marvin E., and Stanford M. Lyman
    1968   "Accounts." *American Sociological Review* 33:46–62.

Scott, Susie
    2005   "The Red, Shaking Fool: Dramaturgical Dilemmas in Shyness." *Symbolic Interaction*, 28:91–110.

Shamir, Ronen
    2005   "Mind the Gap: The Commodification of Corporate Social Responsibility." *Symbolic Interaction* 28:229–53.

Shibutani, Tamotsu
    1955   "Reference Groups As Perspectives." *American Journal of Sociology* 60:562–69.
    1961   *Society and Personality: An Interactionist Approach to Social Psychology.* Englewood Cliffs., NJ: Prentice Hall.
    1978   *The Derelicts of Company K: A Sociological Study of Demoralization.* San Francisco: Jossey-Bass.

Shott, Susan
    1979   "Emotion and Social Life: A Symbolic Interactionist Analysis." *American Journal of Sociology* 84:1317–34.

Silver, Ira
    1996   "Role Transitions, Objects, and Identity." *Symbolic Interaction* 19:1–20.

Smircich, Linda
    1983   "Organizations as Shared Meanings." In Louis R. Pondy et al., Eds, *Organizational Symbolism*, pp. 55–65. Greenwich, CT:JAI Press.

Snow, David A.
    2001   "Extending and Broadening Blumer's Conceptualization of Symbolic Interactionism." *Symbolic Interaction* 24:367–77.

Snow, David A., and Leon Anderson
    1987   "Identity Work among the Homeless: The Verbal Construction and Avowal of Personal Identities." *American Journal of Sociology* 92:1336–71.
    1993   *Down on Their Luck: A Study of Homeless Street People.* Berkeley: University of California Press.

Stets, Jan E., and Peter J. Burke
    2000   "Identity Theory and Social Identity Theory." *Social Psychology Quarterly* 63:224–37.

Stone, Gregory P.
    1962   "Appearance and the Self." In Arnold Rose, Ed., *Human Behavior and Social Processes*, pp. 86–118. Boston: Houghton Mifflin.

Stone, Gregory P., and Harvey A. Farberman
    1970   *Social Psychology through Symbolic Interaction.* Lexington, MA: Ginn.

Strauss, Anselm
    1959   *Mirrors and Masks.* New York: Free Press.
    1964   "Introduction" to *On Social Psychology* by George Herbert Mead. Chicago: University of Chicago Press.

Strauss, Anselm, and Juliet Corbin
    1998   *Basics of Qualitative Research.* Thousand Oaks, CA: Sage.

Stryker, Sheldon
    1959   "Symbolic Interaction As an Approach to Family Research." *Marriage and Family Living* 22:111–19.
    1980   *Symbolic Interactionism.* Menlo Park, CA: Benjamin/Cummings.
    1981   "Symbolic Interactionism: Themes and Variations." In Morris Rosenberg and Ralph Turner, Eds., *Social Psychology*, pp. 1–29. New York: Basic Books.

Stryker, Sheldon, and Peter Burke
    2000   "The Past, Present, and Future of an Identity Theory."*Social Psychology Quarterly* 63:284–97.

Thoits, Peggy A.
    1996   "Managing the Emotions of Others." *Symbolic Interaction* 19:85–109.

Thomas, William I., and Dorothy Thomas
    1928   *The Child in America.* New York: Knopf.

Thrasher, Frederic M.
    1936   *The Gang.* Chicago: University of Chicago Press.

Tillman, Mary Katherine
    1970   "Temporality and Role-taking in G.H. Mead." *Social Research* 37:533–46.

Troyer, William Lewis
    1946   "Mead's Social and Functional Theory of Mind." *American Sociological Review* 11:198–202.

Turner, Ralph H.
    1968   "The Self-Conception in Social Interaction." In Chad Gordon and Kenneth J. Gergen, Eds., *The Self in Social Interaction,* pp. 93–106. New York: Wiley.

Vallacher, Robin R.
    1980   "An Introduction to Self Theory." In Daniel M. Wegner and Robin R. Vallacher, Eds., *The Self in Social Psychology,* pp. 3–30. New York: Oxford University Press.

Wallace, Ruth, and Alison Wolf
    1986   *Contemporary Sociological Theory.* Englewood Cliffs, NJ: Prentice Hall.

Warriner, Charles K.
    1970   *The Emergence of Society.* Homewood, IL: Dorsey Press.

Weber, Max
    1947   *Theory of Social and Economic Organization.* Trans. Talcott Parsons and A. M. Henderson. Glencoe, IL: Free Press.

Weinstein, E. A., and P. Deutschberger
    1963   "Some Dimensions of Altercasting." *Sociometry* 26:454–66.

Weiss, Robert
    1994   *Learning from Strangers: the Art and Method of Qualitative Interview Studies.* New York: Free Press.

Wells, L. Edward, and Gerald Marwell
    1976   *Self Esteem.* Beverly Hills, CA: Sage Publications.

White, Leslie A.
    1940   "The Symbol: The Origin and Basis of Human Behavior." *Philosophy of Science* 7:451–63.

Willey, Norbert
    2003   "The Self as Self-Fulfilling Prophecy." *Symbolic Interaction* 26:501–14.

Wuthnow, Robert
    1994   *Sharing the Journey: Support Groups and America's New Quest for Community.* New York: Free Press.

Zborowski, Mark
    1952   "Cultural Components in Responses to Pain." *Journal of Social Issues* 8:16–30.

Zerubavel, Evitar
    1994   *The Fine Line: Making Distinctions in Everyday Life.* New York: Simon and Schuster.

INDEX

A

Abstract reality, 67–68
Abuse, 212
Accounts, 135
Action, 116–139
  and the act, 138–139
  cause of, 116–117, 126–139
  and communication, 135
  and consummation,
    125, 126
  covert, 119, 121
  and decades, 121
  and decisions, 120
  and definition of the situation,
    117–118, 124, 125, 134,
    138–139
  and direction, 138–139
  as drama, 181–182
  and emotions, 135–137
  and the four stages of the act,
    123–126
  and freedom, 119, 126, 137–138
  and the future, 133, 138
  and goals, 122–123, 124–125,
    133–134, 139
  and human essence, 116–117,
    122, 138–139
  and impulse, 124
  and interpretation, 138
  and manipulation, 125, 126
  and memory, 133
  and mind, 97, 98, 102–103
  and motives, 133–137, 139
  overt, 119
  and the past, 113, 137–138
  and perception, 124–125
  and perspective, 121
  and personality, 122
  and planning, 123, 133
  and the present, 133
  and problem solving,
    124, 125
  and self, 81–82, 86–87, 88–90,
    119, 138
  and self control, 138
  and social environment, 126
  and social interaction,
    117–118, 119
  and social objects, 120–121,
    122–123, 125, 137,
    138–139
  and society, 157, 168
  and the stream of action, 118–122,
    126, 138–139
  and the stream of consciousness,
    119
  summary of, 138–139
  and symbolic interactionism,
    116–139, 192
  and taking the role of the
    other, 108, 111–112,
    113–114
  and thinking, 117–118, 121,
    122, 138
Action, social (See Social Action)
Acts, 120–122, 123–126, 138–139,
    153, 157
Ames, Van Meter, 98–99, 101
Appearance, 175–176
Aronson, Elliot, 23
Asylums, 186
Asch, Solomon, 23
Athens, Lonnie, 163, 195
Attitudes, 39–41
Audience, 176–177
Authority, 14
Autobiography of Malcolm X, 6–9
Averchenko, A., 2–3